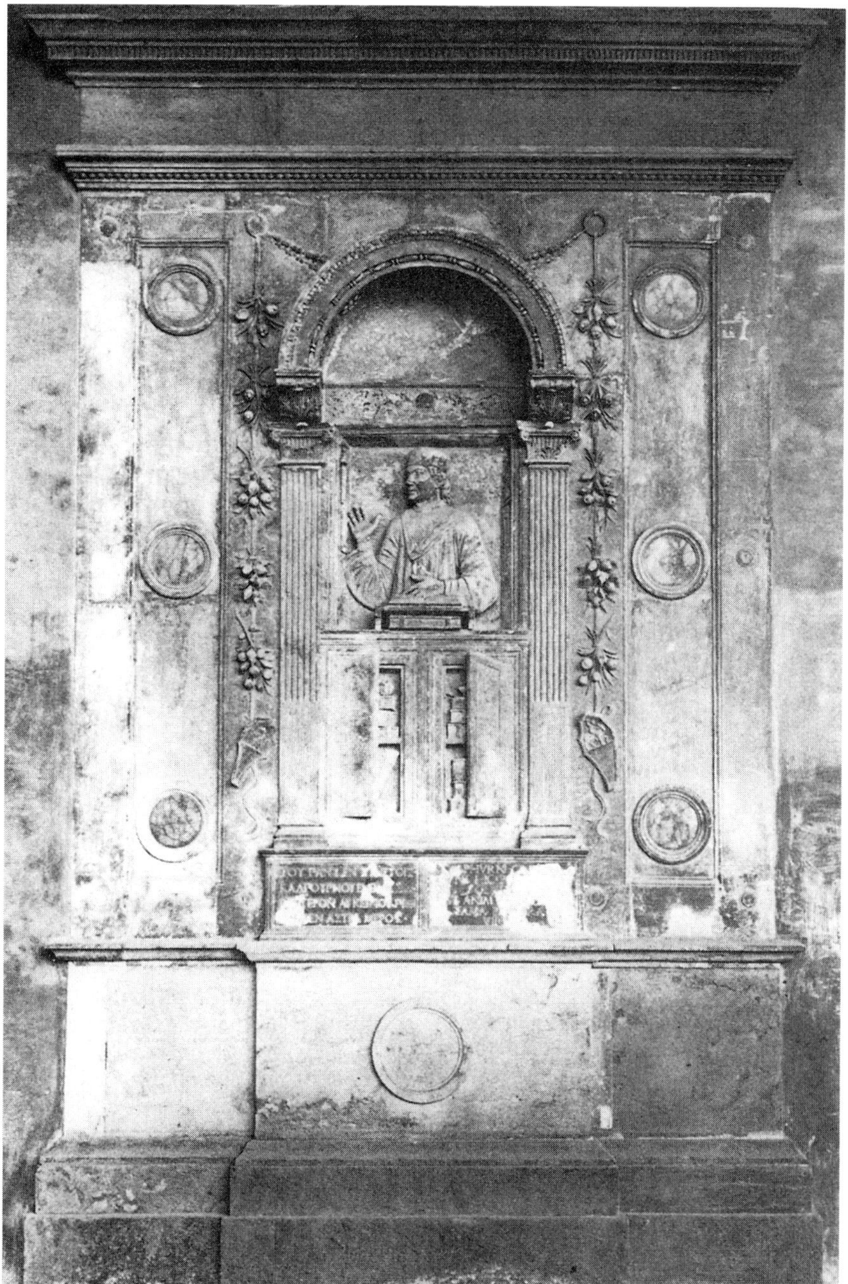

Vainglorious Death:
A Funerary Fracas in
Renaissance Brescia

Cover
Detail of the pavement showing *The Allegory of the Mountain of Virtue*, by Pinturicchio (1454-1513), in the Duomo of Siena, Italy. Reprinted by permission of Scala / Art Resource, NY. See p. 77 (n.75).

Frontispiece
The tomb of the Brescian humanist Giovanni Calfurnio (d. 1503), by Antonio Minelli, in the Chiostro del noviziato, Basilica of St. Antony, Padua. Courtesy of Neri Pozza Editore. See pp. liv–lv.

To the memory of my father,
John Herbert Cullington
(1907-1963)

For
Richard Jones

MEDIEVAL AND RENAISSANCE
TEXTS AND STUDIES

VOLUME 310

Vainglorious Death:
A Funerary Fracas in Renaissance Brescia

Translated and annotated by
J. Donald Cullington

Edited and introduced by
Stephen Bowd

ACMRS
(Arizona Center for Medieval and Renaissance Studies)
Tempe, Arizona
2006

© Copyright 2006
Arizona Board of Regents for Arizona State University

Library of Congress Cataloging-in-Publication Data

Vainglorious death : a funerary fracas in Renaissance Brescia / translated and annotated by J. Donald Cullington ; edited and introduced by Stephen Bowd.
    p. cm. -- (Medieval and Renaissance texts and studies ; v. 310)
    Includes bibliographical references.
    ISBN-13: 978-0-86698-355-6 (alk. paper)
    ISBN-10: 0-86698-355-4 (alk. paper)
    1. Funeral rites and ceremonies--Italy--Brescia--History. 2. Renaissance--Italy--Brescia. 3. Brescia (Italy)--Social life and customs. I. Cullington, J. Donald. II. Bowd, Stephen D. III. Series: Medieval & Renaissance Texts & Studies (Series) ; v. 310.

GT3252.B74 V35 2006
393.0945'26--dc22

2006007477

∞
This book is made to last.
It is set in Adobe Jenson Pro,
smyth-sewn and printed on acid-free paper
to library specifications.
Printed in the United States of America

Contents

Acknowledgments	ix
Abbreviations and Textual Notes	xi
Introduction	xiii
I. Renaissance Brescia	xiv
II. The Dispute	xxvii
III. Elia Capriolo: Author of the *Defensio?*	xxxv
IV. Carlo Valgulio	xl
V. Solidarity between the Living and the Dead	xlvi
VI. Christian Humanism	lii
VII. Sumptuary Legislation and Civic Puritanism	lviii
VIII. Conclusion	lxvi
IX. Note on the Texts	lxix

The Texts

Anonymous [Elia Capriolo?]   1

Defensio statuti Brixianorum de ambitione et sumptibus funerum minuendis

A defense of the Brescians' statute for reducing the rivalry and the expenses of funerals

Carlo Valgulio 89

Statutum Brixianorum de sumptibus funerum optima ratione nullum facere discrimen fortunae inter cives, nec esse honores qui vulgo putantur

That the Brescians' statute about funeral expenditure with perfect logic makes no distinction of rank among citizens, and that what are commonly regarded as honors are not so

Appendix 1 145

Generalis rubrica de funeribus mortuorum

General regulation for funerals of the dead

Appendix 2 153

Quaestio an infrascripta statuta super mortuariis sint contra ecclesiasticam libertatem

An enquiry as to whether the statutes about death disbursements quoted below go against church freedom

Index 225

Acknowledgments

My warmest thanks must be to Stephen Bowd: without his expert guidance and keen involvement this project would never have come to fruition. I am also very grateful to the staff of the British Library, and to the librarians of Queen's University Belfast and my own University of Ulster, for access to the required literary sources, and to Leofranc Holford-Strevens and Vivian Nutton for help in tracing those sources.

JDC

Above all, I am extremely grateful to Donald Cullington for generously bringing these texts to my attention in the first place and for agreeing to work on this project. In particular, I would like to thank him for his significant contribution to the introduction and for his erudite and enlightening textual notes.

The British Academy generously awarded me a research grant in 2003, which allowed me to spend time in Brescia and Venice. My sabbatical leave during 2004–5 was supported by the Manchester European Research Institute, Manchester Metropolitan University, and by my department.

For their advice on a wide range of matters I would like to thank Dr Tricia Allerston, Dott. Ennio Ferraglio, Emeritus Professor Anthony Honoré, Professor Peter Humfrey, Dr. Catherine Kovesi Killerby, Dr. Gabriele Neher, Professor Sharon T. Strocchia, and Professor Nicholas Terpstra. Professor Robert Bjork and Roy Rukkila provided unstinting advice and patient encouragement and they have immeasurably eased the path to publication. I am also grateful to Dr. Leslie MacCoull and the anonymous readers for their very helpful and insightful comments and suggestions.

SDB

Abbreviations

ASB	Archivio di Stato, Brescia
ASC	Archivio Storico Civico
ASV	Archivio di Stato, Venice
BL	British Library, London
CIC	*Corpus iuris canonici*, ed. E. L. Richter and E. Friedberg, 2 vols. (Leipzig: Tauchnitz, 1879–1881)
CICv	*Corpus iuris civilis*, 3 vols. (vol. 1, *Institutiones*, ed P. Krueger, and *Digesta*, ed. T. Mommsen and P. Krueger; vol. 2, *Codex Iustinianus*, ed. P. Krueger; vol. 3, *Novellae*, ed. R. Schoell and W. Kroll) (Dublin and Zürich: Weidmann, 1967–1968)
DBI	*Dizionario biografico degli Italiani*, 45 vols. to date (Rome: Istituto della Enciclopedia italiana, 1960–)
DDC	*Dictionnaire de droit canonique*, ed. R. Naz, 7 vols. (Paris: Letouzey et Ané, 1935–1965)
PL	*Patrologiae cursus completus, series latina*, ed. J. P. Migne, 221 vols. (Paris: 1844–1864)
Sanudo	Marino Sanudo, *I Diarii*, 58 vols. (Venice: F. Visentini, 1879–1903)

Textual Notes

Signature numbers in brackets in the text of the introduction refer to the signature numbers of the original editions of either "Capriolo" or Valgulio.

We have used the Modern Form in all Canon Law citations. For a useful guide see James A. Brundage, *Medieval Canon Law* (Harlow: Longman Group Ltd, 1995), Appendix I.

In this edition of "Capriolo's" and Valgulio's funerary treatises, and of the Brescian funeral statute and the Dominican *Quaestio* contained in the two Appendices, the original spellings of the BL copies have usually been retained, except for the 'normalization' (by classical standards) of certain vowels and diphthongs the rather idiosyncratic use of which, by "Capriolo" in particular (eg., *predae* for *praedae*; *quaeritur* for *queritur*; *praecor* for *precor*), might otherwise cause confusion. Any major emendations have been individually noted. Capitalization and punctuation have been modernized throughout. All italics and quotation marks are editorial. Where other non-classical Latin texts are cited or quoted, the original spelling has not been changed.

Biblical quotations in Latin are taken from the Vulgate.

Introduction

An honorable death needs no funereal pomp, no pallbearers, no escutcheons draped in purple, no turned-down shields and swords, with the whole family weeping for the master, the sobbing wife, and mourning children; nor one with bowed head and clad in black before the hearse, wetting his face with copious tears, nor, last, the orator to eulogize the loved one; no gilded busts of a rich tomb, no titles of the deceased engraved in marble to last until those latter days when death will rend even the stones! But it needs virtue; and the good name of a deserving man, which dominates, without cheap popularity, by its own eminence, not by the rash, blind favor of the people, earned by serious exploits and clean living, active defense of truth and justice, if needed, unto death; and a mind, unafraid and unbending, even under threat of death; and generous confidence.

— Petrarch, *De Remediis* (1366), 2. 122

People will think that many of you would have spent a great deal of money on funeral ceremonies if the law had not prevented it, though in fact their expenditure would have been small and scanty even if no obstacle to free spending had existed. But, I ask, does twenty-four seems to you a small number of priests, this being the maximum number the statute permits each person to bring as a funeral escort? And however small the number of ornamental crosses allowed, a large quantity is excluded in order to prevent the fracture of many bearers' shoulders. To my mind, if the decree errs in anything, it errs in permitting a number of priests and ornamental crosses: one priest and one cross represent and symbolize many. For whether the words prescribed by the Church to be said at burials are said by one

priest or by several, they have the same force, just as with the person who mediates the sacrament of new birth (baptism, that is) and other sacraments: one person mediating them correctly gives as much satisfaction as if a thousand did so, for what matters is numen, not number.

— Carlo Valgulio, *That the Brescians' statute about funeral expenditure with perfect logic makes no distinction of rank among citizens, and that what are commonly regarded as honors are not so* (1509), sig. Avir

In the same company [of foolish Christians] belong those who lay down such precise instructions in their lifetime for the funeral ceremonies they want that they even list in detail the number of candles, black cloaks, singers, and hired mourners they wish to be there as if it were possible for some awareness of this spectacle to return to them, or the dead would be ashamed if their corpses didn't have a splendid burial. They might be newly elected officials planning a public show or banquet, such is their zeal.

— Erasmus, *Praise of Folly* (1511)

Marcolphus: Which man's death seemed more Christian?
Phaedrus: To me, George's seemed more crowned with honor.
Marcolphus: Does even death have its vainglory?

— Erasmus, *The Funeral* (1526)

I. Renaissance Brescia

At the beginning of the sixteenth century the prominent Brescian humanist Carlo Valgulio (ca. 1434–1517) and an anonymous writer, sometimes identified with another local humanist, Elia Capriolo (d. ca. 1523), wrote in defense of a statute which was proposed and enacted so as to avoid the "ruinous costs and useless customs" of many funerals. This statute laid down rules for the use of mourning clothes, regulated

the number of clergy, candles, crosses, and masses for the dead, and also prohibited public displays of grief. The statute might have remained an object of purely local historical interest were it not for the fact that the conventual Dominicans of San Domenico in Brescia, who often attended these funerals, complained about the statute and argued that it infringed ecclesiastical liberty.[1] In turn, the humanists replied with skillful treatises that rose above the narrow confines of a local fracas to address much broader political and philosophical questions. Their pamphlets, which are published in translation here for the first time, demonstrate that in Renaissance Brescia, as in other Italian cities, the funeral was not simply an occasion for easing the passage of the soul with intercessory gestures and expressions of grief but was also a public ritual designed to reflect prevalent civic mores and to reinforce the social status and solidarity of the corpse's family. Funerals offered noble or ruling families the opportunity to enhance their prestige through the richness of their mourning clothes or palls, and through the numbers of mourners who were hired to attend. In the same way, costly and showy funerals allowed parvenus the chance to secure a place for themselves among the social elite and to buy "social respectability."[2]

The rituals of death and burial have always carried meaning in human society, and they were of great significance in early modern Europe.

---

[1] Some of the rubrics in question are printed in the Dominican attack on the statute: *Qu[a]estio an infrascripta statuta super mortuariis sint contra ecclesiasticam libertatem* (Ex conventu S. Dominici Brixie Angelo Britannico Impressore, April 1506), sig. av. They are provided in their entirety in the report of an episcopal commission in July 1507: ASB, ASC 1528, fol. 134r–v. Finally, they appear with minor variations in *Statuta Brixie* (n. p., n. d., but Brescia, 1508). We have also seen the identical rubrics of 1535 and 1621. The former is reprinted from a 1535 edition of *Nonnulla statuta reformata et quaedam de novo condita*, incorporated in the *Reformationes statutorum magnificae civitatis Brixiae* (Brescia, 1621), sig. aviir–v. The statute is printed and translated below, in Appendix 1. The text of the *Quaestio*, with an annotated translation, is found below, in Appendix 2. A fuller account of the dispute is provided below, Section II.

[2] Sharon T. Strocchia, "Death Rites and the Ritual Family in Renaissance Florence," in *Life and Death in Fifteenth-Century Florence*, ed. Marcel Tetel, Ronald G. Witt, and Rona Goffen (Durham, NC: Duke University Press, 1989), 120–45, here 121. See also eadem, *Death and Ritual in Renaissance Florence* (Baltimore and London: Johns Hopkins University Press, 1992), passim.

As many historians have noted, a flourishing genre of *ars moriendi* literature testifies to acute concerns about the final stages of death, when the soul of the dying man or woman would be subject to demonic attacks.[3] The funeral procession that followed was not given the same attention by writers, but there is some evidence, which the works printed here significantly supplement, that these processions changed over the course of the Middle Ages. Before 1350 the funeral procession was "an unobtrusive and secular act in which the honouring of the deceased prevailed over the expression of regret."[4] However, by the late Middle Ages the small group of relatives and friends escorting the body to its place of burial had swollen to "a solemn ecclesiastical procession" comprising priests, monks, the poor, orphaned children, and members of the four mendicant orders: Carmelites, Augustinians, Franciscans, and Dominicans.[5] This elaboration of funerary procedures, including ostentatious displays of grief and costly garments, was a target for disapproving moralists and legislators who frequently tried, as in Brescia in 1505, to limit expenditure on funerals.

The Brescian proposal of 1505 was not a novelty — it appears that an almost identical statute had been enacted in 1473, but remained a dead letter — and like its predecessor its origins lie in the fear that an inflation of funerary expenditure could ruin many Brescians.[6] This inflation in donations and other expenditure was caused by three local factors: a sharp peak in mortality linked to an epidemic of "mazzucho" or "mal di mazucho" flu; the ambition and competitiveness of Brescians; and the greed of the mendicant orders, especially the Dominicans. The "mortuaries" or "death disbursements" made by the testator and his or her family towards the cost of a funeral were vital to provide for prayers and other forms of intercession in order to reduce the time spent in purgatory, and they formed a key part of the income of the poor, of confraternities, and of

---

[3] Michel Vovelle, *La mort et l'occident de 1300 à nos jours* (Paris: Gallimard, 1983), 142–46.

[4] Philippe Ariès, *The Hour of our Death*, trans. H. Weaver (Harmondsworth: Penguin, 1981), 165.

[5] Ariès, *The Hour of our Death*, 165.

[6] See the rubrics printed in *Statuta communis Brixie* (Brescia, 29 June 1473), fols. 8r–9r; and *Leges brixianae* (Brescia, 8 December 1490), sig. aviir–v.

mendicant orders such as the Dominicans and Franciscans. Originally these orders had forbidden the common ownership of property, and members relied upon begging or work for their living. However, by the end of the Middle Ages they had grown rich on the basis of numerous legacies.[7] This disparity between mendicant ideals of poverty and the reality of Dominican or Franciscan wealth was widely resented and it prompted a 'spiritual' or 'observant' mendicant movement which rejected the possession of property or inheritances. Many felt that the 'conventual' Dominicans were too worldly and no longer interested in receiving charity but rather in exacting fees for their services at funerals as mourners or torchbearers. This resentment, possibly coupled with a sense that the duty that the living were expected to pay towards the dead could prove burdensome, finally exploded in Brescia into a bitter and heated dispute focused on sumptuary legislation.

Valgulio and the anonymous author accuse the Dominicans of demanding a "fee" for their services at funerals rather than humbly accepting alms that are freely given. In turn, the Dominicans argue that the statute interferes with the Christian duty to make intercessions for the dead, and therefore threatens their souls. Stung by such Dominican greed and pride, and alarmed by the competitiveness between laypeople, the humanist pamphlets are full of moral censure and hostility towards excessive or false outward displays of piety and wealth. Valgulio and the anonymous author portray themselves as Brescian patriots who wish to strengthen the bonds of civil society and prevent the corrosive spread of vice, avarice, and ambition. While their hope for the purification and renewal of society is based on medieval traditions, notably Augustinianism and the preaching of the spiritual Franciscans (who are praised in the pamphlets), their outlook is also infused with a distinctly humanist emphasis on private and public virtues married to faith in the service of the Ciceronian *res publica*. While the Dominicans have encouraged laypeople to concentrate on externals only, Valgulio and his fellow writer

---

[7] As the anonymous author puts it: "But according to popular rumor you own farms, houses, and many other articles of property. You reap abundant supplies each year and take a share of harvests, vintages, and everything, the fruit and produce belonging to everybody in the abundant territory of Brescia" (*Defense*, sig. Aiiv).

want the Brescians to return to true inner virtue. Valgulio explains why this is so important: "we are striving for moderation, integrity, virtue, and fairness — the sources of true honor and of public and private welfare, and the bonds of civil association and fellowship" (*Statute*, sig. Ar).

Civic concerns of a similar nature prompted the Brescian council to act, and the arguments the two writers made were clearly molded by local conditions, particularly by the tensions and contradictions within the body politic of Brescia itself. Prior to 1426 Brescia was under the rule of dominant local dynasties (who were keen to exploit the Bresciano's rich natural resources and strategic location) such as the Torriani (1266–1290), the della Scala (1332–1337), the Visconti (1337–1403), Pandolfo Malatesta (1403–1404), and Filippo Maria Visconti (1421–1426). However, after the conquest of 1426, Venice imposed a fairly light governing hand on Brescia, and the republican city-state's custom of preserving, and even strengthening, local autonomy stood in contrast with previous signorial restrictions imposed on local autonomy in order to enhance the powers of the feudal lord or duke. Two rectors — a *podestà* (in charge of civil and judicial matters) and a *capitano* (in control of military affairs and finance) — were appointed by Venice, and the republic ensured that the fortifications of this key frontier outpost were repaired after conquest. Major policy decisions, such as the forging of alliances with other states, or the level of taxes and the ways in which fiscal income was employed, rested with Venice, and particularly with the Council of Ten.[8] As a result, there was some Brescian resentment at the amount of taxes collected by the capital, which regarded the city as one of its most lucrative *terraferma* assets.[9] Moreover, Francesco Bragadin, the Venetian-appointed *podestà*

---

[8] Joanne M. Ferraro, *Family and Public Life in Brescia, 1580–1650: The Foundations of Power in the Venetian State* (Cambridge: Cambridge University Press, 1993), chaps. 1–2.

[9] In 1483 the Venetian Marino Sanudo noted that Brescia "in questo tempo, zoè del 1440 in qua, che vene soto el Dominio Veneto, è in mirabile cressimento et opulentia." He also noted that Brescia "è fornida di fontane, campane, et putane"!: *Itinerario di Marin Sanuto per la terraferma veneziana nell'anno MCCCCLXXXIII* (Padua: Dalla Tipografia del Seminario, 1847), 70, 73. In 1504 the Venetian *capi*, or heads, of the Council of Ten asserted that Brescia, above all other cities of the Venetian *terraferma*, "è meglio fornita" with grain: ASV, Capi del Consiglio di Dieci, Lettere, filza 4bis, no.

Introduction xix

in Brescia during 1504 and 1505, was the prime mover behind the statute according to the anonymous author (*Defense*, sigs. Aiiiv–Aivr).[10] In general, though, there is little evidence that Venice attempted to 'centralize' its growing mainland empire, especially the outlying *Bresciano*, *Bergamasco*, or *Trentino* areas, during the fifteenth century, and one historian has noted that the survival of the mainland state must owe a great deal to Venetian diplomatic skill and the autonomy and flexibility of regional government. As John Law says of the roles of the *podestà* and *capitano*: "The aim of their detailed and steadily elaborated commissions was to achieve honest, conscientious but detached government."[11] However, such governance could be hampered by a lack of local knowledge and conflicting legal advice, or even by a clash of values between landholding elites and the commercial class of Venice, and therefore it is possible that the dispute over funerals may have ignited grudges against Venetian interference, and the positions taken by opposing sides may have settled along well-established political or social fault-lines.[12]

Membership of the communal government or council which proposed the statute was closed to Venetian citizens, but under Venetian rule the social range of Brescians who took part in government was initially broadened as those who had participated in the defense of the city against an attack by the Milanese in 1440 were made eligible for membership, while

---

449. The *capitano* of Brescia in 1506 reported that the city was "richissima terra et fidelissima, *maxime* il populo": summary of Marin Zorzi's report given by Alvise Emo on 13 December 1506 in Sanudo, *Diarii*, 6: 508 (all references are to vols. and cols.).

[10] Bragadin was widely praised for his learning: see A. Ventura, "Bragadin, Francesco," *DBI*, 13: 672–74; Elia Capriolo, *Chronica de rebus brixianorum* (Brescia, n. d., but 1505), colophon: "Opus Brixiae diligenter impressum per Arundum de *l* rundis hortatu et auspitio clarissimi D. D. Francisci Bragadini urbis et agri praetoris iusticia pietate et sapientia integerrimi"; and Pietro Bembo to Bragadin, Venice, 1 March 1505, in Pietro Bembo, *Lettere*, ed. E. Travi, 4 vols. (Bologna: Commissione per i testi di lingua, 1987–1993), 1: 187.

[11] John E. Law, "The Venetian Mainland State in the Fifteenth Century," *Transactions of the Royal Historical Society*, 6th ser., 2 (1992): 153–74, here 171.

[12] On the potential for a conflict of maritime or commercial and *terraferma* cultures see Michael Mallett, "La Conquista della Terraferma," in *Storia di Venezia*, IV. *Il Rinascimento: Politica e cultura*, ed. Alberto Tenenti and Ugo Tucci (Rome: Istituto della enciclopedia Italiana, 1996), 181–244, here 214.

others from less ancient families were admitted on the basis of residency, tax and age requirements. However, after 1473 the council moved to tighten up the rules for admission and in 1488 it was, like similar bodies in Venice and Verona, effectively 'closed' to all but those men who came from the oldest families and who met the stringent criteria concerning *civilitas* or legitimacy, lifestyle, and reputation. Thus by the beginning of the sixteenth century the Brescian council was well on the way to completing a process of self-definition as an exclusive governing class with an aristocratic consciousness which mirrors contemporary Venetian developments.[13] An analysis of the applications and admissions for *civilitas* between 1480 and 1508 suggests that they peaked in 1486 and declined thereafter. The pattern of admissions after 1488 indicates that royal, noble, or ecclesiastical sponsorship was a key factor in the process, although a few doctors and teachers, probably considered useful to the city, were admitted without such support. By the middle of the sixteenth century, as one observer of this process has remarked: "There was absolute disdain for applicants associated with commerce or industry."[14]

At a time when the local governing elite was closing ranks against the 'new men' the pamphlets reveal an intersection between fears about the inflation of funeral expenditure and tensions between the factions, 'congeries', or social and religious minorities that made up the commune. For instance, the pretensions of money-grubbing men 'in trade' come in for haughty criticism: Valgulio makes some barbed comments in his pamphlet about honored tax-farmers, "castrators", traitors, and dentists.[15] Brescians, like their Venetian rulers, and indeed most Europeans, would have regarded birth rather than occupation as the basis for

---

[13] Stanley Chojnacki, "Identity and Ideology in Renaissance Venice," in *Venice Reconsidered: The History and Civilization of an Italian City-State, 1297–1797*, ed. John Martin and Dennis Romano (Baltimore and London: Johns Hopkins University Press, 2000), 263–94.

[14] Figures based on an analysis of ASB, ASC 507–521. Quotation in Ferraro, *Family and Public Life*, 61. As Ferraro notes, "The *Accuse date a patrizi di meccanica* (1551–1569) are the oldest such documents in the [Venetian] Terraferma regarding the exclusion of *meccanici* from the [Brescian] council": *Family and Public Life*, 62.

[15] *Statute*, sig. Av^r. Similarly, "meccanici", bakers, artisans, and textile workers awarded knighthoods were attacked in the *trecento* by Franco Sacchetti, *Il Trecentonovelle*, ed. Antonio Lanza (Florence: Sansoni editore, 1984), novella 153, 325–27.

Introduction xxi

virtue, which all philosophers agreed was the best qualification to rule. Venetians prided themselves on the stability of their republic which was governed by a closed aristocratic oligarchy, and they contrasted their happy state with the sink of revolutionary Florence where, as one Venetian ambassador noted scathingly: "the first [among them] who govern the state go to their silk workshops, and throwing their cloaks over their shoulders, and plunging in up to their ankles they work for all of the world to see."[16] These pamphlets are therefore another indication of the ruling elite's resentment towards tradesmen and 'unworthy' social climbers who had been admitted to the council during the fifteenth century but who were increasingly marginalized or excluded by changes to the statutes and council provisions at the turn of the century.[17]

The city was also divided along ancient Guelf and Ghibelline lines. As Niccolò Machiavelli notes in book 20 of *The Prince*: "Although they [the Venetians] never allowed bloodshed, yet they fostered these discords [between Guelfs and Ghibellines in their subject cities] so that the citizens, taken up with their own dissensions, might never combine against them." As in Machiavelli's Florence, it seems that Ghibelline families in Brescia, who were associated with the ousted Visconti regime, were largely excluded from holding public office until the middle of the fifteenth century.[18] Valgulio was a prominent member of an elite

---

[16] "Primi che governano lo stato vanno alle loro botteghe di seta, e gittati li lembi del mantello sopra le spalle, pongonsi alla caviglia e lavorano pubblicamente che ognuno li vede": Ambassador Marco Foscari's 1527 *relazione* to the Venetian senate in E. Albèri, ed., *Relazioni degli ambasciatori veneti al Senato*, 15 vols. (Florence: Società editrice fiorentina, 1839–1863), 2nd ser., 1: 21.

[17] The Veronese orators in Venice successfully contested the grant of citizenship made by the Great Council of Venice to a barber in 1459. See James S. Grubb, "Alla ricerca delle prerogative locali: la cittadinanza a Vicenza, 1404–1509," in *Dentro lo "Stado Italico". Venezia e la Terraferma fra Quattro e Seicento*, ed. G. Cracco and M. Knapton (Trent: Gruppo Culturale Civis, 1984), 24–25. However, Grubb concludes in general that: "Fu l'accomodamento, non il conflitto, a caraterizzare i rapporti fra Venezia e Vicenza in materia di cittadinanza locale," (26).

[18] N. Machiavelli, *The Prince*, trans. George Bull (Harmondsworth: Penguin, 1961), 67. Ghibellines were excluded from office in fourteenth-century Florence, and the political monopoly and social power of the Parte Guelfa was theoretically maintained in the city up until the middle of the fifteenth century. See Alison Brown, "The Guelf

Guelf family, and it may be surmised that his disdain for honored "traitors" must refer to the admittance of Ghibellines into the council despite their association with the Visconti, who besieged the city between 1438 and 1440. Venice had certainly encouraged the participation of Ghibellines in Brescian government, and it may be possible here and elsewhere to read the pamphlets in terms of the tensions created by the clash between Brescian interests and entrenched local particularism, and the priorities of the Venetian government.[19]

The final significant fault-line revealed by the pamphlets is religious: the anonymous author criticizes the Brescian Jews, who were supposedly expelled from the city in the fifteenth century, for lending money to Christians in order to pay for their elaborate funerals. Franciscan preachers who visited the city during the fifteenth century argued that the moral rearmament of Brescia required the expulsion of the Jews, a matter that the council considered comparable to the liberation of the city from the tyranny of the Visconti dukes of Milan.[20] Christians who ran up debts in Brescia to pay for the funerals of their relatives may have had to borrow from the Jewish banks, which had been established in

---

Party in Fifteenth-Century Florence: The Transition from Communal to Medicean State," in eadem, *The Medici in Florence: The Exercise and Language of Power* (Florence and Perth: Leo S. Olschki Editore and University of Western Australia Press, 1992), 103–50. The importance of 'middling' or 'new' men in a fifteenth-century city is explored by eadem, "Lorenzo de' Medici's New Men and their Mores: The Changing Lifestyle of Quattrocento Florence," *Renaissance Studies* 16 (2002): 113–42.

[19] Venice took advantage of the dissensions between the Guelfs and Ghibellines to secure its position in the Valtellina in the *quattrocento*. See Michael Knapton, "Per la storia del dominio veneziano nel Trentino durante il '400: l'annessione e l'inquadramento politico-istituzionale," in Cracco and Knapton, *Dentro lo "Stado Italico"*, 188.

[20] Council provision of 18 April 1494 printed in Agostino Zanelli, "Predicatori a Brescia nel quattrocento," *Archivio storico lombardo*, 3rd ser., 15 (1901): 83–144, 143. Interestingly, in 1503 the special council unanimously approved a contribution to the dowry of Zentilina, a converted Jew. See the *registro* of the *provvisioni del consiglio cittadino* in ASB, ASC 519, fol. 35r–v (27 July 1503, second foliation). Note that the foliation of the *registri* at this period begins on the appointment of each Venetian *podestà*, and since each of the *registri* covers all or part of two calendar years a single volume may contain two or even three different foliations. Occasionally, a modern pencil foliation has been added. We therefore indicate these foliations here and in some cases the original and contemporaneously corrected versions.

Introduction xxiii

the city or its environs by 1463. In order to combat the Jewish hold over the poor (and also in reaction to the perceived threat to Christians from the Jews, who were accused of murder and well-poisoning at this time),[21] alternative banks or *monti* which lent money to Christians at no interest were set up in Italy during the latter half of the fifteenth century. The second *monte di pietà* in northern Italy was established in Brescia in 1489, and over the next few years the city made various attempts to expel its Jews.[22]

In practice, the *monte* proved to be an ineffective alternative to Jewish moneylenders, and the Jews continued to find a living in or around the city. While applicants to the Christian *monte* were obliged to provide proof of their poverty, and were not permitted to cash written bonds, the Jews not only offered a relatively low rate of interest but also imposed fewer restrictions on the borrower than the *monte*, and they accepted both pledges and written bonds. However, in this atmosphere of official anti-semitism, making charitable donations in support of the *monte* was a praiseworthy act. The Franciscan preacher Bernardino da Feltre told the Brescians that such gifts allowed the donor to perform the seven acts of mercy, and they were therefore true alms of the sort praised by the pamphleteers. Dominicans such as Tommaso Vio (Cajetan) questioned the fees that *monte* officals charged, likening them to usurious exactions, and Dominican resentment towards these Franciscan-inspired

---

[21] The torture, execution, or expulsion of the Jewish community in Trent for the alleged ritual murder of a young boy called Simon took place in 1475, and news of this event reached Brescia directly by a letter (quickly published) from the Brescian doctor and prominent council member who examined the body. Moreover, the cult of 'St.' Simon was particularly popular in the Bresciano, and Capriolo himself comments on a miraculous weeping image of Simon at the church of Santa Maria del Carmine in Brescia (where Capriolo would later be buried), which prompted his sister to bear triplets. See R. Po-Chia Hsia, *Trent 1475: Stories of a Ritual Murder Trial* (New Haven: Yale University Press, 1992), esp. 33, 53–57; D. Rigaux, "Antijudaïsme par l'image: l'iconographie de Simon de Trente (+ 1475) dans la région de Brescia," in *Politique et religion dans le judaïsme ancien et médiéval*, ed. D. Tollet (Paris: Desclée, 1989), 309–18; and Capriolo, *Chronica*, fol. LXXIXv.

[22] For example, ASB, ASC 509, fol. 79r (23 June 1486, second foliation); ASB, ASC 511, fol. 58r (4 June 1490, second foliation), "Iudei expellantur de civitate"; ASB, ASC 521, fol. 49r (6 December 1507, second foliation).

institutions may also be a reason why the anonymous author writes in praise of them.[23]

The pamphlets also serve as a reminder that despite (or perhaps because of) Venetian political dominance over the city during the previous eighty years, Brescian cultural life was vibrant and independent, fueled by a booming economy and supported by a flourishing publishing industry.[24] The scope for humanist endeavor and artistic patronage expanded during the fifteenth century when the city became part of the economic and political empire of Venice. However, just as political and economic dominance of Brescia by Venice was not absolute, so the cultural life of the city was characterized by a partnership of Venetian and Brescian traditions. For example, the commune undertook an extensive remodeling of the city fabric in imitation of Venetian styles and structures (the Brescian *Torre d'orologio* was modeled on a gateway standing by the basilica of San Marco in Venice), but the urban space was also shaped by native

---

[23] Brian Pullan, *Rich and Poor in Renaissance Venice: The Social Institutions of a Catholic State, to 1620* (Oxford: Basil Blackwell, 1971), 445, 459, 460, 464–65, 467–68, 474. On the Franciscans and the establishment of the *monti* see generally Vittorino Meneghin, *Bernardino da Feltre e i monti di pietà* (Vicenza: L.I.E.F. edizioni, 1974); Carol Bresnahan Menning, *Charity and State in Late Renaissance Italy: The Monte di Pietà of Florence* (Ithaca and London: Cornell University Press, 1993), chap. 1; and Renata Segrè, "I monti di pietà e i banchi ebraici," *Rivista storica italiana* 90 (1978): 818–33. On Brescia, see Zanelli, "Predicatori," 119–28.

[24] There is a succinct introduction to the geographical, economic, political, and social setting of Brescia in Ferraro, *Family and Public Life*, chaps. 1–2. See also eadem, "Economy and Society in Brescia during the Venetian Domination, 1426–1645" (Ph.D. diss., University of California, Los Angeles, 1983). On Renaissance Brescia see the contributions to *Storia di Brescia. Vol. II: La dominazione veneta (1426–1575)* (Brescia: Morcelliana Editrice, 1963), part 3; and for a more detailed examination of the political and cultural context, see Gabriele Neher, "Moretto and Romanino: Religious Painting in Brescia 1510–1550. Identity in the Shadow of *La Serenissima*" (Ph.D. diss., University of Warwick, 2000). The nature of relations between Venice and its mainland possessions is sketched by Gaetano Cozzi, "Ambiente veneziano, ambiente veneto. Governanti e governati di qua dal Mincio nei secoli XV–XVIII," in *Storia della cultura veneta. Vol. IV/2: Il Seicento* (Vicenza: Neri Pozza, 1984), 495–539. Also useful are the reports of the Venetian rectors in Brescia. These date from 1520 and can be found in *Relazioni dei rettori veneti in Terraferma*, vol. 11, *Brescia* (Milan: A. Giuffré, 1978).

Introduction xxv

Roman traditions and forms distinct from those of Venice: for example, recovered Roman inscriptions were incorporated into some of the prominent new buildings such as the offices of the *monte di pietà*.

The artistic and architectural fabric of the city was also affected by a strong and localized sense of civic piety and sacrality: the city's patron saints, Faustino and Giovità, were credited with having protected Brescia when the Visconti attempted to recapture the city in 1438, and they were given greater iconographic prominence thereafter. The church of the *miracoli* was begun in 1488, and the churches of San Nazaro, San Lorenzo, and Santa Agata were all remodeled after ca. 1470 and received frequent financial support from the council. The foundation of the city hospital and the *monte di pietà* can also be read as exemplifying Brescian pride and pious intent, and it is worth noting that in this matter religion and government, Venice and Brescia, worked hand in hand: the commune paid for the officers who administered the *monte*, and the Venetian-appointed archbishop of Brescia laid the foundation stone of the new hospital in 1447.[25]

Although never as important a center of humanism as its distinguished neighbors Padua and Venice, fifteenth-century Brescia was nevertheless home to a number of classical scholars such as Gabriele Concoreggio, Giovanni Calfurnio, Giovanni Taverio di Rovato, Marino Becichemo, Ubertino Posculo, and Giovanni Britannico who were in touch with humanists elsewhere. For example, there is a letter from Valgulio to Angelo Poliziano,[26] and letters to Valgulio from Marsilio Ficino[27] and Becichemo.[28] Soon after the Venetian conquest the commune of Brescia began to import teachers of grammar and logic to educate and instruct

---

[25] The anonymous writer praises the hospital and *monte* (*Defense*, sigs. Aiiiv, Avr). See Zanelli, "Predicatori," 102.

[26] This letter was written in Arezzo on 18 March 1475, and describes a rather disappointing visit to ancient ruins in the area: Andrea Valentini, *Carlo Valgulio, letterato bresciano del XV secolo* (Brescia: Tipografia Ven. A. Luzzago, 1903), 19.

[27] Ficino to Valgulio, 10 December 1476: Marsilio Ficino, *Epistole M. Ficini Florentini* (Venice, 1495), fol. 71r; and idem, *The Letters of Marsilio Ficino*, translated from the Latin by members of the Language Department of the School of Economic Science, 6 vols. (London: Shepheard-Walwyn, 1978–), 2: 38–39.

[28] M. Becichemo, *Centuria epistolicarum quaestionum* (Venice, 1506), fols. 151v–152v.

its young, and in 1432 the council of the commune appointed Tommaso Seneca di Camerino, who had taught rhetoric and poetry at the schools of Bologna and Perugia, to a generously remunerated post as public teacher of rhetoric and grammar.[29] His successor in 1435 was of equal caliber: Concoreggio, a former pupil of Vittorino da Feltre of Mantua, whom he rejoined during the Venice-Milan clash of 1438, only to return to Brescia in 1441 at the request of the *podestà* Francesco Barbaro.[30] Concoreggio's achievement in producing large numbers of learned pupils was posthumously honored in a resolution of the Council in 1490.[31] Moreover, the humanist boarding school founded by Giovanni Olivieri in nearby Chiari served to educate many Brescian sons, including the brothers of the humanist Laura Cereta whose letters circulated in Brescia at the end of the fifteenth century and testify to a thriving world of salons and intellectual discussion in the city.[32]

The commune was especially keen to foster the learning of Greek, and in 1500 Taverio, a leading Hellenist, was appointed to teach this language.[33] His successor in 1503, Becichemo, born at Scutari but educated in Brescia, may well have stayed in his adoptive city until he moved to Padua in 1517: his commentaries on Pliny, Cicero, Vergil, Livy, Fabius, and Persius earned him the renewal of an unusually lucrative contract in 1505.[34] The commune rewarded scholars in other ways too: by giving money to Francesco Arrigoni in 1508 for his *Panegyric of Brescia*, to Giovanni Britannico in 1482 and 1508 for his commentaries on Persius and Juvenal respectively, and to Panfilo Sasso in 1500 for expounding

---

[29] See C. Pasero, "Il dominio veneto fino all'incendio della Loggia (1426–1575)," in *Storia di Brescia*, 2: 38 and n. 2; E. Caccia, "Cultura e letteratura nei secoli XV e XVI," in *Storia di Brescia*, 2: 501.

[30] G. Busetto, "Concoreggio, Gabriele," in *DBI*, 27: 743–46; Pasero, "Il dominio veneto," 38 and n. 3; V. Cremona, "L'Umanesimo bresciano," in *Storia di Brescia*, 2: 568, n. 3; Valentini, *Carlo Valgulio*, 7.

[31] ASB, ASC 512, fol. 160v (25 June 1490, pencil foliation).

[32] Laura Cereta, *Collected Letters of a Renaissance Feminist*, trans. and ed. Diana Robin (Chicago and London: University of Chicago Press, 1997).

[33] Cremona, "L'Umanesimo bresciano," 556–57; M. Agosti, "La tradizione pedagogica fino al settecento," in *Storia di Brescia*, 3: 303–5; Valentini, *Carlo Valgulio*, 7.

[34] C. H. Clough, "Becichemo, Marino," in *DBI*, 7: 511–15; Cremona, "L'Umanesimo bresciano," 557–61.

Dante and Petrarch; by granting citizenship to Taverio and his descendants in 1486; and by striking a gold medal in honor of the precocious theologian Giovanni Battista Molinari.[35]

Valgulio and Capriolo — if he was indeed the author of one of the pamphlets — were descended from ancient noble families of the Bresciano. They were also among the most prominent of the second wave of Brescian humanists, and they composed their squibs against the Dominicans as privileged players in the lively intellectual and political life of Brescia. As we have seen, the commune regarded such humanist efforts in a positive light, for the publication of classical translations or commentaries enhanced the prestige of the city and confirmed the educational and social exclusivity of the ruling elite. The pamphlets that were hammered into shape in the heat of the funerary controversy and arguments with the Dominicans are therefore worth exploring since they reflect some of the preoccupations and assumptions of the government and the ecclesiastical hierarchy appointed by Venice, and they also provide a striking and unusual instance of the way in which humanists could apply their expertise to a pressing social, political, and religious controversy.

II. The Dispute

The origins of the dispute lie in a proposal made by the Brescian special (or inner) council on 28 June 1505 to cut back on superfluous funereal expenses by observing the existing statute restricting expenditure and behavior, and by adding clauses prohibiting anyone dressed as the poor or any members of a religious confraternity (*scola*) apart from that of the deceased from attending the funeral.[36] The anonymous author attributed the origins of the statute to a local social and economic crisis:

---

[35] Valentini, *Carlo Valgulio*, 8.

[36] "Ad resecandas superfluas expensas, que in funeribus Mortuorum in hac civitate fiunt." See above, n. 1, and the *registro* of the *provvisioni del consiglio cittadino*: ASB, ASC 520, fol. 92r (28 June 1505, first foliation) with a clarification and amplification on fol. 108r (26 August 1505, first foliation) asserting that this provision was not for the prohibition of almsgiving but "pro honore commodo et utilitate civitatis et civium nostrorum." Accordingly, members of the council who transgressed would be deprived

> At a time when the Brescian people were beset by two disastrous and deplorable calamities — an unbearably protracted famine, and a fatally virulent fever which no medical treatment could alleviate — and when funerals were so frequent that wherever in the city you looked you could see funerals, grief, and mourning regardless of sex and age, with lamentation partly for the deceased, partly for those almost starved to death: then it was that, exhausted and afflicted by such calamities, people were seized by an inordinate passion for obsequies. With the competition for funerals growing so increasingly heated that some citizens borrowed money at interest from the Jews and ran up huge debts, because of some custom or other — due to rivalry for a supposed honor — large squads of brothers and the other type of clergy were summoned to these obsequies: a breed so uncompromising that amid the tears and groans of the deceased's relatives, and amid people's deaths, they would sometimes fight with each other (*Defense*, sig. Aiir).[37]

He later specifies that the costs of handing alms (or "fees" as he calls them) to the funeral escort of mendicant "brothers" led many people into debt:

---

of membership. The clauses on "scola" and the poor did not make it into the final statute although they were initially approved by nine votes to one. The accounts of the dispute by A. Cassa, *Funerali, pompe e conviti. Escursione nel vecchio archivio municipale* (Brescia: Stab. Unione Tip. Bresciana, 1887), 42–48; Ennio Sandal, "Autonomie municipali e libertà ecclesiastica. Un episodio di intolleranza a Brescia nel primo Cinquecento," *Commentari dell'Ateneo di Brescia* an. 187 (1988): 375–83; and Catherine Kovesi Killerby, *Sumptuary Law in Italy 1200–1500* (Oxford: Clarendon Press, 2002), 107–8 should be supplemented by this archival material and our discussion. A similar dispute in Parma in 1421 is noted in Kovesi Killerby, *Sumptuary Law*, 106–7, and see below, lx.

[37] Compare the quarreling friars depicted by Erasmus, *The Funeral* (*Funus*), in *The Collected Works of Erasmus*, vol. 40, *Colloquies*, trans. and annot. Craig R. Thompson (Toronto, Buffalo, and London: University of Toronto Press, 1997), 763–95, esp. 769–70. This colloquy was translated into English and published in 1534. See *The dyaloge called Funus, A Translation of Erasmus's Colloquy (1534) & A very pleasaunt & fruitful Dialoge called The Epicure. Gerrard's Translation of Erasmus's Colloquy (1545)*, ed. Robert R. Allen (Chicago: University of Chicago Press for the Newberry Library, 1969), 1–49. Given the religious and political events of that year in England it is perhaps significant that this appears to have been the first Erasmian colloquy thus translated. See below, l–li.

Introduction

> That fee was handed over even by unwilling donors, but owing to a sort of respect for the custom no one wanted to be seen as the prime mover in abolishing it — or rather, no one looked to his own interests, lest he seem less honorable or respectable than someone else to whom he considered himself equal or superior, and day by day rivalry, coupled with expenditure, grew so great that many people ran up a huge debt because of funerals. That this is so is proved by the joy and acclamation with which all orders greeted the decree's proclamation (sig. Aivv).

It is not surprising, therefore, that the conventual Dominicans objected to this apparent attack on their "ecclesiastical liberty" and a lucrative source of their income, and they refused absolution to anyone who observed the law. In April 1506 the Dominicans stated their case in a pamphlet entitled: *Inquiry as to whether the statutes about death disbursements quoted below go against church freedom* (*Questio an infrascripta statuta super mortuariis sint contra ecclesiasticam libertatem*).[38] The anonymous pamphleteer notes the initial Dominican reaction with scorn:

> When the decree was published, these brothers, seeing their profit somewhat diminished (as though pigs were to lose some portion of their usual acorns), first began to grunt and grumble,[39] then made common cause with the wise men of the synagogue and compiled a book which they published, the work of many months and of all the brothers of that order who had any reputation among them for learning (*Defense*, sig. Aiir).

The Dominicans also appealed for support to Pope Julius II at the beginning of February 1507.[40] A few days later the pope granted the bishop of

---

[38] The resort to publication was not unprecedented. The Dominicans, like several other orders in the city, occasionally took advantage of the printing press during the last two decades of the fifteenth century to issue spiritual texts. See Antonio Cistellini, "La vita religiosa nel Quattrocento," in *Storia di Brescia*, 2: 435–36.

[39] "[T]hey [i.e. mendicants squabbling over the deathbed] like hogges grunted I wote not wherfore, of the prefermentes of theyr bulles": Erasmus, *The dyaloge called Funus*, 32.

[40] A copy of their letter to the pope, dated 1 February 1507, is in ASB, ASC 1528, fol. 122v (pencil foliation).

Brescia and his vicar-general Marco Saraco powers to investigate the matter.[41] The commune had already responded to the Dominican objections by appointing five "wise and honest citizens" to determine whether the statute infringed ecclesiastical liberty.[42] These five wise men rapidly came to the conclusion that the statute was good and valid and did not infringe ecclesiastical liberty, and they were granted powers to defend it.[43] Consequently, the amended statute was confirmed by substantial majorities of the general council.[44] The episcopal commission, which moved with "pede plumbeo", as the final report put it, took the syndics' decision into account and held meetings with Fra Girolamo, the Dominican representative. Finally, the archbishop confirmed the statute's validity, declaring that it concerned merely funeral ceremony and not spiritual affairs *per se*.[45] Matters should have rested there, but the Dominican appeal to the pope was found to contain words insulting to the archbishop and to the honor and dignity of the city.[46] The prior of San Domenico, Don Agostino

---

[41] This is noted in ASB, ASC 1528, fol. 122v (4 February 1507, pencil foliation). They met on 13 February 1507 and again on 10 June 1507: ASB, ASC 1528, fols. 123v, 133r (pencil foliation).

[42] The proposal is recorded in ASB, ASC 520, fol. 17r (7 April 1506, second foliation), where it is noted: "Tamen quia multi cives nostri dicunt esse conscientiam factam fuisse per nonnullos religiosos asserentes dictum statutum esse contra libertatem ecclesiasticam & recusare velle eos absolvere" therefore learned citizens are to be appointed. The vote was ten in favor of the proposal, and one against. The proposal to appoint "quinque boni Docti Sincerique cives" to ascertain whether the statute is "validum & bonum" and "non contra libertatem ecclesiasticam" was passed by the general council by forty-eight votes to thirty-eight: ASB, ASC 521, fol. 109v [*correxit* 108] (23 February 1507, first foliation). Five men, including "Tristanus de Valgulio", were duly elected: ASB, ASC 521, fols. 113v–114r [*correxit* 112–113] (11 March 1507, first foliation).

[43] ASB, ASC 521, fol. 123r [*correxit* 112] (7 April 1507, first foliation), where the committee's work is praised ("copiosa ac eleganti relatione facta per sp[ecia]les quinque cives nostros"), and approved by seventy-six votes to eight.

[44] ASB, ASC 521, fol. 138r [*correxit* 127] (15 May 1507), where the decision of 28 June 1505 is approved by sixty-six votes to thirty-six, and the decision of 26 August 1505 by sixty-six votes to twenty-two.

[45] ASB, ASC 1528, fols. 132v–135r (21 July 1507, pencil foliation), quotation at fol. 133r.

[46] ASB, ASC 521, fol. 12r–v (3 August 1507, second foliation), where it is noted that the bishop, following apostolic briefs, has recently confirmed the validity of the statute, and also asserted that the Dominican appeal to the pope was made "verbis

Introduction xxxi

de Moris, was therefore ordered to appear before the Venetians, who supported the decision of the syndics, and he was forced to concede in October 1508 that his fraternity and all the other religious orders in the city would conform to the decree in its final form.[47] The special council seems to have aimed a final dig against the Dominicans two weeks later when it agreed that the names of those tonsured or in holy orders who committed crimes, including "diabolical deceptions", or who led immoral or shameful lives, should be entered in a special book.[48]

The *Defense*'s author — whose work bears an episcopal *imprimatur* — may be making an oblique reference to the Dominican appeal and their impolitic insults when he begins his pamphlet with an ironic reference to the "shining example" the Dominicans have set by their writings and actions:

> They have not, however, done this with the idea and intention of laying bare their own diseased minds, which they take exceptionally great care to conceal by every possible device: rather, they did it in order to accuse the city of Brescia, most moderate, economical, and devotedly supportive of true religion as it is, of an impious and despicable crime, to render it hateful to the apostolic see, and to stir up the whole of Christendom against it (*Defense*, sig. Aiir).

Furthermore, he describes the Dominican book containing these insults as being "sent to every nation" (sig. Aivr), and it survives in a rare copy in London.[49] In the *Quaestio*, the anonymous author (or

---

ignominiosis contra honorem & dignitatem" of the archbishop, his vicar-general, and the city. Approved by eighty-seven votes to ten.

[47] The *oblatio* concerning the Dominican friar is in ASB, ASC 1528, fol. 141r (9 October 1508, pencil foliation). The ducal letter of support to the rectors of Brescia dated 9 October 1508 is in ASB, Ospedale, San Domenico, busta 62, filza 12.

[48] ASB, ASC 521, fol. 6r–v (23 October 1508, third foliation). Approved by seven votes to four.

[49] The full text of the *Quaestio* can be found below, in Appendix 2. Dott. Ennio Ferraglio informs us that there are two other copies known to him: one in the Biblioteca Queriniana, Brescia (collocation number: Cinq.DD.10.m.1), and another in the Biblioteca nazionale, Cremona. The copy of the *Quaestio* which is in the former library is bound with a contemporary work: Martino Codagnello, O.P., *Oratio ad serenissimum Venetorum principem Leonardum Lauredanum*. (Venice, 20 August 1504). The implication is that both works are from the same pen. Having exhorted prudence as the best

authors)[50] quotes the clauses of the statute that outline the penalties for the use of more than twenty-four clergy at funerals and place limits on the number of crosses to be carried. The Dominican argues that the statute has been prompted by a desire to "cheat" or "bind" the clergy.[51] In fact, he argues, laypeople do not have power over churches or any right to alienate ecclesiastical property in this way, and he outlines the grounds for the excommunication of anyone who has drafted, supported, or attempted to enforce the statute. The penalties that are imposed by the statute would prevent the employment of the "balm" of almsgiving — one method for laypeople to make some provision for their souls. The statute also bars clergy from receiving the benefit of charity and interferes with their rightful duty to attend funerals. Finally, and perhaps most outrageously, it permits laypeople to judge their superiors and to second-guess the motives of clerics:

> [G]iven that the extravagance which exists in regard to funerals *did* exist, and that it nevertheless existed in regard to spiritual matters or spiritual adjuncts, still laypeople would by no means be able to deal with funerals. Otherwise it would follow that in everything they could be the judges of clergy and of the supreme pontiff, since they could easily interpret everything as evil and extravagant; and they would become judges of secret thoughts which derive from the mind alone.[52]

The Dominican arguments rest on scripture, which encourages and even enjoins almsgiving,[53] and most importantly on canon law and the

---

virtue for rulers in this latter work, Codagnelli draws attention to the vices and faults of the Brescians: "O perditam urbem. O civitatem desolatam. O patriam destitutam. O corda omni inclementia feritate barbarieque consepulta. Quis non mecum Brixiae calamitatem iacturamque deploret?" Sig. biiir. Cf. below, lxiii-lxiv.

[50] The anonymous humanist author mockingly describes the Dominican book as "the work of many months and of all the brothers of that order who had any reputation among them for learning" (*Defense*, sig. Aiir). Cf. above, xxix.

[51] *Quaestio* (sig. divr): "Nam videntes se non posse ligare clericos directe, per indirectum poenam apposuerunt in fraudem."

[52] *Quaestio*, sig. er. For the biblical allusion, see Romans 2:16.

[53] *Quaestio*, sig. biir–v. Vulgate passages cited are Tobit 4: 7, 11, 17; Daniel 4: 24; Luke 7: 12, 11: 41; Hebrews 13: 16; Ecclesiasticus 3: 33; Proverbs 22: 9.

interpretations of an array of eminent medieval canon and civil lawyers such as Panormitanus (Niccolò de' Tudeschis [1386–1445]), Hostiensis (Henricus de Segusio [1190~1200–1271]), and Alberico da Rosciate of Bergamo (ca. 1290–1360). Parts of three papal decretals are fundamental to the Dominican case: Innocent III's decretal *On ordinances*;[54] the final chapter of the decretal issued at the Fourth Lateran Council *On not alienating the Church's property*;[55] and the decretal defining the four ways of releasing the souls of the departed: by the offerings of priests, by the prayers of saints, by the alms of loved ones, or by the fasting of relatives.[56] Around these pronouncements, and the supporting scholastic glosses, the Dominican case revolves.

The anonymous author (or authors) of the *Quaestio* argues that "death disbursements" for a number of clergy, candles, money, and other matters related to funerals are a form of Aristotelian "munificence" (as in *Nicomachean Ethics* 4.2.1–19) and should be made freely by each testator, without the despotic and unlawful interference of the government. He rebuts the argument that the statute prohibits one and not all types of almsgiving by

---

[54] *Quaestio*, sig. aiir: "We note that laypeople — even devout ones — have been given no power over churches and church members, laypeople who still have the obligation to obey, not the authority to command; and any statute which they make on their own initiative and which also impinges on the convenience and favorable treatment of churches has no standing unless it has been approved by the Church...": X 1. 2. 10; *CIC* 2: 12–14.

[55] *Quaestio*, sig. aiir–v: see below, 159–61.

[56] *Quaestio*, sigs. aivv (quoting the second sentence only), biiir (quoting the first sentence only): "Animae defunctorum quatuor modis solvuntur, aut oblationibus sacerdotum, aut precibus sanctorum, aut karorum elemosinis, aut ieiunio cognatorum. Curatio vero funeris, conditio sepulturae, pompa exequiarum, magis sunt vivorum solatia quam subsidia mortuorum. Si aliquid prodest inpio sepultura preciosa, oberit pio vilis aut nulla. Nec ideo tamen contempnenda sunt corpora et abicienda defunctorum, maximeque iustorum. Ubi et illud salubriter discitur, quanta possit esse remuneratio pro elemosinis, quas viventibus et sentientibus exhibemus si neque hoc apud Deum perit, quod examinis hominum membris offitii diligentia persolvitur": C. 13 q. 2 c. 22; *CIC* 1: 728. Translation below, *Quaestio*, n. 9. Much of this discourse derives from Augustine's *De cura pro mortuis gerenda* (*PL* 40. 591–610), written as a reply to Paulinus of Nola, and is taken verbatim from *De Civitate Dei*, 1.12, 13: see D. E. Trout, *Paulinus of Nola* (Berkeley: University of California Press, 1999), 245–47.

affirming that it is nevertheless an infringement of the general principles laid down by divine, papal, and imperial law, and by pointing out that an inferior power can never legislate against a superior such as the Church. The Dominican, following St. Augustine, admits that extravagant funerals do give more comfort to the living than the dead, but such extravagance, which includes the wearing of black mourning clothes, must be distinguished from the things "conducive to the relief of souls" listed in the decretal. Such "solaces for the living" are discountenanced by the church and are not, in any case, the main focus of the Dominican attack.[57]

The Dominican rejection of the funerary statute was probably made with some confidence of success, since the alienation of church property by the laity was clearly proscribed by canon law and the bishop of Brescia himself had rejected the enforcement of a similar statute of 1473.[58] The Dominicans' intemperate language and their decision to use the printing press as a weapon in the war of words may also be indicative of their sense of self-righteous indignation. However, the Dominican excommunication of any Brescian who proposed or implemented the 1505 statute provoked rage among some inhabitants of the city, and the council was forced to take into account this popular reaction. Moreover, the *Quaestio* may have misjudged its intended audience, for it is a typical piece of scholastic commentary, and often punctuated with pomposity. In short, it is just the type of inelegant and unlettered text that angered humanists trained to express their thoughts in the Ciceronian rhetorical tradition.[59] As we have seen, Brescia was home to many humanist scholars, and two of them rose to the defense of the statute and the reputation of the city with considerable style and panache.

---

[57] *Quaestio*, sigs. divv; bivr–v.

[58] There is a 1479 "Scomunica contro gli usurpatori dei beni del convento" in the Dominican archives which may relate to the earlier dispute: ASB, Ospedale, San Domenico, busta 89, filza 57.

[59] The anonymous author condemns St. Thomas Aquinas's "captious syllogisms" (*Defense*, sig. Aiir); and attacks "the hair-splitting of tub-thumpers" (*Defense*, sig. Aiiiv).

III. Elia Capriolo: Author of the *Defensio?*

There is no evidence in the text itself to link the *Defensio* with Capriolo, but its authorship has been assigned to him in recent years: a plausible tradition given Capriolo's known literary style and his wider interests although Valgulio's comment about going into battle "a second time" (*Statute*, sig. Ar) might indicate *his* authorship as do some similarities of argument.[60] Elia Capriolo was born into a noble and pious Brescian family during the first half of the fifteenth century.[61] He studied philosophy and law and undertook a career in the service of the commune until 1508 when he withdrew from political and intellectual life. This action may have been prompted by old age and prolonged by adverse political conditions, for he supported Venice during the occupation of Brescia by the French after 1509, and he was fined after an unsuccessful uprising against their rule in 1512. Capriolo's literary output is limited and mainly notable for his *De confirmatione Christianae fidei* (published in 1497, and reprinted six times in different parts of Europe by 1519), which is largely a defense of the testimony of the four evangelists concerning the divinity of Christ; and his *Chronica de rebus brixianorum* (published in ca. 1505 and reprinted in Italian in 1585, 1630, and 1744), which is an annalistic production punctuated by outbursts of moral outrage.

The pamphlet on the funerary dispute is undated, but the author claims that it was written in four days, probably at the height of the fracas in 1506, for it is an ironic, mocking, and occasionally rambling rebuttal of the Dominicans' specific arguments. After an introduction, in which the author describes the miseries endured by the Brescians and sets the tone of high moral outrage at their mistreatment by the Dominicans, the

---

[60] The attribution is made by M. Giansante, "Capriolo, Elia," *DBI*, 19: 219, and repeated in the *Index Aureliensis catalogus librorum sedecimo saeculo impressorum*, part 1, vol. 6, *BVO–CARR* (Baden-Baden: Koerner, 1976), 477. However, there is no support for this assertion in older sources such as O. Rossi, *Elogi historici di bresciani illustri. Teatro di Ottavio Rossi* (Brescia: Bartolomeo Fontana, 1620), 183–85, or L. Cozzando, *Libreria bresciana* (Brescia: Rizzardi, 1685), 216–17.

[61] For a useful biographical summary see Ennio Sandal, "Elia Capriolo," in *Uomini di Brescia* (Brescia: Giornale di Brescia, 1987), 149–64.

text falls into three sections. The first section considers the Dominican claim that the banning of one method of almsgiving effectively abolishes divine law and subverts the injunction to give alms. In the second section, the writer examines human law and the argument that the statute overturns an imperial "indult" or concession allowing Christians to bequeath money and property to the Church, holy men, and the needy. In the third and longest section he considers the relationship between the religious and the secular worlds and their respective claims over property.

A clear thread running through the entire text is a belief that the true Christian way of life embraces virtues such as lowliness of heart, tenderness, humanity, pity, charity, modesty, meekness, piety (*pietas*), and compassion (*misericordia*) (*Defense*, sigs. Aiiir, Aivv–Avr, Avr). The Dominicans, by their attack on the Brescians, by their poor conduct at funerals, and by their self-serving definition of alms (amounting to little more than a "fee"), have shown themselves to have no claim to these Christian virtues. Indeed, the author even goes so far as to argue that the Dominicans are harmful to both the human body and the body politic. He notes that during the recent famine they had "full granaries" when everyone else in Brescia was starving, yet they refused to help the people who had already given them so much by way of alms. For this injustice and greed, and lack of civic duty, the Dominicans should be driven into exile (sigs. Aiiir–v, cf. sigs. Aiir–v and Aivr). Moreover, he alleges that the Dominicans tortured and terrorized old women in their inquisitorial activities against witchcraft in the Valcamonica, and that in fact they themselves "may plead and pray for frequent funerals and our deaths, and may achieve them forcibly by means of certain magical prayers!" (sig. Avr).[62] His description of the Dominicans' general behavior is damning:

---

[62] The mountainous Valcamonica region was often the scene of witch-hunting during the fifteenth and sixteenth centuries, with notable outbreaks in 1485–1487 and 1518–1521. The former outbreak stirred up a great deal of controversy in Brescia as the *podestà* tried to restrict the activities of the Dominican inquisitor. Both Venice and the pope were forced to intervene but not before the Dominicans had launched a personal attack on the *podestà*'s vicar for supposed heresy. This Dominican attack on a fellow humanist and the order's appeal to Rome over Brescian and Venetian heads no doubt rankled with the anonymous author and helps to explain his negative comments. See Federico Odorici, *Le streghe di Valtellina e la santa inquisizione* (Milan, Venice, and

Does it seem to you noble, does it please you, that like plump and well-fed flocks wantonly nibbling now these, now those plants in flowery, gentle pastures stretching afar, so *you* are devouring and despoiling all the private property and goods of laypeople in any way you fancy? You are not satisfied with draining away their blood by cutting one vein — or four, or ten — but choose to open the whole lot, and to draw the life out of people with one suck. Blood is what makes blood, and life is what gives life. Such is your brutality and cruelty, so cheap and contemptible are the people of Brescia in your eyes, that because they have for serious and pressing reasons narrowed (not blocked) just one road, with countless others still open, and have dared to confront your greed, like frustrated wild beasts you proceed with such zeal and such effort to rouse the apostolic see and all Christendom against them with false accusations! (sig. Aivv)

The basis for the central argument of the pamphlet is set out in the first section where the author explains that the statute does indeed ban one method of almsgiving. However, he argues that the gift of alms should be made freely and without expectation of anything in return, and bestowed on those who need them: "Alms must be free and gratis, not paid for" (sig. Aiiv).[63] In this way, the money given to the religious orders, which escort a layperson's body to the grave, ought to be considered a fee as it is given in return for work carried out — work the Dominicans would not undertake without payment. If the Dominicans deny this, he

---

Rome: Regio Stabilimento Nazionale di Paolo Ripamonti Carpano, 1862), 125–28, 141–44; the contemporary account of a similar (or possibly identical) case: *Le Cronache bresciane inedite dei secoli XV–XIX*, transcribed and annotated by Paolo Guerrini, vol. 1 (Brescia: Editrice 'Brixia Sacra', 1922), 183–87; and the documents (cited here in chronological order) in Joseph Hansen, *Quellen und Untersuchungen zur Geschichte des Hexenwahns und der Hexenverfolgung im Mittelalter. Mit einer Untersuchung der Geschichte des Wortes Hexe* von Johannes Franck (Bonn: Carl Georgi, Universitäts-Buchdruckerei und Verlag, 1901), 472, 19–20, 29–30, 31, 510–11, 32–33, 320; and ASV, Capi del Consiglio di Dieci, Lettere, filza 5, pezzo 10, 21 May 1487. Very similar tensions resurfaced in 1518: Giorgio Tortelli, "Inquisizione e stregoneria a Brescia e nelle valli. La difficile convivenza fra autorità laiche e religiose nei primi decenni del XVI secolo," in *Scritti in onore di Gaetano Panazza* (Brescia: Stamperia Fratelli Geroldi, 1994), 259–68. See also below, *Defense*, n. 43.

[63] Christ enjoined his disciples: "Freely ye have received, freely give" (Matt. 10: 8).

pointedly asks: "Why do you never escort a pauper's corpse to burial?" (sig. Aiiv). Moreover, the order is hardly worthy to receive alms since it has acquired great wealth through confessions, the "lucrative poaching of wills," and by "trapping widowers and widows."[64] In any case, the statute does not prohibit other ways of giving alms: anyone who has some tenderness, humanity, charity, and pity in their heart will be able to act with true piety and compassion towards those in need. By contrast, the Dominicans want to offer their prayers for the deceased in public places and with due care taken to extract the maximum profit. They are the ones, therefore, who most militate against almsgiving by not practicing it.

In the second section the anonymous writer goes on to refute the argument that the Brescian statute infringes an imperial indult. This indult or concession had been made by the sixth-century emperor Justinian and permitted people to leave any goods they wished to the Church.[65] He explains that by this indult the emperor indulged testators in allowing them to leave their possessions to the Church, especially to "upright, holy men." However, it is contrary to human and divine law for a person to leave money to the Dominicans or some other order and thereby leave his wife and children to starve. Besides, the Brescians are very generous to the poor as the existence of the *monte di pietà*, among other things, demonstrates. In short, the law should agree with divine reason, but it may also be revised to meet new political circumstances. New laws are permitted by the Venetians, so long as they are just, and many valid historical precedents may be found for a law regulating funeral expenditure.

The third section of the argument covers a wide range of matters and contains many digressions and repetitions. The author asserts that the Dominican doctors' interpretation of "death disbursements" as candle-wax, cash, and a group of clergy is far too narrow. It is clear to him that such disbursements consist of *any* bequest to the Church, as the pope intended by his canon prohibiting the use of church property for

---

[64] Testaments containing bequests, requests, and endowments to the Dominican convent of San Domenico survive in ASB, Ospedale, San Domenico, buste 11 and 12. There are two peaks in the numbers of wills held which occur, unsurprisingly, in the years of particularly high mortality: 1478 and 1505 (twelve and six respectively).

[65] See below, *Defense*, n. 17.

secular purposes.[66] Therefore the statute does not prohibit any of the many ways of releasing souls from purgatory, especially as it has been shown that the statute does not prevent *true* almsgiving. There follows an attack on those who argue that all property connected with sacred matters, such as a funeral, should be appropriated by the Church. In this way, he says, the supposedly learned Dominican doctors ignore the examples of Christ and the apostles who gave away their property. He points out that by following this logic "the whole world will be under your jurisdiction — nothing will be ours" (sig. Avir) and the Dominicans would turn themselves into latter-day Midases! In fact, laypeople can arrange funerals and decide on the number of candles and priests escorting the corpse without destroying the Church's freedom or breaking the papal canon. Consequently, this statute affects only the layperson and does not impinge upon religious freedom.

Finally, the pamphleteer asserts that the statute is in the Brescians' best interests. In the *Quaestio* the Dominicans had argued that the government should not intervene to deprive private citizens and ordinary people of the power to decide on their own affairs as they wish:

> [A]lthough Titius[67] can prescribe in his *will* that only twenty-four clergy be invited to his funeral, yet a city in general cannot make a *statute* to this effect, because the first procedure diminishes no one's freedom, as the second does. For power in a city is not the despotic type where masters rule over *slaves*, but the statesmanlike type where masters rule over *citizens*, who in many ways are free as regards nearly all their own affairs.[68]

The anonymous writer brushes this legal finagling aside and retorts:

> No doubt this is to enable you too to say what Florentine moneylenders usually say when they have financial dealings with some

---

[66] See below, 159–61.

[67] A typical name used (especially for the judge) in Roman legal formulae: see A. Borkowski, *Roman Law*, 2nd ed. (London: Blackstone Press Ltd, 1997), 75–76.

[68] *Quaestio*, sig. diiiv. Cf. Aristotle, *Politics*, 1252a7–16, where the statesman (*politikos*) is contrasted with the ruler of a kingdom (*monarkhos*), or of a household (*oikonomikos*), or of a group of slaves (*despotês*).

simple, thick-skulled fellow whom in his ignorance they fleece: "If only there were plenty like you!" He, however, goes away happy, thinking that the moneylender considers him wise (sig. Avv).

It is true, he concludes, that the bishop of Brescia persuaded the Brescian people that it was in their best interests to reject a comparable statute.[69] However, it is probable that he did this with the understanding that the religious would voluntarily accept a lower fee, which is clearly not the case in this instance.

Some aspects of the structure and logic of these arguments betray the haste with which the pamphlet was composed: the author, like Capriolo in some of his other published works, is often repetitious or tendentious, and the reader quickly gains a vivid impression of white-hot rage, indignation, and scornful fury against the Dominicans. That said, the author is an effective and devastating satirist, and his emotions are never allowed to get in the way of his reasonable and accurately aimed intellectual blows. However, his attack is surpassed in cool and calculated intellectual firepower by that of his admired colleague Carlo Valgulio.

IV. Carlo Valgulio

Carlo Valgulio was born in Brescia in ca. 1434 into an ancient and powerful Guelf family. His father Stefano was a prominent lawyer fluent in both Latin and Greek, and this background no doubt helped Carlo to become "excellent in Latin, but without equal in Greek."[70] He may have

---

[69] This may refer to the 1473 statute and to an attempt to enforce it in 1478 or 1479 after 30,000 inhabitants died of the influenza known as the "mal di mazucho." See the chronicle of the notary Giacomo Melga printed in *Le Cronache bresciane inedite*, 15–17. He notes that at that time Brescians did not attend funerals for fear of contagion, and that the Dominicans were exceptional among the religious orders for continuing to bury the dead: *Cronache*, 21–22. Of course, this exceptional service may have been motivated by Dominican greed as much as by charity. Melga may also have been biased: he acted as notary for the Dominicans before the episcopal commission investigating the funerary statute in 1507: ASB, ASC 1528, fol. 133r–v (pencil foliation).

[70] Cremona, "L'Umanesimo bresciano," 563 and n. 1; Valentini, *Carlo Valgulio*, 11. However, neither author names his source; but in a similar vein Becichemo says in his published letter to Valgulio (see n. 28 above) how glad he is to be approved

Introduction xli

studied with Becichemo's teacher, Calfurnio, as well as with Concoreggio, and may later have opened his own humanist school in Brescia, with Andrea Marone as a rather disgruntled pupil.[71] The climax of his scholarly career came just before a ceremonial visit to the city by the exiled queen of Cyprus, Caterina Cornaro, in 1497: with the publication in Brescia, from the press of Bernardino Misinta "at the expense of Angelo Britannico," of a single volume containing his Latin versions of Greek works by Cleomedes (*De contemplatione orbium excelsorum disputatio*), Aelius Aristides (*Oratio ad Rhodienses de concordia*), Dio Chrysostom (*Oratio ad Nicomedios de concordia cum Nicenis componenda* and *De concordia oratio Niceae habita, seditione sedata*), and Plutarch (*De virtute morum* and *Praecepta connubialia*).[72] Valgulio had previously spent some time in Florence, meeting and befriending such leading lights of humanism as the poet and

---

by so learned a friend: "qui, ut patriam linguam omittam, in graeca adeo excellis ut inter latinos, quum a Hieronymo Donato et Daniele Renerio discesserim, quem tibi praeponam habeo neminem." This is high praise, for both the Venetian patricians Donato and Renerio were distinguished intellectuals and Hellenists close to Aldus Manutius: see M. E. Cosenza, *Biographical and Bibliographical Dictionary of the Classical Humanists and of the World of Classical Scholarship in Italy (1300–1800)*, 5 vols. (Boston: G. K. Hall, 1962), 2: 1253–55; 4: 3010.

[71] Rossi, *Elogi historici*, 204 (*recte*, 205).

[72] C. V. Palisca, *Humanism in Italian Renaissance Musical Thought* (New Haven and London: Yale University Press, 1985), 89; idem, "Carlo Valgulio: The Proem on Plutarch's *Musica* to Titus Pyrrhinus," in *The Florentine Camerata: Documentary Studies and Translations* (New Haven and London: Yale University Press, 1989), 15–16; and Valentini, *Carlo Valgulio*, 12, 20–23. These writers credit Valgulio with translation of only one speech by Dio Chrysostom, but it is clear that there were two (the first occupying eleven pages of the volume, fols. 46a–51a; the second only three, fols. 51b–52b), and that both were dedicated to Francesco Todeschini Piccolomini: see L. F. T. Hain, *Repertorium bibliographicum*, vol. 1, pt. 2 (Stuttgart and Paris: J. G. Cotta, 1826–1838, repr. Milan: Görlich, 1948), no. 5450; P. O. Kristeller, *Supplementum Ficinianum*, vol. 1 (Florence: Olschki, 1937), 114–15; Cosenza, *Biographical and Bibliographical Dictionary*, 4: 3544. Confusion was no doubt caused by the similar titles of what are in fact successive items in Dio's oeuvre (*Orationes XXXVIII / XXXIX*), and by the extreme brevity of the second. Capriolo, relating the events of 1497 in Brescia, notes with approval these translations by Valgulio in *Chronica*, Book 12, fol. LXXIIr (*recte*, LXXIIIr): "Per quae tempora Carolus Valgulius civis noster utraque lingua peritissimus Cleomedem de contemplatione orbium excelsorum: Aristidem Dionem de concordia: & Plutarchi praecepta connubialia cum quibusdam aliis e graeco in latinum vertit."

textual scholar Poliziano, Plato's chief translator and interpreter Ficino, Pietro Gravina, Antonio Calderini, Benedetto Accolti, and Giovanni Cavalcanti.[73] After a spell as tutor to the sons of Tommaso Minerbetti, he served as secretary to the papal treasurer Falco Sinibaldo between 1481 and 1485, and later (from about 1492) to Cardinal Cesare Borgia, gratefully dedicating the above-mentioned translation of Cleomedes to him, and the two of Plutarch to Rodrigo (Pope Alexander VI) and Giovanni Borgia respectively.[74] He is known to have borrowed Greek texts from the Vatican Library in 1481, 1483, 1484, 1495, and 1498.[75] Back in Brescia — the date of his return is uncertain[76] — he was apparently appointed to the post of apostolic protonotary and to two church benefices,[77] and, like Capriolo, became a member of the city's oldest *accademia*, the "Vertunni", named after a mythic pagan deity and founded in ca. 1479 by the Benedictine monk Bartolomeo Averoldi, later abbot of Leno and archbishop of Spalato.[78] According to Capriolo, Valgulio withdrew from public life in 1506 and devoted his remaining years to philosophical contemplation and to further translation and essay writing.[79] Contemporary

---

[73] Cremona, "L'Umanesimo bresciano," 563, n. 2; Valentini, *Carlo Valgulio*, 13.

[74] Palisca, *Humanism*, 89; Kristeller, *Supplementum*, 1: 114–15; Valentini, *Carlo Valgulio*, 20–21.

[75] Palisca, *Humanism*, 89 and n. 3; idem, "Carlo Valgulio: The Proem," 15 and n. 9; Kristeller, *Supplementum*, 1: 114; A. Zanelli, review of Valentini, *Carlo Valgulio*, *Archivio storico lombardo*, 4th ser., 1 (1904): 132 and n. 1.

[76] Cremona, "L'Umanesimo bresciano," 563, n. 2.

[77] Sanudo, *Diarii*, 23: 596. Sanudo mentions the reassignment "of two benefices in Brescian territory left vacant by the death of Master Carlo Valgulio, apostolic protonotary." A post held by Valgulio until 1502, when he resigned it for somewhat mercenary reasons, was that of "arciprete" (high priest) of the then wealthy parish of S. Andrea, Iseo: see P. Guerrini, "Carlo Valgulio, arciprete di Iseo," in *Memorie storiche della diocesi di Brescia*, vol. 3 (Brescia: Istituto figli di Maria Immacolata, 1932), 217–19.

[78] Caccia, "Cultura e letteratura," 509; Valentini, *Carlo Valgulio*, 13.

[79] Elia Capriolo, *Chronicorum de rebus brixianorum libri quatuordecim*, in *Thesaurus antiquitatum et historiarum Italiae* ... ed. J. G. Graevius, vol. 9, part 7 (Leiden: Petrus Vander, 1723), book 13, col. 136: "Verum enim vero cum *Carolus Valgulius* civis noster, & stemmate, & virtute praeclarus, multa fortunae commoda & ornamenta sprevisset, ut sacratissimae philosophiae expeditior, quietusque magis vacaret, quo nihil gratius, nihilque magis homini expetendum seculo censuit: *Isocratem* de pace, *Plutarchi* musicam, *Arianum* de gestis *Alexandri & Atticis* in Romanam linguam, praeter multas alias

Introduction *xliii*

records indicate that he was murdered on 7 January 1517 by the notorious gangster Filipino de' Sali,[80] perhaps for political reasons connected with his support of the Guelf party,[81] but more likely because he complained about some of de' Sali's depredations.[82] Valgulio's literary output during his retirement was undiminished, and four of his works were published. Two were translations: Pseudo-Plutarch's *De musica* with a *Proem* by Valgulio, printed in Brescia by Angelo Britannico in 1507;[83] and Arrian's *Anabasis*, printed in Venice by Bernardinus de Vitalibus for the publisher Antonio Moreto in 1508.[84] The other two were the essays *De sumptibus funerum* and *Contra vituperatorem musicae*, published together in 1509.

Valgulio's *De sumptibus funerum*, which was written several years after the publication of the Dominican book and probably just before the order finally gave up the struggle in October 1508, is much less concerned with replying to the specific arguments of the *Quaestio*, and it therefore

---

celeberrimas elocutiones suas, & scite, & fidelissime convertit." This edition of Capriolo's Brescian history includes the last two unpublished books of Capriolo's work taken from manuscripts in Brescia ("P. P. Oratorii" [i.e. the Oratory of St. Philip Neri], now in Brescia, Biblioteca Queriniana) and the Vatican Library: Vat. Lat. Ottoboniano 2272.

[80] "Diario di Bartolomeo Palazzo," in *Le Cronache bresciane*, 301, giving Palazzo's first diary entry for January 1517. The Brescian *podestà*'s report of Valgulio's murder was noted in Venice on 21 February 1517: Sanudo, *Diarii*, 23: 596.

[81] Valentini, *Carlo Valgulio*, 14–15, takes this view.

[82] Pasero, "Il dominio veneto," 308–9.

[83] Palisca, *Humanism*, 89–100, 106–10; idem, "Carlo Valgulio: The Proem," 13–44; Kristeller, *Supplementum*, 1: 115; Valentini, *Carlo Valgulio*, 23–24. Valgulio's translation was published two years before the Greek text of this work — which, if not by Plutarch (ca. 50–ca. 120), probably dates from his era — was printed: see again Palisca, *Humanism*, 105; and idem, "Carlo Valgulio: The Proem," 14, where he adds: "The dialogue was more informative regarding Greek musical culture than any previously translated writing, and it became the most widely read of any of the Greek sources. Moreover, it preserved fragments by Heracleides Ponticus, Glaucus of Rhegium, Pratinas, Lamprocles of Athens, Aristoxenus, and various anonymous authors. Valgulio's translation was accurate and literal and rendered the musical terminology intelligently."

[84] L. W. Daly, "Charolus Valgulius' Latin Version of Arrian's 'Anabasis,'" *Library Chronicle of the University of Pennsylvania* 17 (1951): 83–89; Palisca, "Carlo Valgulio: The Proem," 16 and n. 13; Kristeller, *Supplementum*, 1: 115; Valentini, *Carlo Valgulio*, 24–25.

perfectly complements the earlier pamphlet. Valgulio turns his attention to those who, "battling for a silly, false notion of honor" (*Statute*, sig. Ar), argue that rich and poor should not be buried in the same way and at the same expense. In doing so Valgulio aims many shafts against the Dominicans whom he accuses of giving "weight to their cause by a religious manner, title, and appearance" only, and "deceitfully indoctrinating the ignorant crowd and some simple-minded, superstitious citizens" (sig. Ar). Later in his treatise, Valgulio refers to the "devout scorner of the world" (sig. Aiiiv), those "encased in the shell of religion's outer clothing" but lacking an inner religious sense (sigs Aiiiiv–Avr), and in a similar fashion to "false brothers," and especially one man whose "name and garb [alone] are religious" (sig. Aviv).[85] However, these attacks should not be understood simply as anti-clerical statements, but must be interpreted as an introduction to the principal theme of his pamphlet: the uselessness of external honor in comparison with inner virtue. Valgulio asks the reader to consider whether the expense of funerals bears any relation to the true virtue of the deceased. To make his point, he contrasts the corpse, which is merely "food for worms" (sig. Avir), with the lavish spending on prayers, priests, and other ornaments at its burial. He argues that no honor or virtue can be acquired simply by purchasing multiple masses.

Valgulio outlines in three distinct sections the Christian, natural, and legal bases for his view that there is no rank or distinction among the dead. In the first section he attacks wealth and describes how the will of Christ was opposed to worldly honor. In his view, therefore, funeral expenditure is "more truly commerce and usury than alms, since it demands and expects things greater than itself: it demands honor and praise, as being greater" (sig. Av). In the second section he explains that all men are equal by nature, and the proof of this lies in the fact that men are all physically alike, mortal, and endowed with reason and speech. Therefore, no one is allowed "what another is not" (sig. A2r), and no one should take precedence over anyone else. In the third section Valgulio traces the development of civil laws

---

[85] Perhaps he had Fra Girolamo, who represented the Dominicans before the episcopal commission, or the Dominican prior of San Domenico in mind here. Compare Erasmus's colloquy *The Funeral*, in which one interlocutor declares: "Or do you believe the world is still so stupid that whenever it sees the garb of Dominic or Francis it thinks their sanctity is present too?": *Collected Works*, 40: 768.

Introduction xlv

under the pressure of human evil. He argues that while all men are endowed with reason, this quality is not evenly distributed among men, and there are some who cannot achieve virtue by the free development of their reason. Laws are necessary to check these men who rebel or do not otherwise follow reason and nature. All force for good in human affairs arises from the use of reason — from the "mental virtues which are willed and natural" (sig. A2v). By contrast, external elements, such as the expenditure at issue, are not good or evil in themselves but should only be appraised according to the extent that they are used for good or evil. Therefore, wealth, possessions, "knightly gold", countships, kingdoms, and therefore funeral expenditure cannot "confer praise or censure on their owners and masters: for nothing gives what it does not have" (sig. A2v).

Finally, Valgulio elaborates on his concept of honor and its relationship with virtue. Virtue — which includes loyalty (*pietas*), faith, hope, charity, justice, temperance, and compassion (*misericordia*) — is its own reward and does not seek honor. Men may choose to exercise virtue or vice; and honor will be bestowed upon a virtuous man by others when they observe him acting in a virtuous way. In a Stoic or Augustinian fashion Valgulio explains that many things such as wealth or poverty are not within men's control and therefore should not be praised or blamed. In fact, there is no "bliss during life" (sig. Aiiir) according to Christ's principles, so that externals should not be honored, except perhaps when performed for the benefit of others, especially the needy (sig. Aiiir-v). The rest of the treatise is a fairly consistent variation upon these principal themes. Valgulio contrasts emptiness in prayers, masses, and the outward show of funerals with true inner virtue and the honor that it incidentally brings.[86] The climax of his discourse is reached

---

[86] A similar emphasis on true inner virtue rather than worldly honors can be found in the letters and public lectures of the *quattrocento* Brescian humanist Laura Cereta: see Cereta, *Collected Letters*, e.g. 106 ("The snares of our age are higher things, which are set by our own perceptions in the darkness and error that leads us to strive for worldly honors"), and 168 ("Virtue is more fulfilling than any amount of money; it outlasts life and it replaces years of anguish in the end with the inviolate restitution of eternal peace. What mental turmoil so gnaws away at you, therefore, that you constantly lust after loathsome profit as though you were on fire, when among human beings praise is more precious than any coin?").

when he lists the absurd figures on whom empty outward honors have been showered. Some citizens have done what neither God nor nature can and have made the "unlearned learned and bastards legitimate" (sig. Avr). To make matters worse, honors have been conferred on such low-lifes as tax farmers, castrators, dentists, trumpeters, flautists, and traitors. Valgulio believes that it would be better to scorn those "who have virtue's sign on display but lack virtue" (sig. Avv), particularly as such false distinctions lead to social disruption — as the case of costly funerals has demonstrated (sigs Avv–Avir).

V. Solidarity Between the Living and the Dead

The general questions about honor, the proper use of wealth, and the relationship between the living and the dead emerge and interlink in the two humanist pamphlets. The relationships at stake in this dispute — between the laity and the clergy, and the living and the dead — were based on traditional Christian notions of reciprocity and gift-giving (particularly alms). Like most Renaissance Italians, Valgulio and his fellow writer accepted that the living owed the dead a service, and that a proper funeral and prayers of intercession were good works which would also gain spiritual benefits for those left behind. Charity was one of the cardinal Christian virtues, and it consisted especially of the seven corporal acts of mercy, which included burying the dead. Such acts were supposed be made freely to those most in need and with no thought of any immediate benefit to the donor except in terms of the contribution they made to one's salvation. Such charity was often linked with — or indistinguishable from — noble generosity, liberality, and magnificence.[87]

As Valgulio and the anonymous author recognize, solidarity between the living and the dead was strengthened in a variety of ways in early modern Europe. For example, confraternities or lay religious companies

---

[87] 'Generosity' (*generositas*) and 'nobility' (*nobilitas*) were classical and Renaissance synonyms. However, the recipients of this liberality were most often friends and clients of political and social significance rather than the truly needy. On notions of charity and noble munificence as 'gifts' see Natalie Zemon Davis, *The Gift in Sixteenth-Century France* (Oxford: Oxford University Press, 2000), esp. chaps. 1–2.

made some provision for the burial of members, especially those too poor to afford a decent funeral. Such confraternal "solaces" were canonically approved, and animated by a strong sense of charity.[88] Confraternities received many bequests and donations in return for their presence at funerals, and it also appears that an increasing amount of their income was spent on commemorative masses. This phenomenon forms part of a general trend in northern Italy after the Black Death towards more elaborate funerals and forms of memorialization such as tombs, humanist speeches and consolatory works, and printed epitaphs.[89] Testamentary evidence suggests that the number of religious stipulated to attend the body on its way to burial could vary from one or two, to forty Franciscan friars and forty Dominicans, or even an entire monastery.[90] By ca. 1370 Florentine funerals had become comparatively more elaborate affairs, and a century later the number of clergy involved in funerals had markedly increased as observant Franciscans and Dominicans were drawn in from across the city rather than simply from the local parish. By the early sixteenth century it was not uncommon to find hundreds of clergy involved in the public rites of notable Florentines, and elaborate tombs of the sort condemned by the anonymous pamphleteer — who

---

[88] On this, see John Henderson, *Piety and Charity in Late Medieval Florence* (Oxford: Clarendon Press, 1994); and, for some Bolognese cases, Nicholas Terpstra, "Death and Dying in Renaissance Confraternities," in *Crossing the Boundaries: Christian Piety and the Arts in Italian Medieval and Renaissance Confraternities*, ed. K. Eisenbichler (Kalamazoo: Medieval Institute Publications, Western Michigan University, 1991), 179–200.

[89] Samuel K. Cohn, Jr., *The Cult of Remembrance and the Black Death: Six Renaissance Cities in Central Italy* (Baltimore and London: Johns Hopkins University Press, 1992), 122–33; George W. McClure, "The Art of Mourning: Autobiographical Writings on the Loss of a Son in Italian Humanist Thought (1400–1461)," *Renaissance Quarterly* 39 (1986): 440–75; and idem, *Sorrow and Consolation in Italian Humanism* (Princeton: Princeton University Press, 1990).

[90] For example, at one extreme, the testament of the Brescian noble Sandrino quo. Giacomo de Cucchi, dated 27 September 1477, requests at least 144 religious to accompany the body to burial in the monastery of San Domenico: ASB, Ospedale, San Domenico, busta 11, no. 114. At the other end of the social scale, the Venetian second-hand clothes dealer Zuane Strazzarol asked to be dressed in Capuchin robes and his funeral to be held in their church, but without "pompa": ASV, Notarile, Testamenti, busta 199, no. 319 (17 November 1579). We are grateful to Tricia Allerston for this reference.

points out that pictures and statues of Christ were hardly permitted in churches by the early ecclesiastical authorities (*Defense*, sig. Avv) — grace almost every northern Italian church.[91]

Some Florentines viewed the brigades of friars as a form of "gloria mundana", while others saw their presence as an indicator of great piety. In 1508 Cosimo Pazzi's episcopal constitutions denounced clerics who deliberately flocked to burials in search of alms.[92] In 1526 Erasmus satirized a pompous and elaborate funeral in which the body was accompanied by forty-five mendicants, thirty torchbearers, and twelve professional mourners. In addition, the deceased's horse was draped in black, his arms were on display, and his body was placed in an imposing marble tomb.[93] Funerals probably reached their grandest scale in Italy, and indeed Spain, during the Counter-Reformation, and few were more spectacular than that for Giovanni Battista Borghese in 1610, which was attended by more than twenty cardinals and comprised some extremely elaborate and costly decorations and processions.[94]

It was probably the growing disparity between the funerals of rich and poor, and the marked growth of clerical income from these rites, that led Valgulio to argue that while the dead should not simply be forgotten, the rituals associated with death may nevertheless be of more

---

[91] After 1400 wild mourning figures appear on tombs, in contrast to an early medieval disdain for violent and uncontrolled gesticulation, especially in mourning, which was often attributed to pagans, Jews, devils, and sinners. This Stoic moderation only gradually gave way to the "new emotionalism" of late medieval art (especially evident in depictions of the Lamentation over Christ and the Entombment). On this and the "expressive tendencies" in fourteenth- and fifteenth-century art see Moshe Barasch, *Gestures of Despair in Medieval and Early Renaissance Art* (New York: New York University Press, 1976).

[92] Strocchia, *Death and Ritual*, 61–63, 201–5, 210–12, 225, 232.

[93] Erasmus, *The Funeral*, in *Collected Works*, 40: 772–73.

[94] M. Schraven, "Giovanni Battista Borghese's Funeral 'apparato' of 1610 in S. Maria Maggiore, Rome," *The Burlington Magazine* 143 (2001): 23–28. See also Kathryn B. Hiesinger, "The Fregoso Monument: A Study in Sixteenth-Century Tomb Monuments and Catholic Reform," *The Burlington Magazine* 118 (1976): 283–93. On the marked rise in the number of elaborate funerals in Madrid after 1561 for the purpose of "impressing God and neighbor" see Carlos M. N. Eire, *From Madrid to Purgatory: The Art and Craft of Dying in Sixteenth-Century Spain* (Cambridge: Cambridge University Press, 1995), chap. 4.

Introduction   *xlix*

use to the living than the dead, especially as the living seem very keen to dispose of the corpse underground as quickly as possible. If the dead were really as much revered as the multiplication of priests and prayers indicates, surely the Brescians would lay the bodies out in their houses (*Statute*, sig. Avir) like the ancient Persians and Egyptians (sig. Aiiiiv). Characteristically, Valgulio argues that nature does not want such public obsequies, for "rot and decay" set in to all corpses almost immediately (sig. Aiiiiv). Of course, for all his anticlericalism, Valgulio (who was an apostolic protonotary and a "high priest") does not go so far as to call for the abolition of all organized religious ceremony. Although he dismisses much almsgiving, he is careful to distinguish the money spent on self-glorification from alms given freely and without thought of personal honor (sigs Av, Aiiir–v). Similarly, he raises the question of whether saying a prayer is any good for "purging the souls of the deceased" (sig. Aiiiir). In an echo of the mystical writings of the Neoplatonist ps.-Dionysius the Areopagite (ca. 500), Valgulio asserts that prayers "are no good for the dead," although he does accept that "such charity and compassion (*misericordia*) is good for the living, and very pleasing to God."[95] He objects to prayers said in public by hired priests with "lips and words" alone. This does not mean that priestly intercession should be abolished, for priests may still come to escort corpses for burial as long as both clerics and laypeople remember their duty to the needy. While such Stoic conceptions could appear cold, rigid, or legalistic, equally they could encourage personal contemplation and inner development. Like Epictetus (*fl.* A.D. 100), whose work he probably knew,[96] Valgulio deprecated the "honors" bestowed upon men by others or by external conditions, and he therefore emphasized the action of inner virtue. As he wrote: "Virtue is reason that is perfect in itself and taken to its peak; from it always flow each person's just, brave, controlled, and generous actions, due respect shown to God, to country, to

---

[95] On ps.-Dionysius see below, Valgulio, *Statute*, n. 36.

[96] Valgulio's debt to Epictetus is signaled throughout our edition of his text. He was not alone in his high regard for the philosopher whose newly discovered *Enchiridion* of Stoic philosophy was translated into Latin by Niccolò Perotti, circulated in at least thirteen manuscripts, was retranslated by Angelo Poliziano, and went through many editions after 1497.

parents, in short to all mankind (observing the proper priorities) and, of course, towards themselves" (sig. A2v).

However, within fifteen years of the Brescian dispute Protestant reformers north of the Alps had largely disrupted the power of gift relations in the economy of salvation and notions of divine obligation and reciprocity embodied in the mass, purgatory, or payments to clergy and confraternal brothers for funeral duties.[97] Martin Luther (1483–1546) argued that masses for the dead had simply become opportunities for making money, and he contrasted the "true Christian work" of serving one's neighbor with the useless endowment of masses encouraged by the "pope's pseudo-priesthood."[98] Luther and other early reformers in Germany, Switzerland, and England accused the Catholic clergy of *Totenfresserei* (feeding on the dead) and argued that endowing intercessions for the dead impoverished widows and children, as well as the poor. In Nikolaus Manuel's satirical play *Die Totenfresser*, which was performed in Bern during Lent in 1523, one of the devourers of the dead is identified as the pope, who exclaims: "Church offerings, weekly, monthly, and annual masses for the dead / Bring us more than enough. / Pity the hardship it inflicts upon the children of the givers!", while a sacristan declares: "I like dead people better than fighting and screwing / They are our food and pay."[99] As part of their assault on purgatory in England in the 1530s evangelicals such as John Bale deplored priests, canons, and monks who "do but fyll their bely / With my swett and labour for

---

[97] Zemon Davis, *The Gift*, chap. 7.

[98] Martin Luther, *The Babylonian Captivity of the Church* (1520), in *Luther's Works*, gen. ed. Helmut T. Lehman, vol. 36, *Word and Sacrament II*, ed. Abdel Ross Wentz (Philadelphia: Muhlenberg Press, 1959), 25–36; and idem, *The Misuse of the Mass* (1521), in *Works*, 36: 203. See also idem, *A Treatise on the New Testament, That is, The Holy Mass* (1520), in *Works*, 35, *Word and Sacrament I*, ed. E. Theodore Bachman (Philadelphia: Muhlenberg Press, 1960), esp. 93–94, 96.

[99] Quoted in Steven E. Ozment, *The Reformation in the Cities: The Appeal of Protestantism to Sixteenth-Century Germany and Switzerland* (New Haven and London: Yale University Press, 1975), 112–13. Pamphilius Gengenbach published a dramatic poem also titled *Totenfresser* in 1521. It features a mendicant among the seven "devourers of the dead": 111. In the same year Johann Eberlin von Günzburg, an ex-Franciscan preacher, published a description of a utopian Protestant community where the dead were to be accompanied to the cemetery by friends and neighbors, mourning clothes were to be worn for only one week, and alms and prayers might commemorate the deceased: 100–1.

Introduction   li

ther popych purgatory."[100] A recent study has shown that the funeral, and especially ducal attempts to enforce burial outside the city walls rather than in the crowded and unhealthy mendicant churches, became a flashpoint for anticlericalism and subsequently confessional conflict in Leipzig in 1536. Similar disputes arose in other parts of the empire at the beginning of the sixteenth century. However, even in Protestant Germany or England the evidence for a simplification or purification of funeral rites is mixed. Upper-class funerals in England were certainly scaled down after ca. 1580, and the Puritans were critical of any wasteful extravagance, but in Germany and England the desire for an 'honorable' burial meant that bells, palls, candles, crosses, and processions including paupers and guild members persisted with some variations according to social status. The difference was that such rites were solely for the benefit of the living community — not the dead.[101]

While they share many of the same concerns about the exploitation of popular fears about death and the afterlife, it would be wrong to depict Valgulio and the anonymous author simply as Lutherans *avant la lettre*. They never rejected the existence of purgatory, as Luther did by 1522, nor the right of members of the mendicant orders to be present at funerals. However, like many Lutherans they emphasized that the "solaces" associated with funerals were most important as a form of charity towards the living needy rather than as a form of intercession for the dead. In this way, they were in agreement with Augustine that funeral ceremonies "are more for the comfort of the survivors than to assist the dead."[102] They would have despised the assertion made by one Spanish writer in 1536 that the size of a funeral procession was directly related to the time the soul of the deceased spent in purgatory.[103] Above all, they

---

[100] Quoted in Peter Marshall, *Beliefs and the Dead in Reformation England* (Oxford: Oxford University Press, 2002), 55. See also 56–64.

[101] Craig M. Koslofsky, *The Reformation of the Dead: Death and Ritual in Early Modern Germany, 1450–1700* (Basingstoke: Macmillan Press Ltd., 2000), chaps. 3, 4; and Ralph Houlbrooke, *Death, Religion, and the Family in England, 1480–1750* (Oxford: Clarendon Press, 1998), chap. 9, esp. 270–71.

[102] Augustine, *De Civitate Dei*, 1.12. This passage was also used by sixteenth-century English evangelicals in their attacks on purgatory and the organization of communion. See Marshall, *Beliefs and the Dead*, 52, 144–45, 150, 268.

[103] Cited in Eire, *From Madrid to Purgatory*, 123.

sought to preserve and strengthen the reciprocal relationship between God and men through simpler and more pious devotions and less grasping and public priestly intercessions. The two men wrote in defense of Brescia and outlined the ways in which the loyal Brescian citizen could ensure a fitting and decent Christian burial. Their arguments in favor of streamlining or simplifying the ceremony, and their emphasis on inner virtue and loyalty, are made with the examples of Christ, the apostles, and the primitive Church in mind. However, to modern eyes, the most striking and obvious support for their Christianity and their sense of civic solidarity is their humanism.

VI. Christian Humanism

The possession and use of wealth and sacramentals was a key point of debate for Christians and humanists concerned with renewing and reforming the church and popular piety throughout the Middle Ages. The anonymous pamphleteer's comment about Christians being forced to borrow from the Jews reveals that the material burden placed upon the living by the dead could be intolerable — especially at times of increased mortality such as 1505. At the heart of the Christian humanism expressed by Valgulio and his colleague is the fear that laypeople, and indeed the clergy, have been distracted from true and simple faith by such outward observances and trappings. As Hans Baron has shown, early humanist ideas in Italy about the philosopher's independence from the blows of fortune owed a great deal to the Franciscan ideal of voluntary poverty and ascetic renunciation of worldly goods. The presiding spirit of the early Renaissance, Francesco Petrarch (1304–1374), was "in many respects an ally of the Franciscan spirit" who epitomized this sense of worldly pessimism and despair. Petrarch was initially attracted to "poverty in honor and moderation," but his Christian asceticism was gradually tempered by the recognition that such poverty and unsatisfied needs were only suitable for a few, and that wealth could actually aid the wise man.[104] However, Petrarch believed that an attitude of indifference

---

[104] Hans Baron, "Franciscan Poverty and Civic Wealth as Factors in the Rise of Humanistic Thought," *Speculum* 13 (1938): 1–37, here, 1, 7 (quoting Petrarch).

Introduction

to external fortune was the best course to take since death *had* dominion — it entirely vitiated earthly affairs. At the end of his life he wrote: "Death does not know *imperium*, does not recognize princes, and is the greatest leveler of all."[105] Therefore, he wrote in the dialogue *Insepultus abiiciar* ('Dying in fear of being cast away unburied'), "all rites of burial are designed for the sake of the living,"[106] and elsewhere he notes:

> An honorable death needs no funereal pomp, no pallbearers, no escutcheons draped in purple, no turned-down shields and swords, with the whole family weeping for the master, the sobbing wife, and mourning children; nor one with bowed head and clad in black before the hearse, wetting his face with copious tears, nor, last, the orator to eulogize the loved one; no gilded busts of a rich tomb, no titles of the deceased engraved in marble to last until those latter days when death will rend even the stones![107]

Rather, it is the case that the virtue and good name of a man established through his wise and just actions will be a sufficient memorial.[108]

Hans Baron also argued that the ascetic ideals of Franciscan and Stoic poverty which permeated society after ca. 1250, and strongly influenced

---

[105] Petrarch, *De Remediis*, 2. 119. For an English translation see *Petrarch's Remedies for Fortune Fair and Foul: A Modern English Translation of* De remediis utriusque Fortune, *with a Commentary* by Conrad H. Rawski, 5 vols. (Bloomington and Indianapolis: Indiana University Press, 1991), 3: 302. Compare Petrarch's description of the death as the great leveler in *Triumphus mortis*, 1: 'U' sono or le ricchezze? u' son gli onori? / e le gemme e gli scettri e le corone, / e le mitre e i purpurei colori? / Miser chi speme in cosa mortal pone / (ma chi non ve la pone?), e se si trova / alla fine ingannato è ben ragione": Francesco Petrarca, *Rime e trionfi*, ed. Ferdinando Neri, with notes by Enrico Carrara, 2nd ed. rev. by Ettore Bonora (Turin: Unione Tipografico-Editrice Torinese, 1963), 558, lines 82–87.

[106] Petrarch, *De Remediis*, 2. 132; trans. Rawski, *Petrarch's Remedies*, 3:335 (English title as rendered by translator).

[107] Petrarch, *De Remediis*, 2. 122; trans. Rawski, *Petrarch's Remedies*, 3:312–13. The rest of the passage is quoted in the epigraph to this introduction.

[108] Petrarch, *De Remediis*, 2. 122. Compare this exchange in 130 ("Dying anxious about one's fame after death"): "Fear: 'What kind of fame will I have once I am gone?' Reason: 'Your fame will be just like the life you led before you died, and at the time you died'": trans. Rawski, *Petrarch's Remedies*, 3:331.

humanist thought in the fourteenth century, were challenged by a new justification and praise of 'civic' wealth in the fifteenth century. Leonardo Bruni (ca. 1370–1444), chancellor of Florence, translated the *Economics* attributed to Aristotle and in this way helped to bolster arguments in favor of the moral and intellectual value of wealth and worldly affairs. Poggio Bracciolini (1380–1459) asserted in his work *De vera nobilitate* that the Stoic virtue of the wise man was "naked" (*nuda*) and "partial" or "needy" (*egens*) since "it does not permeate the civic community, it appears deserted, hermit-like."[109] Many humanists subsequently agreed that the well-rounded human being and active citizen could not live by strict Stoic principles, and fifteenth-century civic funeral orations in Florence began to include praise of the deceased on account of his acquisition and use of wealth, rather than for his renunciation of "vain worldly goods."[110] Art historians have identified a parallel change of outlook in funerary sculpture: there was "a rejection of Christian concern for the future in favor of pagan glorification of the past." The Renaissance sanctioned "the principle of individual commemoration," and extended such commemoration to the soldier and humanist, as well as to the bishop.[111] Indeed, Leonardo Bruni's wish for a simple tomb was ignored by a grateful city, and his tomb in the Franciscan church of Santa Croce has young cherubs holding garlands of vines and fruit over a triumphal arch with Bruni himself in his chancellor's robes holding a copy of his history of Florence. In a similar fashion, the 1503 tomb of the Bergamasco humanist Giovanni Calfurnio in Padua exhibits the iconographic innovations symptomatic of this "international rage" by the inclusion of personal biographical elements (an open bookcase, indicating Calfurnio's humanist achievements) and roundels depicting the seven virtues as "character witnesses."[112]

---

[109] Baron, "Franciscan Poverty," 33.

[110] Baron, "Franciscan Poverty," 22. See also John M. McManamon, *Funeral Oratory and the Cultural Ideals of Italian Humanism* (Chapel Hill, NC: University of North Carolina Press, 1989).

[111] Erwin Panofsky, *Tomb Sculpture: Four Lectures on its Changing Aspects from Ancient Egypt to Bernini*, ed. H. W. Janson, foreword by Martin Warnke (London: Phaidon Press Ltd., 1992), 67.

[112] Panofsky, *Tomb Sculpture*, 75. There is a photograph of Calfurnio's tomb in the Basilica del Santo, Padua, in *Storia di Brescia*, 2: 548. See above, Frontispiece.

Humanists in early sixteenth-century Italy were sharply divided over the spiritual and philosophical benefits of wealth and worldly concerns. In Paolo Cortesi's reform treatise *De Cardinalatu* of 1510, the humanist Roman writer prescribed a large household and palace for the average cardinal. For Cortesi, liberality, magnificence, and charity were virtues in that they led to the employment of learned men, the promotion of study, and the relief of the poor through the building of hospitals and monasteries.[113] However, contempt for the world and for worldliness in a civic or ecclesiastical setting could also be compatible with *cinquecento* humanism. For example, the Venetian humanists and hermits Vincenzo Querini (Fra Pietro) and Tommaso Giustiniani (Fra Paolo) took a tougher line than Cortesi towards church wealth in their reform treatise of 1513, the so-called *Libellus ad Leonem Decem*. The hermits wanted the papal household to provide an example of good conduct for Rome, and indeed for the whole world.[114] Querini asserted that ecclesiastical reform should begin with the papal household, which was the largest of the Roman courts, comprising some seven hundred people by this time (it had doubled in size since Pius III's reign ten years previously).[115] The members of Pope Leo's household who were not in necessary occupations, particularly women, should return home, and his entire household be reduced to one-third of its present size. Leo should also remove all gold and silk hangings from private and public rooms and his own bed, and give them up for holy purposes.

---

[113] John F. D'Amico, *Renaissance Humanism in Papal Rome: Humanists and Churchmen on the Eve of the Reformation* (Baltimore and London: Johns Hopkins University Press, 1983), 230–31. Compare P. V. Murphy, "A Worldly Reform: Honor and Pastoral Practice in the Career of Cardinal Ercole Gonzaga (1505–63)," *Sixteenth Century Journal* 31 (2000): 399–418.

[114] J. B. Mittarelli and A. Costadoni, eds., *Annales Camaldulenses ordinis Sancti Benedicti*, 9 vols. (Venice, 1755–1773), 9: col. 699; and see the draft manuscript related to this proposal by Querini in the Sacro Eremo Tuscolano, Frascati, cod. F II A, fols. 348r–349r. This has been published by Hubert Jedin, "Vincenzo Quirini und Pietro Bembo," in idem, *Kirche des Glaubens — Kirche der Geschichte: ausgewählte Aufsätze und Vorträge*, 2 vols. (Freiburg i. B.: Herder, 1966), 1: 165–66; and discussed in Stephen D. Bowd, *Reform before the Reformation: Vincenzo Querini and the Religious Renaissance in Italy*, Studies in Medieval and Reformation Thought 87 (Leiden, Boston, and Cologne: Brill, 2002), 165–79.

[115] D'Amico, *Renaissance Humanism*, 41–44.

The Dutch humanist Erasmus articulated a similar concern for more simplicity and holiness among laypeople and clergy. In his first will of 1527 he forbade an expensive, vulgar, or ostentatious burial for himself, but asked for one in accordance with ecclesiastical rites, "so that nobody could complain."[116] In his satirical dialogue *The Funeral*, he depicts the good Christian refusing special masses because he has total faith (*tota fiducia*) in Christ's sacrifice, which means that there are enough merits accumulated to cleanse the human soul.[117] Valgulio closely resembles Erasmus in his deprecation of outward forms of observance (especially in his comment that what matters about candles at funerals is "*numen*, not number" [*Statute*, sig. Avir]) and of the intervention of priests and religious; in his hope for civil unity; and in his faith in the perfectibility of man if he followed the rational laws of his own nature. Just like Valgulio, Erasmus wrote: "All living things strive to develop according to their proper nature. What is the proper nature of man? Surely it is to live the life of reason, for reason is the peculiar prerogative of man."[118] Just as Valgulio sarcastically referred to his Dominican opponent as the "devout scorner of the world" (*Statute*, sig. Aiiiv), so Erasmus lacerated monks in his *Praise of Folly* (published in Venice in 1515). He points out that these monks are not so solitary as their name suggests, "and wherever you go these so-called solitaries are the people you're likely to meet." Elsewhere, Erasmus allowed for the existence of learned monks living lives of piety, but he did not accept that monasticism in itself was a form of piety; rather it was a way of living, "either useful or useless in proportion to one's moral and physical disposition."[119]

---

[116] Erasmus, *The Funeral*, in *Collected Works*, 40: 794 n. 110.

[117] *Collected Works*, 40: 777–78.

[118] Quoted in W. J. Bouwsma, "The Two Faces of Humanism: Stoicism and Augustinianism in Renaissance Thought," in *Itinerarium Italicum*, ed. H. A. Oberman and T. A. Brady Jr. (Leiden: E. J. Brill, 1975), 3–60, here 21–22.

[119] Erasmus, *Praise of Folly and Letter to Martin Dorp 1515*, trans. B. Radice, intro. and notes A. H. T. Levi (London: Penguin Books, 1971), 164–67; the second quotation from the 1501 *Encheiridion militis christiani* is in C. Trinkaus, "Humanist Treatises on the Status of the Religious: Petrarch, Salutati, Valla," *Studies in the Renaissance* 11 (1964): 7–45, here 45. Neither Capriolo nor Valgulio appears in Erasmus's surviving correspondence, but the Brescian humanist Marino Becichemo was part of an Erasmian circle in Padua in the 1520s, and he had lived and worked in Brescia between 1501 and

Introduction

The common inheritance of Christian humanists such as Petrarch, Bruni, Valgulio, and Erasmus was the body of writing left by the ancient Stoic philosophers, and Valgulio's pamphlet contains many Stoic elements such as disdain for external fortune; the idea of virtue as its own reward; and the assumption that the divinely-ordered universe is accessible to human understanding, so that man's perception of the rational order of the universe tells him a good deal about the nature and will of God, and consequently that man's reason forms the main link between himself and God. It is notable then that Valgulio does not write in the guise of a new Isaiah or Ezekiel, or even in the strict tradition of Augustine. The tone and substance of his pamphlet is more humanist and Stoic than Augustinian: thus, the reference to God's hatred of sin, especially pride, which Valgulio makes at the end of his treatise, is uncharacteristic, and reads more like an afterthought than the coda to an exhortatory sermon (*Statute*, sig. Avir). Rather, writing as a humanist and a Brescian patriot Valgulio seeks to bond civil society together in recognition of the pre-eminence of virtue, which is the perfection of reason. Valgulio's debt to Cicero is clear here: he argues that the exercise of virtue must encourage fellowship among men, as well as brave, controlled, and generous actions, and the due respect shown to God, to country, to parents, and to all humanity (sigs Av–A2v). For Valgulio, loyalty (*pietas*) heads the list of virtues, and such societal obligations or "considered action" in a civic setting was considered by Cicero superior to "prudent reflection" (sig. Aiiir).[120] In a similar fashion, the anonymous writer echoes Cicero's discussion of Solon's tough funerary laws, and emphasizes the beneficial effects of such just and reasonable laws on society (*Defense*, sig. Aivr). The anonymous author and Valgulio agree that the Dominicans and ambitious Brescians have become prey to vice and that there is a danger that this will lead to civil dissolution. As Valgulio says:

> For what is an unwillingness to live on equal terms with the rest, and according to the same decrees and ordinances of the city whose parts and members you are — what else is it but a rupturing of civic

1508. See Clough, "Becichemo, Marino;" and Silvana Seidel Menchi, *Erasmo in Italia, 1520–1580* (Turin: Bollati Boringhieri, 1987), 35–37.
    [120] Valgulio's debt to Cicero is signaled throughout our edition of his text.

association, a rending of parts from their whole, and of members from their body, and a desire to lord it over others as wild beasts do, relying on brute strength? (*Statute*, sig. Avv)

However, a concern with civil unity was not the sole preserve of humanists. In fact, there were numerous medieval legal precedents in Brescia and elsewhere in Europe which showed a concern for binding civil society together into a harmonious and virtuous unity. Notable among the statutory precedents that sharpened the moral cutting edge of Christian humanism was sumptuary legislation.

VII. Sumptuary Legislation and Civic Puritanism

The framers of medieval sumptuary laws in Europe aimed to prevent political quarrels, preserve local trade, and enforce the moral and social order. In general, sumptuary legislation regulated costly (especially female) clothing, and the conduct of men and women at weddings and funerals. Funerals featured high on the list of concerns of Italian legislators between 1200 and 1500.[121] Statutes prohibited uncontrolled weeping at funerals, the tolling of bells, the carrying of excessive numbers of torches or candles, and the misuse of shrouds. For example, in fifteenth-century Florence limits were set on the number of clergy permitted to attend funerals, and the number of multiple masses for the soul of the deceased.[122] Such limitations on the numbers, behavior, and dress of those attending weddings and funerals in medieval Italy have been closely related to attempts to control noble gatherings and to defuse potentially disruptive political, social, or economic ambitions. These checks were made in the context of relatively rapid economic changes and the consequent upward mobility on the part of the wealthy *popolani* families who were muscling in on communal government during the Middle Ages.[123] Immoderate mourning gestures and the excessive use of mourning clothes and candles

---

[121] A table illustrating the range and number of Italian sumptuary concerns between 1200 and 1500 is provided in Kovesi Killerby, *Sumptuary Law*, 38.

[122] Strocchia, *Death and Ritual*, 212.

[123] Kovesi Killerby, *Sumptuary Law*, 71–76, 80–81, 89.

Introduction lix

were also singled out for condemnation by medieval Spanish synods and were prohibited by sumptuary legislation issued by King Ferdinand and Queen Isabella in 1502 on the grounds that they led to "inordinate superfluous spending." The monarchs also provided an explanation as to why such excesses were dangerous: they showed a lack of faith in the Christian doctrine of the Resurrection. They state:

> All these gestures of weakness and dolorous cries were devised only for the solace of the living. But we Catholic Christians believe that there is another life beyond this, where our souls will enjoy eternal life; and we should endeavor to earn this life through meritorious works, not through vain and transitory gestures such as excessive spending on mourning clothes, or the inordinate burning of candles ... Instead, it would be much better for all that money so vainly spent to be used for masses, alms, and other meritorious works.[124]

However, for all its spiritual motives such sumptuary legislation also aimed to reinforce the social order by differentiating between men and women, and among royalty, titled nobility, and the rest in terms of numbers of candles, and mourning dress permitted.[125] Similar aims were behind the attempts by the Brescian ruling elite to restrict entry to the council from 1473, and in both funerary pamphlets — written by members of the governing class in defense of the statute — it is not hard to detect a correlation between support for sumptuary legislation and social control.

Sumptuary legislation was also a feature of the relationship between episcopal and communal authority. City governments and bishops could work together to enforce laws, as in Perugia in 1485 when women who broke the sumptuary legislation were made liable to excommunication

---

[124] Quoted in Eire, *From Madrid to Purgatory*, 153–54. In a letter to Francesco de Carrara, Petrarch expresses disgust with the throngs of weeping and wailing matrons who attend noble and plebeian funerals, and he advises Francesco to make them stay indoors and away from churches, and to put an end to "Hunc morem, quia gravi et nobili contrarium politie tuoque regimine indignum": *Senilium rerum libri*, 14. 1.

[125] "zentihomini de Venezia, cavalieri ... [and] dottori" were exempt from Brescian sumptuary legislation in 1477: Cassa, *Funerali, pompe*, 71–72. See also Kovesi Killerby, *Sumptuary Law*, 87–88; and Strocchia, *Death and Ritual*, 212.

and other penalties.[126] However, the potential for conflicts between the Church and the state was great in the case of funerary legislation where "the line of demarcation [between lay and ecclesiastical matters] became more obscure."[127] Milanese funeral *capitoli* adopted by Bergamo in the middle of the fourteenth century varied the number of clergy who could assist at funerals depending on the proximity of the burial to a mendicant convent. Similar restrictions on numbers of clergy are found in Pisa, Aquila, Padua, and Faenza in the fourteenth and fifteenth centuries. Despite this, there is very little evidence of clerical protests against the infringement of ecclesiastical liberty. Besides Brescia, it seems that the only other Italian dispute along these lines occurred at Parma in 1421 in response to a statute prohibiting excessive funeral expenditure.[128] This statute was examined by the *Collegio de' Giudici*, and approved in its amended form by Filippo-Maria Visconti. The statute noted that many laypeople had spent inordinate amounts on funerals — some willingly, but others through a sense of duty or in order to avoid embarrassment and not to appear greedy. Henceforth the bier was to be accompanied through the street and adorned in the church with no more than four candles of less than three pounds in weight, and only parish clergy with one cross could attend while the bell of the parish church, and no others, rang out.[129]

Brescia's first surviving sumptuary legislation, passed sometime between 1200 and 1276, concerns funeral ceremonies. These laws limited the number of candles permitted at funerals to two and the number of crosses to one, and condemned the useless expenses incurred for mourning clothes. Subsequent legislation restricted expenditure on mourning clothes; numbers of large crosses; and the numbers of clerics and religious attending funerals.[130] The anonymous author was well aware that there had been previous attempts to limit funeral expenditure in Brescia:

---

[126] Kovesi Killerby, *Sumptuary Law*, 101–2.

[127] Kovesi Killerby, *Sumptuary Law*, 106.

[128] The Leipzig example is noted above, li.

[129] Kovesi Killerby, *Sumptuary Law*, 107; Angelo Pezzana, *Storia della città di Parma*, vol. 2, *1401–1449* (Parma: Dalla ducale tipografia, 1842), 239, 239–40 n. 3.

[130] Cassa, *Funerali, pompe*, 36–41.

Introduction lxi

And the fact that the bishop of Brescia (whether De Monte or De Dominicis[131]) writes that by his own influence he got the Brescians to reject the same statute has little bearing on the case. They yielded (assuming that what people say was true) to the influence of an outstanding bishop who brings great benefits to the people, and I think that perhaps (as is very likely) the bishop promised to use the same influence to ensure that religious would voluntarily accept the city's forthcoming limit on funeral expenses, not by reducing the number of funeral attendants, but by agreeing to be satisfied with less than the usual fee. The hoped-for result was that, with the expenditure supposedly determined by the statute's intention being weighed against whatever the number of religious might be, due account would be taken of the Brescians' intention and of the churchmen's honor and dignity (*Defense*, sig. Aiv).

While the city did not match Florence or Venice in absolute numbers of sumptuary laws passed between 1200 and 1500 (sixty-one and forty-three respectively), nevertheless it ranks somewhere in the upper part of the league of legislators with eleven known acts.[132] The Brescian council approved sumptuary legislation covering beards, scent, ornaments, jewellery, and male and female clothing in 1503 and again in April and May 1505 (on account of "la difficulta [*sic*] di Tempi"), just a month or two before the funerary statute was first proposed.[133] However, the regularity with which Italian cities such as Brescia enacted such legislation (attempts were still being made in Brescia in 1648 to control

---

[131] De Monte, according to the *Quaestio*, sig. Ciir–v.

[132] Figures from Kovesi Killerby, *Sumptuary Law*, 34, and see Table 2.1.

[133] ASB, ASC 519, fols. 172v–174r (special council, 28 April 1503, first foliation); ASC 519, fols. 7r–8r (special council, 12 May 1503, second foliation), clauses approved unanimously or by nine votes to one; ASB, ASC 520, fols. 62r–65r (general council, 23 and 28 April 1505, first foliation), seventeen clauses approved unanimously for the most part. The "difficulta" doubtless included the ongoing wars and the local outbreaks of flu or "pestis": ASV, Capi del Consiglio di Dieci, Lettere di rettori e di altre cariche, Brescia (1477–1533), busta 19, no. 63 (Brescian rectors to Doge and *capi*, 5 December 1507); ASB, ASC 520, fol. 118r (6 October 1505, first foliation); and the comment "qui in Bressa morivano de feveroni," in the diary of Bartolomeo Palazzo, August 1505: Guerrini, *Cronache Bresciane*, 1: 257.

excessive expenditure on funerary items) suggests that women, or their husbands and fathers, routinely ignored injunctions to remove gold and pearls from dress material, and to keep dowries within manageable limits, as well as to limit the numbers of clergy attending funerals.[134] This is not surprising given Italy's economic prosperity, the cosmopolitanism of its towns, and the close links that existed among images, clothing, and social identity during this period. In the morally tense atmosphere of Renaissance Brescia, Venice, or Florence seemingly trivial matters such as furs and funerals could become the flashpoints for intense social and political conflict and civic puritanism or purification fueled by a heady mixture of Christian humanism, observant Franciscan spirituality, and millenarianism.

The persistence of sumptuary legislation can therefore be related to fears about the decline in lay and clerical morals, imminent divine chastisement, and political failure. Many early Christian writers such as Tertullian, Cyprian, Jerome, and Augustine criticized luxury. Medieval and early modern church synods and councils repeatedly condemned clerics who indulged in sumptuousness, and supported secular moves against malefactors by means of excommunication.[135] While the economic arguments in favor of restraint were repeated in civic council chambers, the council often invited preachers to the city where they forcefully made the moral case against luxury in the churches and piazzas. Many of the preachers who were foremost in attacking lay vices were the spiritual or observant Franciscans and Dominicans, who in the late Middle Ages renewed their vows of apostolic poverty and reliance upon public charity as part of a return to the purity of their orders' original rules. A number of influential preachers emerged from these movements: the Franciscan preacher St. Bernardino of Siena (1380–1444), the observant friar Bernardino da Feltre, and the Dominican preacher and prophet Fra Girolamo Savonarola (1452–1498), who all lacerated excesses in public expenditure, fashion, and habit, especially among the

---

[134] Cassa, *Funerali, pompe*, 41. Materials relating to some late sixteenth-century cases of sumptuary transgression are in ASB, ASC 166, filza 182.

[135] On this, see Kovesi Killerby, *Sumptuary Law*, chap. 5; and Eire, *From Madrid to Purgatory*, 148–53.

Introduction lxiii

young.[136] Savonarola's vision of the imminent apocalypse meant that the Florentines had to arm themselves morally for the final judgement by destroying lascivious or luxurious clothes, books, and pictures. On the basis of this eschatology, Savonarola managed for a brief time to erect a sort of theocracy in the city until he was excommunicated and burnt in 1498.[137]

Such 'civic puritan' movements in the Renaissance were not confined to Florence; and Brescia was certainly not exempt from religious, prophetic, and mystical stirrings. Bernardino of Siena preached against luxury in Brescia in 1422, and in 1442 the Brescians were urged by seven preachers to give up their superfluous and satanic excesses in clothing.[138] Indeed, it is alleged that Savonarola preached in Brescia during Lent 1489 and received a vision of future destruction there.[139] Once again, Bernardino da Feltre inspired bonfires of books (including the Talmud) and feminine attire by his preaching in Brescia in 1492 and in both subsequent years.[140] In this regard, it is notable that Elia Capriolo's chronicle of Brescian history is frequently interspersed with descriptions of portents and prodigies, usually interpreted as providential signs or dire warnings of the calamities destined to fall upon the impious and loose-living. Thus,

---

[136] Relevant sermons by Bernardino of Siena are in *S. Bernardini Senensis ordinis fratrum minorum opera omnia*, vol. II, *Quadragesimales de Christiana religione sermones XLI–LXVI* (Ad claras aquas, Florentiae; Quaracchi-Florence: Ex typographia collegii S. Bonaventurae, 1950), 45–48 (sermon XLIV), 73–85 (sermon XLVI), 86–99 (sermon XLVII).

[137] On the reaction against funereal pomp in Florence after ca. 1480 see Strocchia, *Death and Ritual*, 210. See generally Donald Weinstein, *Savonarola and Florence: Prophecy and Patriotism in the Renaissance* (Princeton: Princeton University Press, 1970). The influence of Savonarolan ideals in Florence after 1498 is demonstrated by Lorenzo Polizzotto, *The Elect Nation: The Savonarolan Movement in Florence, 1494–1545* (Oxford: Clarendon Press, 1994). There has been little discussion of the influence of Savonarola outside Florence, but see Bowd, *Reform before the Reformation*, 180–200.

[138] Zanelli, "Predicatori."

[139] Roberto Ridolfi, *The Life of Girolamo Savonarola*, trans. Cecil Grayson (London: Routledge and Kegan Paul, 1959), 26–27.

[140] His activities are noted by Capriolo, *Chronica*, fol. LXXXv (*recte*, LXXIv). See also Cassa, *Funerali, pompe*, 82–83; and Zanelli, "Predicatori."

Capriolo condemns (while describing in extravagant detail) the luxurious festivities that took place on the occasion of a papal visit to Brescia in 1502.[141]

---

[141] Capriolo, *Chronicorum* (Book 13, cols. 129–31) (with contemporary editorial interventions in brackets preceded by *recte*, and our corrections followed by a question mark): "Anno igitur sequenti cum *Anna* Regina *Hungariae* ex *Francia* ad jugalem thorum accederet, ei *Brixia* transiturae Pontifex & Sacerdotes cum omni civitatis concursu obviam accessere: atque sub aurea umbella per Jurisconsultos sericis vestibus, & pelliceis magno pretio orariis collo pendentibus ornatos in urbem pompabiliter ea tribus suscepta est diebus. Qua majestate tanto luxu abundavit civitas nostra, ut *M. Scauri* libido eam invasisse videretur, ut & nos conqueri possimus, didicisse hominem provocare naturam, & auxisse artem, vitiorum irritamenta. In poculis libidines celare juvit, & chrystallinis auratisque bibere calicibus, vera luxuriae gloria aestimata est, quod posset statim totum deperire. Mensae quoque, vel disci ex olivarum radicibus tuberibusque variis multarum rerum figuris suapte natura signati, civibus nostris tam frequenti, tamque grato usui venere, ut non modo citreis & cupressinis, verum etiam eburneis pretio plerumque compararentur. Insuper & abaci visi sunt argenteis auratisque ornati plurimum vasis, malluviis, gutturniis, trulleisve, & manalibus [,] urceis, cadis, candelabris, cyathis, salinis, cochlearibus, crateris, ampullis, capidibus, phialis, aliisque bifruculis [for bifurculis?], & epitrapetiis. Missos facio parietes, columnas & structuras marmoreas, non tantum aereis & argenteis, sed aureis saepissime comparatas. Praetereo etiam bullas, armillas, moniliave, coronas, reticula aurea, gemmas, margaritas, & annulos, quorum tanta incessit libido, ut a mortalibus numina, aut reges a populo, aut a plebe patricii & senatores (ut antiquitus servabatur) minime discernantur. At plebeja fere quaeque virgo, dum nuberet [*recte*, nubat], ad millenas, nobilis ad vicies usque millenas libras nostrates, & ultra aliquando magnatum aliqua nomine daret [*recte*, dedat]: quod quidem in omni terrarum orbe maximum matrimonii aestimatum est patrimonium. Lineae aut laneae vestes non modo, sed sericae, argenteaeque, & aureae ad omne etiam barbaricum schema, interulae vel subuculae tam virorum, quam mulierum, orificiis alias collaribus serico & auro crispis, jugatisque ad talos fere usque protensae, latissimaeque, ac manicatae, ut non unum, sed plura earum singulis corpora tegerentur. Suppara diploides posthac gestantur, & caligae [*recte*, caligae braccatae], quibus licet pudenda [*recte*, pudenda intus] tegantur, non tamen celantur, sed ejus forma extra percipitur, quod intus celatur. Renones quoque, quos *rotonos* vocitant, saraballa, mastrucaeve, togae, pallia, quae nunc *sterniae*, chiroditae, vel tunicae, etiam caudatae, virgataeque, laticlavi, celotia, chalases, epitogia, chlamydes, zonae, lora, & omnia tam peregrina, quam domestica indumentorum genera, insuetis etiam nominibus appellata, adjectis quoque fimbriis, quae quidem omnium facilius depingi possent, quam latinis dictionibus exarari, ita usui, immo abusui evenere, ut profestis quoque diebus non modo primates & nobiles, verum & populares ipsi plebeique & rustici ea

Introduction   lxv

Since Brescia stood in the midst of the field of battle, it was inevitable that the War of the League of Cambrai (1508–1517) against Venice affected the tenor and urgency of the debate about funeral expenditure in the city. Throughout 1507 and 1508 Brescian rectors sent reports back to Venice describing the build-up of German troops over the border, and the city itself soon came under bombardment. The Brescians formally affirmed their loyalty to the republic, but as soon as the French invaded their territory, many Brescians opportunistically changed their political colors.[142] When the forces of the pope, the French king, the emperor, and the king of Spain defeated the Venetians at Agnadello in May 1509, some people placed the blame for the defeat squarely on the richly-attired shoulders of the effete Venetian nobility, whose sins had provoked God to punish the city. It was in response to a feeling that divine chastisement had fallen on the city that the raft of sumptuary legislation was re-enacted and preachers drew large crowds to hear the spread of vice in Venice condemned.[143] Brescia, as one of the republic's subject cities lost to the French, became the focus of "horrible signs" associated with the defeat: in 1511 an "impious and fierce serpent" was sighted in the air between Brescia and Cremona. In a speech calling for

---

frequenti aemulatione induerent. Sed omissis instar Mercurialis galeri capititiis [for capitiis?], inter hujuscemodi deliramenta hoc fuit maximopere damnandum, quod cujuslibet generis panno in frustula de industria lacerato, ad caligas & indumenta ipsa conficienda, illa diversis coloribus consuebatur [for consuebantur?]." Wonders and portents are noted in Capriolo, *Chronica*, fols. LXXIv (*recte*, LXXIIv), LXXIIv (*recte*, LXXIIIv), LXXIIIr (*recte*, LXXIVr). Capriolo asserts the veracity of miracles and marvels and defends them as proof of Christian tenets in his *De Confirmatione Christianae Fidei* (Brescia, 1497), sigs. avr–avv.

[142] Sanudo, *Diarii*, 7: 282, 590.

[143] Girolamo Priuli, *I diarii di Girolamo Priuli [AA. 1499–1512]*, ed. Arturo Segrè and Roberto Cessi, Rerum Italicarum Scriptores 24. 3, vols. 1, 2, 4 (Bologna and Città di Castello: S. Lapi, 1912–1938), 4: 112. Venetian sumptuary legislation of the period has been printed in G. Bistort, *Il magistrato alle pompe nella republica [sic] di Venezia, studio storico* (Venice: Società, 1912; facsimile ed. Bologna: Forni, 1969). See also Sanudo, *Diarii*, 11: 796–99; 12: 79–85, 87; and Felix Gilbert, "Venice in the Crisis of the League of Cambrai," in *Renaissance Venice*, ed. John R. Hale (London: Faber and Faber Ltd., 1973), chap. 10, which considers the link made by Venetian patricians between moral corruption and political failure, the pressures acting on the government between 1509 and 1517, and the splits that arose within the patriciate as a result.

the reform of Christendom made at the opening of the first session of the Fifth Lateran Council in 1512, Egidio of Viterbo, the general of the Augustinian Hermits, even went so far as to cite the battle of Brescia as a portent and a disaster for the whole of Italy.[144]

VIII. Conclusion

Like Egidio of Viterbo and many other Italians, Elia Capriolo thought that the portents for Italy were far from good, and he believed that the fault for the French occupation of Brescia lay not only in the stars but in the Venetians themselves, who were neglecting their ancestral virtues of justice, generosity, and faith.[145] As their contributions to the funerary fracas demonstrate, Valgulio and his fellow pamphleteer abhorred the way in which the demands of a conventionally 'good' burial could lead to clerical exploitation, the commemoration of false virtues, and the spread of vice. The anonymous author argued that the Dominicans employed "the tunnels of guile and trickery, and the catapults of hell-fear"

---

[144] Ottavia Niccoli, *Prophecy and People in Renaissance Italy*, trans. Lydia G. Cochrane (Princeton: Princeton University Press, 1990), 28, 46–47. See also the helpful scene-setting by Nelson H. Minnich, "Prophecy and the Fifth Lateran Council (1512–1517)," in *Prophetic Rome in the High Renaissance Period: Essays*, ed. Marjorie Reeves (Oxford: Clarendon Press, 1992), chap. 4. On Egidio of Viterbo's eschatology see John W. O'Malley, *Giles of Viterbo on Church and Reform* (Leiden, Boston, and Cologne: Brill, 1968).

[145] Capriolo, *Chronicorum* (Book 14, cols. 139–40): Capriolo notes the entry of Louis XII into Brescia on 23 May 1509 and adds: "Quod faustum, felixque sit semper, & procul a *Venetorum* lapsu, qui si maiorum suorum virtutem, justitiam, benignitatem, & fidem in omnes continuo prosequuti essent, praesentem status sui cladem cum tanta subditorum inopinata mutatione forte non sentirent. Uti enim virtutibus ipsis regna surgunt, crescunt, & servantur; ita etiam contra cadunt, ruunt, & funditus evertuntur; eo praecipue quod principum gesta tempore pacis, subditorum documenta sunt tempore belli. Quare tanti *Venetorum* interitus sola causa fuisse videretur eorum a parentibus, & maioribus suis degeneratio: quamquam ea omnia caelorum influxu contigisse aliqui arbitrentur; cum praecipue Mars in revolutione in angulo contentiones, & bella significaverit, & Luna Virgine hora oppositionis luminorum [for luminum?] ante solis adventum in Arietem in domo inimicorum inventa, sanguinis effusionem, & oppidorum, villarumque depopulationem portenderit."

(*Defense*, sig. Aiiv), and that they were encouraging corrosive ambition and competition for false honors among the Brescians: in short, they had fallen far away from the original intentions of St. Dominic and were threatening both the city of man and the city of God. In contrast, he promoted the true Christian virtues of lowliness of heart, tenderness, humanity, pity, charity, modesty, meekness, piety, and compassion, and he punningly praised the observant Franciscans for their "angelic" way of life (sig. Aiiiv).

These Christian virtues were also supported by humanist studies: in particular, Stoic philosophy, and the concept of a Ciceronian *res publica* in which virtuous men, loyal towards Brescia and Venice, could live well and achieve happiness in public life.[146] The anonymous author therefore praised the Brescians for their good public works such as the foundation of the *monte di pietà* and hospital, while in his pamphlet Valgulio offered more obviously Ciceronian virtues such as loyalty, faith, justice, and magnanimity in support of the funerary statute and its aims. Both men agreed that these virtues could be expressed through a moderate attachment to the solaces of prayer and almsgiving at funerals, and that in this way civil society would be well-ordered, pious, and secure. However, the image of integration, balance, and order promoted, for example, by the severe architectonic simplicity of the Renaissance tomb masked deeper anxieties about disorder. In this way, such Christian humanist concerns

---

[146] Indeed, it is possible to gauge the strength of Elia Capriolo's humanism from his ostensibly religious work *On the establishment of Christian faith* where the wisdom of the apostles is judged by the standards of Socrates!: "For who among them [i.e. the apostles] can be condemned for stupidity or weak-mindedness? What did any of them do that would not also befit a true and very wise philosopher? Socrates, who was judged the wisest of all men not only by the testimony of great philosophers but also by Apollo's oracle, disdained personal advantage, hated pride, favored gentleness and kindness above all else, ruled out self-seeking claims to knowledge, always relied on divine testimonies and clung faithfully to them, was satisfied with virtuous and righteous conduct and — a wonderful quality — hoped for no human reward for such an onerous service. Rather, submitting himself to certain danger and death because of it, he declared that he had been sent by God for this sole purpose, and said that he preferred to obey God rather than men. Consider, then, whether the deeds of our authors seem divergent from those of people who are called wise": Capriolo, *De Confirmatione Christianae fidei*, sig. aiiiir–v. Translation by J. Donald Cullington.

with loyalty, civic duty, and purity were also compatible with the normative drive of sumptuary legislation and civic puritanism. Legislators and preachers prohibited social practices which led to luxury and other vices, and in a few dramatic instances such as Savonarolan Florence they tried to realize a theocratic vision of government which was highly inimical to conflict or change.

In a similar way, the Brescians' strong sense of civic duty was underscored by a commitment to a narrowing of the social base, or closure of the ranks of the governing elite. Although Valgulio attacks the "disloyal, unjust, proud, grasping, greedy, cruel, insolent, and ignorant" man, whether he is a knight, count, or king, and he scorns those who hand out the "badges" of virtue (*Statute*, sig. Avr), he also lambastes the tax farmers, dentists, musicians, and traitors on whom such badges of honor have been conferred. It seems highly probable that the concepts of duty, piety, and honor outlined in both pamphlets were identical to the ideals and actions expected of members of the increasingly restricted governing elite of Brescia. Both authors therefore ridicule the rigidity of social conventions in funerary practice, but their pamphlets also contain considerable evidence of a backlash against any loosening up of the social hierarchy.[147]

These attitudes undoubtedly reflected concerns expressed in Venice, and indeed across the whole of Europe more generally, and in some ways they are a testimony to the strength and independence of Brescian cultural life and its precocious reforming piety.[148] Such social rigidity — in theory and practice — may have helped the city to weather a potentially destabilizing, if relatively minor, conflict over funerals, but a few years later the "constitutional pact" with Venice, predicated as it was on trust in the Venetian virtues and Brescian loyalty, collapsed like a house

---

[147] An analysis of the grants of *civilitas* between 1480 and 1508 shows that the period 1500–1508 saw an annual average of approximately two admissions per year, rising to 11 in 1508: ASB, ASC 507–521.

[148] See Gabriele Neher, "Moretto and the Congregation of S. Giorgio in Alga 1540–1550: Fashioning a Visual Identity of a Religious Congregation," in *Fashioning Identities in Renaissance Art*, ed. Mary Rogers (Aldershot, 2000), 131–48. Professor Peter Humfrey is writing a study of Venetian art and religious reform which will touch on these matters.

Introduction

of cards, weakened by unsustainable internal social conflicts and blown apart by the guns of France.[149]

These pamphlets do not simply open a window on to a forgotten funerary fracas; they also reveal a great deal about Renaissance funerary practices, the relationship between clergy and laity on the eve of the Reformation, and the nature of elite political, social, and religious attitudes during the Renaissance. They also hint at the considerable tensions that existed within the social and political body of Brescia as it struggled to define and defend its ideology and identity and maintain some degree of regional autonomy in the shadow of Venice on the eve of war: in short, they tell us a great deal about the meaning of death and life during the Renaissance.[150]

IX. Note on the Texts

The unattributed *Defensio statuti Brixianorum de ambitione: et sumptibus funerum minuendis* and one of the surviving copies of Carlo Valgulio, *Statutum Brixianorum de sumptibus funerum optima ratione nullum facere discrimen fortunae inter cives: Nec esse honores qui vulgo putantur* (Io. Antonius de Gandino dictus de Caegulis Apud portam Sancti Stephani: Brescia, 10 February 1509) are bound together in one volume in the British Library, London, with Elia Capriolo's *Chronica de rebus Brixianorum* (Arundus de Arundis: Brescia, n. d., but 1505) (pressmark 662. g.13 [1–3]).[151]

---

[149] Ann Katherine Isaacs, "States in Tuscany and Veneto, 1200–1500," in *Resistance, Representation, and Community*, ed. Peter Blickle (Cambridge: Cambridge University Press, 1997), 291–304, here 302, 303.

[150] The debate on the significance of regionality and autonomy in Renaissance Italy has been outlined by Elena Fasano Guarini, "Center and Periphery," in *The Origins of the State in Italy, 1300–1600*, ed. Julius Kirshner (Chicago: University of Chicago Press, 1996), chap. 4. The editor intends to return to this matter, as well as the nature of identity and ideology in fifteenth-century Brescia, in a future study.

[151] Palisca, *Humanism*, 100, n. 27, suggests that Giovanni Vincenzo Pinelli's copy of Valgulio's treatises on funerals and music "may now be in Milan, Biblioteca Ambrosiana." However, we have established that a copy is held not there but at the Biblioteca Nazionale Braidense.

According to the anonymous author of the *Defensio*, he composed the work in four days (sig. Aiir). The colophon (at sig. Aviv) notes that it was published at the command and expense of the Republic of Brescia, and was viewed and approved by the archbishop apparently acting as vicar-general for the bishop of Brescia. Ennio Sandal has speculated (on the basis of uncited English sources) that this work was published in Venice by Giorgio de' Rusconi because members of the Britannico family, who held the monopoly for printing in Brescia at the time, were in the Dominican order and therefore unlikely to print such a hostile piece of writing.[152]

The two pamphlets by Valgulio are printed in a different type, and more spaciously: *Statutum Brixianorum* (sigs Ar–Aviv) and *Contra vituperatorem musicae* (sigs Aviv–Aviiir).[153] This is the first printed text to bear the name of Giovanni Antonio Bresciano, who seems to have been Angelo Britannico's main rival as a printer of humanist literature in Brescia prior to the sack of the city in February 1512, issuing eight further editions in 1510 and 1511. The two 'extra' surnames may represent a move from his hometown, Gandino, to the Brescian district of Cigole.[154] On the back of the final leaf (sig. Aviiiv) is printed in a large and bold typeface: "DE: STATUTO: FU/NERARIO: BRI/XIANORUM".

---

[152] Sandal, "Autonomie municipali," 381.

[153] On the musical treatise see Stephen Bowd and J. Donald Cullington, "Two Renaissance Treatises: Carlo Valgulio of Brescia on Funerals and Music," *Annali Queriniani* 3 (2002): 131–71. An edition of the text can be found in Aegidius Carlerius, Johannes Tinctoris, Carlo Valgulio, *"That liberal and virtuous art": Three Humanist Treatises on Music*, trans., annot. and ed. J. Donald Cullington, intro. Reinhard Strohm and idem (Newtownabbey: University of Ulster, 2001).

[154] P. Veneziani, "La stampa a Brescia e nel Bresciano, 1472–1511," in *I primordi della stampa a Brescia 1472–1511, Atti del convegno, Brescia 6–8 June 1984*, ed. Ennio Sandal (Padua: Editrice Antenore, 1986), 1–24, here 22–23; Fernanda Ascarelli and Marco Menato, *La tipografia del '500 in Italia* (Florence: Leo S. Olschki, 1989), 170.

Anonymous [Elia Capriolo?]

Defensio statuti Brixianorum de ambitione et sumptibus funerum minuendis

▦

A defense of the Brescians' statute for reducing the rivalry and the expenses of funerals

Anonymous [Elia Capriolo?]

[sig. Aiir]

Defensio populi Brixiani rei violatae ecclesiasticae libertatis ob decretum ab eo factum de ambitione[a] et sumptibus funerum minuendis, accusantibus Fratribus Sancti Dominici.

[Prologus]

Si quis antea forte dubitavit quanta cupiditate atque avaritia pectora eorum hominum ardeant, qui se ab inani quodam animi tumore Fratres Praedicatores vocant, perfectum iam tandem per eos ipsos est, ut nulli amplius hominum sit dubitationi locus. Praeclarum namque specimen earum dedere, et amplissima monumenta eiusce rei condidere, quae ne in ulla parte orbis ignota forent ingentem numerum eorum formis aeneis confici curaverunt, ut cunctis mortalibus copia esset. Quanquam non eo animo eoque consilio id fecere, ut suos morbos animorum nudarent, quos nulla non arte contegendi magnam praecipuamque curam gerunt, verum ut moderatissimam, frugalissimam veraeque religionis diligentissimam cultricem Brixianam civitatem impio atque nefario crimine accusarent, sedique apostolicae invisam redderent, et universum Christianum genus adversus ipsam concitarent. Sed ea est vitiorum vis atque natura, avaritiae praesertim parentis omnium, ut aciem mentis obstupefaciant praecipitesque agant cultores et possessores suos. Ea demum est divinae iustitiae ratio de inimicis suis, suos ut inimicos ulciscatur. Vitia enim imprimis inimici Dei sunt, quibus ministris accipit poenas ab iis

---

[a] *correxi*: ambitiones *cod.*

Anonymous [Elia Capriolo?]

A DEFENSE OF THE BRESCIANS' STATUTE FOR REDUCING THE RIVALRY AND THE EXPENSES OF FUNERALS.

A defense of the Brescian people, accused by the Dominican brothers of infringing church freedom by the decree they made for reducing the rivalry and the expenses of funerals.

[Introduction]

If anyone previously doubted how great is the lust and greed that fires the hearts of those people who from some vain motive of pride style themselves "preaching brothers", they themselves have at long last ensured that no one has any further room for doubt. They have given a shining example of the two former qualities, and set up impressive monuments to their vanity, a large number of which they have had cast in brazen images, thus providing plenty for all mankind to see, so that no part of the world may be unacquainted with them. They have not, however, done this with the idea and intention of laying bare their own diseased minds, which they take exceptionally great care to conceal by every possible device: rather, they did it in order to accuse the city of Brescia, most moderate, economical, and devotedly supportive of true religion as it is, of an impious and despicable crime, to render it hateful to the apostolic see, and to stir up the whole of Christendom against it. But such is the power and nature of vices, especially of greed, which is mother to them all, that they paralyze mental perception and infatuate their adherents and possessors: that, after all, is divine justice's way with its enemies, to avenge its enemies. (For vices are particularly God's enemies,

qui illis utuntur inimicis et ipsis Dei. At quid dico avaritiam suam hos homines patefecisse? Nec minus quidem ingratitudinem atque immanitatem prae se tulerunt, inhumanissima omnium scelera, quae non modo charitatem funditus tollunt, sed omnem omnino societatem humanam evertunt. Sed quanta vecordia aut potius impudentia atque temeritate agitantur, ut quos impietatis accusant, quos indignos communione hominum praedicant, quibus tantam notam dedecoris, infamiae, ignominiae apud omnes nationes inurunt, id se ad eorum honorem et gloriam facere profiteri audeant. Atque utinam hoc sit! Aliud esse haud dubie reor, quod superat omnes indignitates. Usque adeo enim nos hebetes, adeo tardos esse existimant, quia elenchos Sancti Thomae — captiosos opinor esse syllogismos[1] — ignoramus, ut tenebras pro luce, nigrum pro candido per ludibrium atque contemptum se nobis persuadere posse putent. Quid facerent si Scottum scirent?[2]

Quare ne nobilissima civitas antiquum decus fidei, religionis, pietatis — quo perpetuo tenore excelluit excellitque — amittat et falsis criminibus opprimatur, defensione opus est, et obiecta crimina sunt diluenda. Ego pro virili parte mea in tanto discrimine versanti patriae deesse nefas putavi, nullo quidem ingenio meo doctrinave ulla aut eloquentia fretus sed apertissimae veritati fidens, cuius ope quatriduo uno defensionem hanc composui adversus accusationem complexam volumine formis impresso editam[3] ab iis a quibus minime oportebat. Precor igitur Christianos omnes, ad quorum manus accusatorius liber ille pervenit, ut aequis et attentis animis hanc quoque defensionem legant: efficiet profecto ut si quod odium et adversam voluntatem in Brixianos conceperunt falsis

A defense of the Brescians' statute

and with their help he punishes the practitioners of those very enemies of his.) But why do I say that these men have revealed their greed? They have displayed just as much ingratitude and brutality, the most inhuman of all crimes, which not only utterly destroy charity but also completely subvert all human society. But what great madness — or rather shamelessness and recklessness — it is that drives them daringly to claim they are doing this *for the honor and glory* of those they accuse of impiety, declare unfit for human company, and brand with such a worldwide stigma of shame, disgrace, and infamy! If only *this* could be the outcome! But I firmly believe it is something else: the deepest possible humiliation. Just because we do not know St. Thomas's critical inquiries (I consider them captious syllogisms),[1] they consider us so dull, so stupid, that they think they can with mocking scorn persuade us darkness is light and black is white. What would they be doing if they knew Scotus?[2]

Therefore, lest our noble city lose the ancient prestige of faith, religion, and piety which has eternally distinguished it — and still does — and be overwhelmed by false charges, we must defend it and dispel the charges hurled at it. I thought it would be wrong if I failed to do my utmost for my native city when its situation is so critical. With no talent, learning, or eloquence to rely on, I put my trust in the obvious truth, with whose aid I have within four days written this defense against a complex accusation issued in a printed volume[3] by those who ought least to have done so. I therefore beg all Christians into whose hands the accusing book has come to read this defense no less fairly and carefully. Its effect will surely be to make them renounce any hatred and ill-will

---

[1] In two encyclopedic syntheses, the *Summa contra gentiles* and the *Summa theologiae*, Thomas Aquinas (ca. 1225–1274) attempted to combine Aristotelian rationalism with Christian doctrine. He is mentioned here because he was a much-revered former member, and father-figure, of the Dominican Order (Ordo Praedicatorum) which the anonymous author is attacking.

[2] In commentaries on the Bible, Aristotle, and Peter Lombard's *Sentences*, the Franciscan Johannes Duns Scotus (ca. 1265–1308) reacted against both Aristotle and Aquinas, his rival as the most influential theologian of the Middle Ages. The subtlety of his arguments, however, led sixteenth-century humanists and Reformers to ridicule the Scotists as mere "Dunses" or "Dunsmen" — hence the word 'dunce'.

[3] *Quaestio an infrascripta statuta super mortuariis sint contra ecclesiasticam libertatem* (hereafter *Quaestio*): see Appendix 2.

criminibus persuasi, eam omnem abiiciant, et in ipsos accusatores cognita veritate graviorem atque vehementiorem convertant.

 Cum populus Brixianus duobus calamitosissimis ac miserandis malis premeretur, diutina atque intolleranda fame et exitiali urentique morbo quodam qui nulla ope medica levari poterat, tam frequentia funera essent ut quamcunque in partem urbis circumvertisses oculos, funera, luctus, gemitus omnis sexus atque aetatis partim moerore mortuorum, partim prope enecti fame populi conspicerentur, ingruebat inde haud mediocris fessis et conflictatis tantis malis hominibus exequiarum cura, ad quas, exardescente in dies magis atque magis adeo ambitione funerum ut cives aliqui grande aes alienum accepta a Iudaeis faenori pecunia conflarent,[4] consuetudine nescio qua per aemulationem existimati honoris convocabantur magna agmina Fratrum et alterius generis clericorum,[5] gens adeo intractabilis ut inter ploratus et gemitus defuncti propinquorum ac inter mortes quandoque proelia inter se consererent. Cum haec ita essent, expressit necessitas senatui Brixiano ut cui parti[b] malorum posset, ei mederetur. Decretum itaque factum est comprobantibus dominis rectoribus urbis, quo decreto non modo sumptus funerum minuuntur, verum etiam ambitio et sollicitudines atque molestiae curantibus funera levantur, quando quidem caetera mala nullo humano consilio levari posse videbantur. Hoc publicato decreto hi Fratres, quia aliquid de suo quaestu imminutum videbant, quasi suibus detracta de glandibus consuetis portio aliqua foret, primo grunnire ac fremere coeperunt, deinde consiliis inter sapientes synagogae communicatis librum composuere, ipsumque

---

[b] *correxi:* partim *cod.*

A defense of the Brescians' statute

they have conceived towards the Brescians through the influence of false charges, and turn it in a deeper and stronger form — when they learn the truth — upon the accusers themselves.

At a time when the Brescian people were beset by two disastrous and deplorable calamities — an unbearably protracted famine, and a fatally virulent fever which no medical treatment could alleviate — and when funerals were so frequent that wherever in the city you looked you could see funerals, grief, and mourning regardless of sex and age, with lamentation partly for the deceased, partly for those almost starved to death: then it was that, exhausted and afflicted by such calamities, people were seized by an inordinate passion for obsequies. With the competition for funerals growing so increasingly heated that some citizens borrowed money at interest from the Jews and ran up huge debts,[4] because of some custom or other — due to rivalry for a supposed honor — large squads of brothers and the other type of clergy[5] were summoned to these obsequies: a breed so uncompromising that amid the tears and groans of the deceased's relatives, and amid people's deaths, they would sometimes fight with each other. The Brescian senate was therefore forced by circumstances to remedy whatever part of these calamities it could. So, with the approval of the city's ruling masters, a decree was passed not only cutting expenditure on funerals, but also reducing the competition, the worries, and the troubles of those arranging them — since, of course, the other calamities seemed incapable of reduction by any human device. When the decree was published, these brothers, seeing their profit somewhat diminished (as though pigs were to lose some portion of their usual acorns), first began to grunt and grumble, then made common cause with the wise men of the synagogue and compiled a book which they published, the work of

---

[4] Though the New Testament does not specifically condemn the exaction of interest, various church councils outlawed it: first for clerics (Arles, 314; Nicaea, 325), later for laypeople as well (the Third Lateran Council, 1179; the Second of Lyons, 1274). But the Fourth Lateran Council (1215) allowed it to the Jews, who therefore found moneylending one of their most reliable sources of income in Italy until the establishment of *monti di pietà* in the fifteenth century: see Pullan, *Rich and Poor in Renaissance Venice*, 431–75. (See also n. 21 below.)

[5] The secular clergy, i.e., priests living 'in the world' rather than as members of a religious order.

edidere multorum opus mensium Fratrumque omnium eius ordinis qui in aliqua sunt opinione apud ipsos doctrinae.

Continet liber ille gravissimam atque atrocissimam accusationem: id decretum Brixianorum tollere libertatem Ecclesiae et iura pontificia atque imperatoria infringere ac violare,[6] Brixianos omnes a sacris, a societate et communione caeterorum hominum esse reiiciendos contendunt. Adeoque suas omnis exercent opes ut, si minus prudentem aliquem ac levem Pontificem sortiti forent, haud dubium est quin magnum aliquod dedecus magnumque incommodum populo Brixiano accipiendum fuerit. Sed providentia superum constantem prudentemque habemus.[7] O impiam, O immanem et ingratam atque avaram gentem! Haeccine est charitas praedicantium verbum Dei? Haeccine est misericordia erga populum tantis oppressum malis religiosorum hominum? Haeccine est gratitudo erga eam civitatem a qua tot tantaque commoda semper accepistis accipitisque, quae duo vobis opportunissimis locis praeclara monasteria condidit cum pulcherrimis templis eaque magnifice paravit et exornavit, quae vos vestit, vos pascit, tam avidam gentem tantumque numerum, cuius benignitate nihil vobis deest praeter moderationem et aequitatem,

many months and of all the brothers of that order who had any reputation among them for learning.

The book contains a grave and cruel charge: they maintain that the Brescians' decree abolishes the Church's freedom, and tramples and trespasses on the rights of pope and emperor,[6] so all the Brescians should be excluded from the sacraments and from other people's society and company. They use all their resources so well that if luck had given them some imprudent and unreliable pope, the Brescian people would without any doubt have had to endure much disgrace and much inconvenience. But by heavenly providence we have a firm and prudent one.[7] You godless, monstrous, ungrateful, and greedy folk! Is this the charity of those who preach God's word? Is this the compassion religious show to a people stricken by such misfortunes? Is this the gratitude you show to a city from which you have always received — and still receive — so many great benefits? One that founded two splendid monasteries in very convenient places for you, with beautiful churches which it superbly equipped and adorned? The city that clothes and feeds you, who are so greedy and so numerous? Through whose kindness you lack nothing except moderation

---

[6] *Quaestio* (sig. br–v): ". . . illud statutum dicitur esse contra libertatem ecclesiasticam quod est contra privilegia indulta Ecclesiae universali sive a domino deo, sive a papa, sive ab imperatore . . ."

[7] Julius II, b. Giuliano della Rovere (1443–1513, pope from 1503), is remembered more for his military enterprises — attacked, together with his luxurious life-style, by Erasmus in *Moriae encomium* (*Praise of Folly*) (1509) (see Erasmus, *Collected Works*, vol. 27, ed. A. H. T. Levi [Toronto: University of Toronto Press, 1986], 138–39) and throughout *Julius exclusus de caelo* (ca. 1513) (*Collected Works*, 27: 168–97) — and for his patronage of Bramante, Raphael, and Michelangelo, than for his ecclesiastical reforms. Ironically, the first of these was the constitution "De fratrum nostrorum" (1503) which, immediately after his own use of simony to gain the papacy, invalidated future pontifical elections achieved by that means. The anonymous author's praise of him here stems mainly from his refusal of the Dominicans' request to excommunicate the people of Brescia (see Cassa, *Funerali, pompe*, 44–47 and above, xxix–xxx), but may also owe something to the fact that (under the influence of his uncle Francesco della Rovere, later Sixtus IV) Julius had for a time lived with members of the Order of Friars Minor, and had acted as its protector from 1474: see J. Moorman, *A History of the Franciscan Order from its Origins to the Year 1517* (Oxford: The Clarendon Press, 1968), 573. See also Christine Shaw, *Julius II: The Warrior Pope* (Oxford: Clarendon Press, 1993).

quae ab aliis dari nequeunt? Vestrisne precibus utentur Brixiani ad pacem Dei impetrandam, qui impia bella seritis adversus eos? Ad iramne molliendam ac deprecandam caelestium vestras orationes adhibebunt, qui tantas ipsi volvitis moles irarum ut perdere altricem vestram praeclaram civitatem falsis criminibus modici lucelli gratia quaeritis? Si censetis et compertum vobis esse praedicatis persuadereque omnibus hominibus conamini Brixianos [sig. Aiiv] esse excommunicatos, cur habitatis, cur versamini cum ipsis? Quid sermonem communicatis? Quid eorum bona capitis? Abite igitur ne contagio obsit; nolite temnere sanctiones vestras; docete exemplo vestro vos vera dicere et integre consulere. Fugite Brixianos quos fugiendos esse censetis, ne fallere atque decipere homines aliud agendo et aliud praedicando videamini. Quid praeterea de tanto numero librorum nomen vestrum desecuistis? Quid lapidem iecistis et abscondistis manum, si fraudem calumniamque nullam in negocio esse putatis? Cur vos pudet auctores et consultores apertos esse veritatis, praesertim cum vocari velitis Praedicatores, hoc est, nuntii ipsius veritatis nudi, simplices, non simulantes nec dissimulantes, non fucati, intrepidi, magnanimi (tales namque Deus amat esse suos oratores)? Verum conscientia et metu[c] impuri consilii perturbatus animus inconstansque mens vestra incertos animi atque dissimulantes facit, ut quod maxime agitis minime id agere videamini. Sed nihil id erat opus: ipse liber avaritiam atque cupiditatem olens vos et vestra ingenia prodit et accusat.

 Descendamus iam tandem ad certamen rationum, in quibus cognoscendis et veritate iudicanda oratos omnes velim ut deposito odio, quo plurimo apud omne genus tam ecclesasticorum quam saecularium hanc gentem constat laborare, liberis et aequis utrique parti animis utantur. Nec erit magni operis res propter clarissimam atque apertissimam planitiem veritatis. Eorum ambages aliquas praetermittam, nec ego meas ullas volvam, et valere sinam rationes quasdam in favorem statuti nostri collectas a quodam Albrico[8] et ab accusatoribus ordine propositas: sponte illas reiicio.

[c] *correxi*: metus *cod.*

and fairness, things that others cannot give you? Will the Brescians use your prayers to gain peace with God if you are waging an unholy war against them? Will they employ your petitions to appease and avert heaven's wrath if you yourselves are piling up such huge loads of wrath, as you seek to ruin the famous city that nurtures you by falsely accusing it for the sake of a tiny profit? If you believe — even declaring how sure you are, and trying to convince all the world — that the Brescians are excommunicate, why do you live and associate with them, why make conversation with them, why take their goods? Go away then lest the pollution harm you, do not despise your penal sanctions, show by your example that you speak and rigorously observe the truth! Shun the Brescians whom you believe should be shunned, lest you seem to cheat and deceive people by doing one thing and preaching another! Why, moreover, have you excised your name from so many books? Why have you thrown a stone and hidden your hand if you think there is no deception or slander involved? Why are you ashamed to be open advisers and espousers of the truth, especially as you wish to be called preachers (that is, messengers) of truth itself — men who are naked and artless, not pretending or dissembling, genuine, fearless, and magnanimous, for that is how God likes his spokesmen to be. But the fear-racked consciousness of foul intent upsets your thoughts and renders your minds unstable, making you dither and dissemble, so that what you do most you appear to do least. But there was no need for that: the book itself, reeking of greed and lust, betrays and impugns you and your propensities.

Let us now at last proceed to argue the issues: in examining them and determining the truth I would ask everyone to put away the hatred which, it is agreed, sorely afflicts our people of every class, whether religious or lay, and to give frank and fair consideration to both sides. This will not be too demanding, because of the blindingly obvious clarity of the truth. Some of their digressions I shall omit, nor shall I reel off any of my own. I shall also rule out certain points favorable to our statute gathered by one Alberico[8] and set out in order by the accusers: I purposely

---

[8] He is identified as the legal writer Alberico da Rosciate of Bergamo (ca. 1290–1360) in *Quaestio* (sigs aiiir–aivr), where ten points drawn from his *Quaestiones statutorum* are listed as possible arguments for the Brescian statute. For further details of Alberico, see L. Prosdocimi, "Alberico da Rosate," *DBI*, 1: 656–57.

Nullum tamen praetermittens argumentum rationemve ullam adversariorum nec verbum quidem, quod vel minimam momenti speciem causae eorum facere videatur, planissime demonstraturum profiteor esse me non modo statutum seu decretum nostrum nihil comminuere ecclesiasticam libertatem, id quod adversarii ostendere conantur, sed ipsos accusatores ipsam permanifesto oppugnare, hocque per omnia capita argumentationum illorum quae robur et fundamentum totius causae putantur efficiam. Quorum primum sumitur a iure divino, quod quidem est huiusmodi.

[I]

Tolli contendunt per nostrum decretum ius divinum, quod modum unum conferendae elemosynae ad quam ab divis suademur et aliquando iubemur prohibeat, non semper ergo ut in hac causa.[9] Ut concedamus nullam speciem elemosynae esse reiiciendam modumve ullum spernendum, nego elemosynae nomen mereri, nec re vera elemosynam esse, quod alicui datur ut ab eo aliud accipias — quod quidem ni reciperes tu id non tribuas — aut quod minime calamitosis, miseris, egentibusque confertur. Elemosynam Graeci, nos misericordiam recte dicimus: ea est cum aegritudinem in animo suscipimus calamitatibus alienis commoti, et illis pro nostra facultate opem ferimus, nullam aut operam aut officium aliamve omnino repensionem exposcentes sperantesve ab eo cui auxilium tulimus. Gratuita namque et libera esse debet elemosyna, non mercenaria.

Cum itaque vobis religiosis aliquid impenditur officii causa vestri et operae quam exhibetis comitando alicuius saecularis funus, quodque labore vestro viae iactura insuper temporis promeremini, id nullo pacto elemosyna censeri potest, sed merces, sed praemium impensae operae iure vocari debet. Argumento est quod nemo vestrum adibit funus cuiusquam seu vocatus seu non vocatus ni se sciat recepturum praemium, quo praemio si casu aliquo fraudati sitis altas querimonias excitare soletis,

reject them. But by passing over no argument or point made by our opponents — not even one word which seems to give the least impression of bearing on their case — I promise to show very clearly not only that our statute or decree in no way destroys church freedom, as our opponents try to prove, but that the accusers themselves blatantly attack it. I shall achieve this in relation to all those points of their presentation which are considered the core and basis of the whole case. The first of these centers on divine law and is as follows.

[I]

They maintain that divine law is abolished by our decree because it bans one method of almsgiving (something we are divinely urged and at times commanded to do), so does not *always* ban it, as alleged here.[9] Let us admit that no type of alms should be rejected, no method spurned. I deny, however, that it is worthy of the name 'alms', or is *really* alms, if something is given to someone with a view to your getting from him something else, failure to receive which would cause you not to make the gift, or if the alms are bestowed on those who are not at all afflicted, wretched, or needy. What the Greeks properly call "alms" (*elemosyna*) and we call "compassion" (*misericordia*) is that when, moved by the afflictions of others, we feel sick at heart, and bring them all the help we can, not requiring or hoping for any work or service or any other repayment whatever from the person we have helped — for alms must be free and gratis, not paid for.

When, therefore, you religious are paid something for the service and work you do in escorting the funeral of some layperson, and for kindly toiling along the road and sacrificing your time as well, in no way can that be considered alms: it ought rightly to be called a fee, a reward for work carried out. Proof lies in the fact that none of you, whether invited or not, will go to anyone's funeral unless he knows he will get a reward, and if by any chance you are cheated of it you usually utter

---

[9] *Quaestio* (sig. biir): "Nec valet si dicatur: 'Non prohibemus elemosinas fieri, sed hanc specialem,' quia haec est elemosina, ergo prohibetur elemosina, et nullam possunt prohibere."

nec unquam amplius ad eundem curantem aliud funus (memores retentae in superiore funere mercedis) vel plurimum rogati accedetis. Ac si quando de funere aliquo perpetrato forte loquimini, hanc candelam, hanc pecuniam sum lucratus in funere huius vel illius dicere soletis. Igitur si porrigere suam humanitatem usque ad sepulturam mortuorum elemosyna et misericordia est, id quod profecto est teste Augustino in libro *De Moribus Ecclesiae*,[10] utri tandem elemosynam tollunt, saecularesne qui magna mercede magnaque iactura rei familiaris ad misericordiae vos munus non alliciunt, an vos qui ad nullius unquam funus spe incisa praemii vaditis? Si hoc negatis, cur nunquam comitamini cadaver inopis ad sepulturam?

At neque elemosyna est quod datur non indigenti et nulla miseratione digno, quales estis vos. Curnam per Deum immortalem vobis sit miserendum? Num egestas admonet, qui latifundia, domos aliasque possessiones multas — ut fama est hominum — in bonis habetis, qui amplos proventus annuos percipitis, qui messium, vindemiarum et rerum omnium fructuum ac frugum mortalium omnium Brixianae terrae amplissimae portionem capitis, ad quam accipiendam (quasi iure quodam hereditario vobis debitam) quotannis mittitis et destinatis ad illud exequendum munus Praedicatores, cuius rei gratia ut magnum numerum eorum habeatis praecipuo studio procuratis, quoniam id genus dialecticum ac litteratum ad agricolas persuadendos ut largius praebeant quam eorum esset voluntas aptius esse existimatis? Taceo ditia confessionum retia, sileo opulentissima aucupia testamentorum, praeterquam quod

loud complaints, and you will never again, however earnestly requested, approach the same person when he arranges another funeral, because you remember the fee withheld at the previous one. And if ever you happen to mention some funeral you have performed, you usually say: "I've gained this candle, this money at so-and-so's funeral." If, therefore, alms and compassion consist in extending one's humanity to the burial of the dead, as they certainly do according to Augustine in his book *On the conduct of the Church*,[10] then *who* are abolishing alms: the laypeople who fail to attract you to your duty of compassion with a large fee and a large outlay of family property, or you who never attend anyone's funeral when your hope of a reward is cut off? If you deny this, why do you never escort a pauper's corpse to burial?

But neither is it alms that is given to someone who, like you, is not in need and deserves no pity. Why indeed, for God's sake, should you be pitied? Does your poverty urge it? But according to popular rumor you own farms, houses, and many other articles of property. You reap abundant supplies each year and take a share of harvests, vintages, and everything, the fruit and produce belonging to everybody in the abundant territory of Brescia; and to receive it — as though owed to you by some inherited right — you send people out each year, detailing preachers to perform that task. For this purpose you take special pains to have a good number of them, since you think that type of logician and learned man is more adept at persuading farmers to provide more than they would wish. I do not mention your nets bulging with confessions, and I say nothing about your lucrative poaching of wills, except that always,

---

[10] Augustine, *De moribus Ecclesiae catholicae et de moribus Manichaeorum libri duo* 1. 27. 53 (*PL* 32. 1333): "Quare illa omnia, quibus huiuscemodi malis incommodisve resistitur, qui officiose atque humiliter praebent, misericordes vocantur, etiamsi sapientes usque adeo sint, ut iam nullo animi dolore turbentur; nam quis ignoret ex eo appellatam esse misericordiam, quod miserum cor faciat condolescentis alieno malo?" Augustine wrote at greater length on the importance of almsgiving in his *De sermone Domini in monte* 2. 2. 5–9, and throughout his *Sermones* 60, 61 and 72: see *Writings of Saint Augustine*, vol. 3, trans. D. J. Kavanagh, Fathers of the Church 11 (Washington, DC: Catholic University of America Press, 1951), 113–18, 259–73, 275–86, 287–92. See A. Fitzgerald, "Mercy, Works of Mercy," in *Augustine Through the Ages*, ed. idem (Grand Rapids: Eerdmans, 1999), 557–61.

privatae vobis semper quacunque hora patent domus unde quasi de penoribus vestris quicquid usui ad vescendum esse potest promendi potestas est. Pudet referre diligentiam atque sedulitatem quibus in captando orbos et orbas hi Fratres utuntur, quos omnes accuratissime in tabella descriptos ante oculos semper habent, mittunturque domo — ut quidem in populo frequens est fama — quasi in provincias legati aptissimi quique ad blandiendum, assentandum captandumque atque omnino instructi omnibus artibus, omnibus machinis bellicis operibusque quibus orbos illos et orbas oppugnent. Cumque omni genere machinarum pro natura ingenioque expugnandorum utantur, nullum tamen foelicius admovent quam cuniculos fraudum et astus et catapultas inferni metus. Reversi ad monasterium quisque exponit gesta in legatione sive potius in oppugnatione sibi destinati orbi vel orbae; qui praeclarius negocium transegit, is in maiore honore apud caeteros Fratres habetur. An aegris, infirmis attenuatisque corporibus vestris miserebimur, quorum torosa valentiaque membra et aptas certaminibus vires cum admiratione spectamus? At tamen fateor ingentibus vos premi calamitatibus quibus profecto est miserendum, quae calamitates conscientia tantae ingratitudinis et tantae avaritiae animam vestram depopulantur. Sed quaenam ratio miserendi et opitulandi vobis iniri potest, qui morbos vestros non modo non cognoscitis, verum medici sanorum ultro esse vultis; qui simulatione quadam animae nostrae miserationis, qui [sig. Aiiir] in diras excommunicationis inciderimus, crudelitatem in nos exercetis?

Quod etsi mercedem hanc elemosynam esse concedamus, an cum innumeri sint — ut vosmet inquitis — conferendae elemosynae modi et indigentibus subveniendi,[11] si unum civitas aliquem propter magnos usus rei publicae praeclusit liberis atque patentibus caeteris omnibus, humana atque divina miscenda vobis fuerunt, infames et accusatores libelli spargendi per omnes partes orbis terrarum? Si omnes divi qui homines ad munera elemosynae cohortantur, unde ius istud divinum petitis, in corporibus adessent, haud dubie non se hortari nec se sentire

whatever the time, private houses lie open to you from which you are able to take, as though from your own larders, whatever can serve you for sustenance. It is shameful to report the trouble and effort these brothers devote to trapping widowers and widows: they keep in constant view a carefully compiled list of them all on a tablet, and common rumor has it that from their house are sent out — like ambassadors sent to the provinces — all the men most adept at flattery, obsequiousness, and enticement, those fully trained in all the skills, assault-weapons, and devices needed for attacking those widowers and widows. And although they use every sort of weapon, according to the character and intelligence of their intended victims, no weapon do they apply more successfully than the tunnels of guile and trickery, and the catapults of hell-fear. Returning to the monastery, each outlines his exploits in the embassy, or rather in the attack on the widower or widow assigned to him. The one who has done a more impressive job is held in greater esteem by the other brothers. Or shall we pity your sick, feeble and weakened bodies, you at whose brawny, healthy limbs and athletic strength we gaze admiringly? And yet I admit that you are beset by great afflictions which should arouse pity, afflictions which ravage your souls with the consciousness of such ingratitude and greed. But what means of pity and help can be devised for you, who not only do not recognize your own diseases, but wish to be healthy people's doctors into the bargain? By a certain pretense of pity for our souls you show cruelty towards us, who have fallen prey to the curses of excommunication.

But even if we admit that this funeral fee is alms, since (as you yourselves say) there are countless ways of giving alms and aiding the needy,[11] if the city has for pressing political reasons blocked a particular one but all the others are freely available, did you *have* to confound things earthly and heavenly? Did you *have* to scatter discreditable and defamatory pamphlets all over the face of the earth? If all the gods who urge men to the duty of alms, from which you derive that holy law of yours, were present in the flesh, surely they would protest that they did not urge or

---

[11] *Quaestio* (sig. biiir): "Et quum innumerabiles quasi sint modi elemosinas faciendi, diversique diversis placeant, velle limitare modos, et clericis favorabiles prohibere, est homines ab elemosinis retrahere et divinis inspirationibus resistere ... et sic ecclesiasticam libertatem violare."

exclamarent per universos elemosynarum modos esse egentibus auxiliandum — hoc namque locupletare egenum esset et locupletem exinanire atque egenum facere — sed per eos modos suppetias calamitosis eundum esse qui maxime commodi opem danti forent. Si ipsi quoque egeni rogentur quo elemosynae modo sibi subveniri velint, nullo alio respondebunt nisi opitulanti commodissimo.

Caeterum quid de varietate modorum miserendi verba facimus? Unicus omnino miserendi modus et unica ratio est, mens videlicet pia et cor mite atque humile. Quoniam autem variae res sunt quibus mortales egere possunt, variae quoque calamitates quibus naturae infirmitas humanae conflictatur, per abusum complures dicimus esse elemosynae atque misericordiae modos. Non enim res quae datur — cera, pecunia et caetera huiusmodi — est elemosyna, sed cordis humilitas, mansuetudo, humanitas et miseratio et charitas. Quare, cum nostrum decretum modum mensuramque sumptibus funerum statuit, non imperat ut corda immitia sint et dura, ac de corde pellatur miseratio et charitas. Quod enim pectus misericors ac mite in funere non faciet, alia ratione quapiam suum officium suumque munus obibit; nescit vera pietas, vera misericordia veraque virtus — nec potest — parere nisi iustis imperiis iustisque legibus, nec ullis quit vinculis coerceri nec ulla vi contineri aut impediri. Immensae sunt potestatis atque libertatis: non mulctam, non poenam, non supplicia legibus, decretis, indulctis seu pontificia seu imperatoria seu regia sint — si forte illas a suo munere prohibere velint — intentata perhorrescunt. Testes sunt martyres quorum fides, pietas, charitas, animi magnitudo ullaque pars virtutis Christianae nullis tormentis, nullis cruciatibus vel minimum inflecti potuerunt. Quae cum[d] ita sint — et sunt luce solis clariora — decretum nostrum non est contra ius divinum, sed vos ipsum non a cornu nec a lateribus sed recta fronte oppugnatis, qui avaritia, ingratitudine, effrenato studio habendi armati et instructi charitatem et misericordiam de vestris pectoribus expulistis.

"Prohibet," inquiunt, "decretum non elemosynas modo, verum orationes ac preces religiosorum pro defunctis, vetans eos vocari ad prosequendum funus."[12] An opportuniora vobis videntur orationibus ac precibus

---

[d] *correxi*: cmu *cod.*

A defense of the Brescians' statute

feel that one should succor the needy with *every* type of alms, for that would mean enriching the poor man while squeezing and impoverishing the rich one. Rather they would say that one should assist the afflicted by the means most convenient for the person providing help. If, moreover, the poor are asked what type of alms assistance they would like, they will reply: "Only what is most convenient for the helper."

Yet why do we speak about the diversity of means to show pity? It has only one means and one method: a devout mind, that is, and a gentle, lowly heart. But since there are different things that people can be in need of, and different afflictions that weak human nature is distressed by, we inaccurately say there are several types of alms and compassion. For it is not what is given — a candle, money, and other such things — that constitutes alms, but lowliness of heart, tenderness, humanity, pity, and charity. So when our decree places a check and a limit on funeral expenditure, it does not order hearts to be harsh and cruel, or pity and charity to be banished from the heart, for a compassionate and gentle soul will find some other way to discharge the obligation and duty it will not fulfill at a funeral. True piety, true compassion, and true virtue will not and cannot obey any unjust authorities or laws, or be confined by any chains, or be repressed or hindered by any force. Their power and freedom are boundless, and they tremble at no fine, punishment, or penalties threatened by laws, decrees, or indulgences, and laid down by pope, emperor, or king, should they wish to prevent them from doing their duty. The martyrs bear witness to this, people whose faith, piety, charity, magnanimity, and any other facet of Christian virtue no torment, no torture could even slightly deflect. These things being so — and they are clearer than daylight — our decree does not contravene divine law: you are the ones who attack it, not from the wing or from the flanks but head-on, since, armed and equipped with greed, ingratitude, and unbridled lust for ownership, you have driven charity and compassion out of your hearts.

"The decree," they say, "bans not just alms, but prayers and petitions for the departed by religious, since it forbids their being invited to escort a funeral."[12] Do places filled with the noise of workshops and with the

---

[12] *Quaestio* (sig. divv): "Dicitur etiam quod quanto plures (praesertim religiosi) conveniunt, tanto plures dicuntur orationes — et tanto plures etiam saeculares conveniunt, et euntes ad domum luctus monentur de fine cunctorum."

esse loca quae strepitu officinarum, concursibus negociantium civium et plebis, quae stridore plaustrorum omnique tumultus genere sunt plena, quam vestrae cellae, sacella, chorus, tota ecclesia proprie dicata orationibus loca, in quibus orare pro defunctis nihil vos prohibet et nihil orantes interpellat? Sed esto: tumultus urbani non impediunt vestras preces. At cereus candelave ardens impedit avarissimas mentes, quam ante oculos vestros spectantes continenter minorem ardendo fieri, et longitudinem execrantes viae, quae minuendo cereo spacium dat, gressusque lentos funeris increpantes, nihil minus quam ad orationes atque preces apti estis. Non enim eadem mente Deo ac mamone servitur.[13] Atque etiam conficto casu aliquo saepe candelam extinguitis, cumque in vos convertit oculos is qui funus ornat ac dirigit iterum illam accenditis, verentes ne vos alta voce increpet et integram operam navare atque praestare compellat, aut mercede privet quam non promeriti sitis.

Caeterum isthaec misericordia animarum haud quaquam vos movet; movet quod non vocati stipem non capitis. Si hoc est falsum — non vetet decretum quemlibet ullum numerum religiosorum ad funus vocari, sed tollat praemium — quis vestrum ea misericordia atque humanitate capietur ut funus cuiusquam mercede sublata prosequatur? "Vententur prosequi et advocari omnes, pecunia vero ad monasteria ad eos mittatur." Quis vestrum non admitti ad funera queretur? Quis libros pro libertate Ecclesiae componet? Quis eripi ac violari iura divina, pontificia atque imperatoria vociferabitur? Quis Brixianos excommunicatos esse proclamabit? Vos: vos igitur contra libertatem Ecclesiae tenditis, qui iuri divino obviam itis haud prohibendo quidem verbis munia misericordiae, sed re ipsa atque operibus abiiciendo ea et contemnendo; qui nunquam prosequimini cuiusquam funera humanitate atque misericordia commoti, sed precio empti. Et est misericordiae munus prosequi ad sepulturam funus, ut auctoritate divi Augustini demonstravimus: proinde et excommunicati vestrismet rationibus estis. Quisnam verius prohibet rem quampiam

A defense of the Brescians' statute

hustle and bustle of tradesmen and common people, with the screeching of carts and with every sort of din, seem to you more appropriate for prayers and petitions than your cells, shrines, choir, and whole church, places specially dedicated to prayer, where nothing stops you praying for the deceased and nothing interrupts you as you pray? But let us grant that the city's noises do not obstruct your petitions: yet a taper or burning candle *does* obstruct your greedy minds, for you see it getting gradually smaller before your eyes as it burns, you curse the length of the route which allows time for the taper to diminish, you complain about the slow pace of the funeral procession, and there is nothing you are less suited for than prayers and petitions. The same mind cannot serve God and mammon![13] Also you often fake some accident and snuff out a candle, lighting it again when the funeral arranger and director looks in your direction, for fear that he will loudly reprove you and force you to make an effort and carry out the work not done, or else deprive you of a fee you have not earned.

But the compassion for souls you speak of stirs you not at all: what stirs you is that if not invited you get no tip. If this argument is wrong — that the decree does not forbid anyone to invite any number of religious to a funeral, but removes the reward — which of you will feel such compassion and humanity that he will escort anyone's funeral when his fee is removed? "Let them all be forbidden to escort and be invited to funerals, but let the money be sent to them in their monasteries." Which of you will complain at being excluded from funerals? Who will write books to defend the Church's freedom? Who will protest that divine, papal, and imperial rights are being seized and smashed? Who will proclaim that the Brescians are excommunicate? It is you, *you* who therefore oppose the Church's freedom, who fly in the face of divine law, not by banning the duties of compassion in words, but by rejecting and despising them in actual fact and in your deeds. You never escort anyone's funeral because you are moved by humanity and compassion, but because you are hired at a price. And since, as we have shown on divine Augustine's authority, it is compassion's duty to escort a funeral to burial, so by your own arguments you are also excommunicate. Who more truly bans something

---

[13] Cf. Matthew 6: 24 and Luke 16: 13: "Non potestis Deo servire et mammonae."

quam is qui ab ea perpetuo et constanti tenore abstinet? Quis efficacius imperat eandem quam qui summa fide exercet eam? Nam haec volumus coram tribunali ipsius veritatis agitari: "Efficacissime ille iubet misericordiam et elemosynam qui misericorditer agit; ille vere prohibet eandem qui nunquam utitur ea." Non enim qui dicunt "Domine, Domine", sed qui verbum Dei opere custodit, et reliqua. . . .[14] Certum scimus Christum legittimosque ipsius sectatores plus multo contulisse agendo quam loquendo. Efficacissima verissimaque doctrina est in utramque partem, cum agendo docemus potius quam disserendo (de praeceptis degendae vitae loquor). Vis continentiam docere? Age tu vive continenter. Vis elemosynam hortari et iubere? Fac ipse frequens et ardenter illam. Vis elemosynam tollere ac prohibere? Ne tu utare unquam ea, id quod vos summa fide facitis, qui nunquam cadaver destitutum pauperis ad sepulturam comitamini quia non sit unde mercedem impensi officii accepturi sitis — nihili facientes aeterna atque amplissima praemia illa caelestia quae parata sunt pietatem, humanitatem, charitatem et misericordiam (non mercenariam sed sinceram) colentibus quae neminem frustrantur[15] — et qui nunquam divitis nisi empti. Ah, quanto decentius, quanto convenientius vobis erat, praesertim cum religiosorum nomen usurpetis, et eorum qui excellentia quadam oratores Christi vocari [sig. Aiiiv] volunt, misereri afflictae tantis malis civitati, nutricique vestrae auxilio indigenti quacunque poteratis ope subvenire. Et certe poteratis, atque ea maxime ope quae tum opportunissima erat, quibus orrea plena vi magna frumenti (frequenti fama populi id celebrante) erant. Id erat profecto munus pietatis, id misericordiae et elemosynae verum officium, quin potius gratitudinis atque iustitiae vestrum; id fuerat munus iustitiae — inquam — non modo divinae sed naturalis et civilis, quod gratis acceperatis a Brixianis et vobis abundabat supervacuumque erat, id quod furtiva venditio declarabat, semienectis fame restituere, aut saltem mensura pari

A defense of the Brescians' statute

than he who constantly and continually avoids doing it? Who more effectively commands something than he who most reliably implements it? We want the following motion to be debated before the bar of truth itself: "He most effectively orders compassion and almsgiving who acts compassionately; he truly prevents it who never practices it." For it is not those who say "Lord, Lord", but he who keeps God's word in deed ... etc.[14] We are quite sure that Christ and his genuine followers achieved much more by doing than by talking. The most effective and the truest teaching is two-sided, when we teach by doing rather than by lecturing (I speak of ethical principles). You wish to teach temperateness? Well then, live temperately. You wish to urge and order almsgiving? Perform it frequently and zealously. You wish to abolish and ban almsgiving? Never practice it, as is absolutely typical of you, for you never escort a poor man's abandoned corpse to burial, since it is not something which will bring you a fee for performing a service. You set at nought the eternal and bountiful heavenly rewards prepared for those who observe piety, humanity, charity, and compassion (the real sort, not paid for), virtues which disappoint nobody.[15] You never escort a rich man's funeral either, unless you are hired!

How much more fitting and appropriate it would have been for you, especially as you use the name of 'religious', and of those who for some outstanding quality wish to be called Christ's spokesmen, to have pity on a city beset by such calamities, and to provide your nurturer, who needed your help, with whatever aid you could — and you certainly could have given it, especially the aid easily available then to those whose granaries were full to the brim with corn, according to a widely circulated popular rumor. That would indeed have been a duty of piety, a true service of compassion and almsgiving. Even more, it would have been a duty of gratitude and justice on your part — justice, I say, not only divine but also natural and civic — to restore to the half-starved Brescians, or at least exchange for an equal amount in more prosperous times, what you had received free from them, and possessed in plenty and in excess of

---

[14] Cf. Matthew 7: 21: "Non omnis qui dicit mihi, Domine, Domine, intrabit in regnum caelorum: sed qui facit voluntatem Patris mei, qui in caelis est, ipse intrabit in regnum caelorum."

[15] Cf. 1 Corinthians 2: 14.

pensandum foelicioribus annis. At vos ultro libris compositis falsa crimina continentibus permanifestisque calumniis vexatis eos. O ingratitudinem inauditam, O avaritiam execrandam et feralem immanitatem! Vere istud est evertere iura divina, istud[e] est tollere ecclesiasticam libertatem, istud vos dignos facit qui non modo ab humano consortio pellamini, sed aqua, igni atque omnibus elementis interdicamini![16]

[II]

Perfecte iam hunc locum conclusum esse arbitror, statutum videlicet Brixianum non esse contra ius divinum, quod erat primum fundamentum accusationis. Planissimeque demonstratum est ipsos accusatores idem ipsum ius et ecclesiasticam libertatem oppugnare, proinde et excommunicatos esse. Pari facilitate reliqua fundamenta eorum clarissimis argumentis verissimisque rationibus evertemus, quorum sequens est quod nostrum decretum est adversus quoddam indulctum Imperatoris,[17] quare et contra libertatem Ecclesiae, nosque propterea excommunicatos. Quam severitas aptior graviorisque sit momenti ad continendum non modo cives in officio verum etiam ipsos religiosos in disciplina quam indulgentia, praetermittendum in praesentia esse arbitror. Scimus certe omnes quam saepe indulgentia parentum liberis officiat. Inquiunt itaque: "Imperator indulget ut unicuique liceat decedenti relinquere Catholico et Sanctissimo Concilio de bonis quot optaverit." Quid erat opus ea indulgentia Imperatoris, si nullis antea vinclis legum cohercita erat voluntas

---

[e] *correxi*: istuc *cod.*

A defense of the Brescians' statute

your needs, as shown by your secret sale of it. Yet you actually harass them with books you have written containing false charges, and with outright slander. What unheard-of ingratitude! What despicable greed, what monstrous cruelty! *That* is truly subversion of divine laws; *that* is abolition of church freedom; *that* justifies your being driven out of human society and deprived of water, fire, and all the elements.[16]

[II]

I think this point has now been completely proved: that, contrary to the first main charge, the Brescian statute does not go against divine law. It has also been quite clearly shown that it is the accusers themselves who attack that same law and church freedom, so they are also excommunicate. With equal ease, using clear deductions and true explanations, we shall overturn their other main charges, the next one being that our decree contravenes a certain indult of the emperor,[17] so it also goes against the Church's freedom, and we are therefore excommunicate. I think that at present I should omit to mention how much more fitting and efficacious sternness is than indulgence in keeping not only citizens to their duty but also religious to their vocation: surely we all know how often parental indulgence spoils children. They say, then: "The emperor is indulgent in allowing each person at his death to bequeath as much of his property as he chooses to the holy catholic council." What need was there for that indulgence of the emperor if there were no previous legal

---

[16] In the Roman Republic, before a capital sentence was executed the condemned person was given time to escape into exile, but when he departed a decree of *interdictio aquae et ignis* ('denial of water and fire') made him an outlaw. For this and other features of Roman and later law relating to exile (and its spiritual equivalent, excommunication), see Randolph Starn, *Contrary Commonwealth: The Theme of Exile in Medieval and Renaissance Italy* (Berkeley, Los Angeles and London: University of California Press, 1982), 18–24.

[17] *Quaestio* (sig. biiv, citing a law from the Justinian's *Code, On the inviolability of churches*: Cod. 1. 2. 1; CICv 2: 12): "Habeat unusquisque licentiam sanctissimo catholicoque concilio decedens bonorum quod optaverit relinquere." The word 'indult' (*indultum*) normally refers to a faculty granted by the Holy See allowing a specified deviation from the Church's common law, but here it is used in a wider sense to mean 'concession', 'privilege'.

testantium quominus bona sua legarent cuicunque collibuisset, ac praesertim bonis ac sanctis viris, ut exprimit indulctum? Verum non modo prohibitum id non erat, sed ab illa aeterna et praepotenti lege Dei iubemur, quae est summa ratio, a qua lex naturae nunquam deviat, nec ab ea humanae leges discrepare debent, alioquin iniustae nec verae leges censendae erunt, iubemur — inquam — non solum probis ac sanctis viris, verum omnino et absolute egentibus res nostras impartiri vel invitis imperatoribus atque pontificibus, si modo id vetarent, quod non faciunt. Potius enim parere Deo debemus quam hominibus.[18]

"At vestrum decretum id tollit."[19] Apertissimum et audacissimum mendacium est. Neque enim alia civitas facile comperietur benignior beneficentiorque in pauperes, quaeque magis bonos viros virtuteque praeditos colat, et eos si ope egeant magis iuvet, quam nostra. Testis est tanta vis pauperum, qui vitam elemosynis substentant, aliunde confluentium in nostram urbem. Testis est tantus numerus religiosorum mendicantium omniumque ordinum magnifica monasteria et geminata aliquorum, quibus omnibus abundantissime victus suppeditatur: sed utinam non etiam nimius! Testantur id hospitalia.[20] Declarat idem Mons Pietatis.[21]

A defense of the Brescians' statute

restrictions preventing testators from leaving their property to anyone they wished, especially to "good, holy men", as the indult phrases it? Yet not only was it not banned, but we are commanded by God's eternal and almighty law — which is supreme reason, from which nature's law never swerves, nor should human laws clash with it, or else they will have to be considered unjust and untrue — we are, I say, commanded to share our goods not only with upright, holy men, but purely and simply with the needy, even against the will of emperors and popes (supposing they forbade it, which they do not). For we should obey God rather than men.[18]

"But your decree abolishes that indult."[19] That is a blatant and barefaced lie, for no other city will easily be found that is kinder and more generous to the poor, or one that respects good, virtuous men more, and gives them more help if they need it, than ours. Witness so large a mass of poor people subsisting on alms, who flock to our city from elsewhere. Witness so large a number of religious mendicants, and the splendid monasteries of all the orders — some even have two — for all of which food is supplied in great plenty, though one wishes it were not also in excess! Witness the hospitals.[20] The *monte di pietà* makes the same point.[21]

---

[18] Cf. Acts 5: 29 (the opening words of the response made by Peter and the other apostles to the high priest in the Sanhedrin): "Oboedire oportet Deo magis quam hominibus."

[19] *Quaestio* (sigs biiv–biiir): "Ergo statutum irrationabile est, ut destructivum ultimarum piarum voluntatum et contra ecclesiasticam libertatem attributam ab imperatoribus."

[20] The Third Order of St. Francis often took on charitable work, which at Brescia included a 'house of mercy' containing "a number of sick persons for whose care and comfort the brethren supplied servants" (Moorman, *History*, 426–27).

[21] Since money-lending at interest was allowed only to Jews (see n. 4 above), the need for loans to indigent debtors in the European Middle Ages was met partly by private pawnbrokers, partly by publicly licensed pawnshops, and partly by *monti di pietà* which were established in Italy from 1462 (the date of the first, at Perugia) by the Order of Friars Minor (Franciscans) to provide the poor with interest-free loans secured by pledges and financed by gifts or bequests from their richer neighbors. The one at Brescia dated from 1489, was soon afterwards reorganized by the influential Franciscan preacher Bernardino da Feltre, and gained extra support from the foundation of a local Fraternity of San Bernardino by another Franciscan, Michele d'Acqui, in the 1490s: see Pullan, *Rich and Poor*, 464–65, 474.

Quid dicam de tanto studio universi populi quo usus est ad impetrandum Capitulum in sua urbe Generale Fratrum Minorum, ad quod conveniet incredibilis numerus Fratrum qui sumptibus omnes nostris alentur, nec aliter eos expectamus quam aliquam legionem angelorum,[22] et profecto angelica eorum vita est, eorumque dux Franciscus vere Seraphin.[23] Non igitur Brixiani decreto ullo potestatem adimunt cuiquam utendi officio benignitatis, beneficentiae, misericordiae erga bonos et indigos viros, quandoquidem ipsi, re et opere, et sine intermissione animis propensissimis eas virtutes amplectuntur.

"Quod heres," inquiunt, "pro anima defuncti facit, per defunctum fieri dicitur."[24] Rabularum istae sunt vafritates. A quibusnam id dicitur? A quibusve creditur? A Deone et a veritate, an a callidis et contentiosis litigatoribus? Quot scimus nos faenore, rapinis omnibusque malis artibus potitos magnis divitiis ne obolum quidem in diebus ultimi fati pro anima sua legare voluisse, rogantibus id etiam heredibus, vobisque in primis eiusmodi operum magnis magistris importune instantibus, qui apud pauperes quoque homines studiose et diligenter hoc officio charitatis fungimini ut eorum proposita animae salute vestram cupiditatem saginetis; ac tamen heredes pro anima defuncti aliquid erogasse quod ipse ne in summo quidem terrore mortis adduci potuerat ut faceret, nec forte quidem ea credebat quae fideles Christiani credunt, aut forte animam mortalem esse existimarat? Et dicetis perinde id valere pro invito quod heredes fecerint atque ipsemet fecisset volens? Sed esto ut vultis. Haud tamen Imperator per illud indulctum nec quidem per ullas

A defense of the Brescians' statute

What shall I say about the *so* earnest desire of the whole people to get within their city the chapter-general of Friars Minor, where an incredible number of brothers will gather, all to be maintained at our expense? We await them just as we would some host of angels,[22] and indeed their way of life is angelic and their founder is the truly Seraphic Francis.[23] The Brescians do not, therefore, by any decree deprive anyone of the power to fulfill their duty of kindness, generosity, and compassion towards good, needy men, since they themselves most eagerly embrace those virtues in fact, in deed, and without ceasing.

"What an heir does for a deceased person's soul," they say, "is said to be done *through* the deceased."[24] That is the hair-splitting of tub-thumpers! By whom is it said? By whom believed? By God? By the truth? Or by cunning and argumentative disputants? How many people do we know who by usury, plunder, and every evil device have gained great wealth, but in their last days have not wished to bequeath even a cent for their soul's sake, despite the pleas of their heirs and despite the relentless threats of *you* in particular, the mighty lords of such schemes, who keenly and conscientiously perform this charitable service even among poor people so that, by promising their soul's salvation, you may sate your lust? And yet the heirs have paid out money for a deceased man's soul — something he himself could not be induced to do even when in the utmost dread of death, and perhaps he did not even believe what faithful Christians believe, or perhaps he had thought that the soul was mortal. So will you say that what the heirs may have done for an unwilling person has the same force as if he himself had done it willingly? But let it be as you wish: the emperor, however, has not by that indult, nor

---

[22] Cf. Matthew 26: 53.

[23] The Franciscan Order was also known as the Seraphic Order because its founder, Francis of Assisi (ca. 1181–1226), had a vision in which a crucified seraph from heaven imprinted on him the marks of crucifixion (stigmata) so clearly that he himself seemed to have been crucified: see *Jacobi a Voragine Legenda Aurea vulgo Historia Lombardica dicta*, ed. T. Graesse, 2nd ed. (Leipzig: Impensis librariae Arnoldianae, 1850), 667; *Jacobus de Voragine: The Golden Legend (Selections)*, trans. C. Stace (Harmondsworth: Penguin, 1998), 262. The expression "angelica vita" is a commonplace for the religious life.

[24] *Quaestio* (sig. biiv), citing the chapter "A nobis" from one of the *Decretals* of Gregory IX, *On the sentence of excommunication*: X 5. 39. 28; CIC 2: 899–900.

leges suas ulli civitati ademit potestatem quominus condere sibi statuta seu decreta seu particulares leges proprias particularibus rebus, easque abrogare aut novas rogare, ac de integro eas antiquare rursusque easdem asciscere,[f] aliasve figere atque refigere, prout tempora desiderent et praesens status civitatis postulet. Idque situm positumque est in arbitrio atque deliberatione bonorum et aequorum civium qui senatus vocatur, eaque deliberatio a iure sive a iusto naturali ingenito in mentibus optimatum qui tali iudicio praesunt proficiscitur. Illa namque est recta ratio cum ratione divina consentiens, quam nullus imperator, nullus rex unquam — nisi tyranni esse velint — prohibebit. Atque ideo nostra civitas caeteraeque aliae sua statuta et leges particulares habent. A nostris dominis Venetis[25] quippe iustis nunquam impeditae, multo minus ab aliis prohibentur, nec ullo tempore ab illis imminuentur nisi cum coeperint esse iniusti, nec ab ipsis civitatibus infringentur nisi cum tempora ususve statusque rerum suadebunt atque docebunt earum immutandarum necessitatem.

Nam cum res humanae plenae sint mutabilitatis instabilesque sint tanquam navigemus in salo, ut aliter in secunda, aliter in adversa tempestate administranda est navis: sic ratio rerum publicarum administrandarum temporibus est accommodanda. Nostra civitas cum ingentibus procellis et periculosis fluctibus volveretur dirae famis et exitialis morbi, visum est senatui nostro comprobantibus rectoribus urbis, quorum Franciscus [sig. Aivr] Bragadenus,[26] egregius philosophus atque

---

[f] *correxi*: assiscere *cod.*

A defense of the Brescians' statute   31

even by any laws of his, deprived any city of the power to establish for itself statutes or decrees, or special laws suited to special circumstances, and to rescind them or table new ones, and again reject those and re-adopt the former ones, or frame and reframe others, as the times require and a city's current situation demands. *That* matter rests squarely on the considered decision of good, fair-minded citizens — called a senate — and *that* consideration proceeds from law or from the natural justice inherent in the minds of those eminent men responsible for such judgment; for it is right reason, consonant with divine reason, which no emperor and no king — unless they want to be despots — will ever ban. Our city, therefore, and the other remaining ones, have their own statutes and special laws; these are not blocked by our rulers, the Venetians,[25] who are just, and much less are they banned by others. They will never be eroded by the Venetians unless they start being unjust, nor will they be annulled by the cities themselves unless the times, or experience and current circumstances, urge and demonstrate the need to change them.

Since human affairs are as full of uncertainty and as liable to change as a voyage on the open sea, just as a ship must be controlled in one way when the weather is good, in another when it is bad, so the system of controlling public affairs must be adapted to the times. When our city was tossed about by the severe storms and dangerous currents of a terrible famine and a deadly plague, our senate — with the approval of the city's governors, led by the outstanding philosopher and theologian

---

[25] Venice had gained Brescia from the Visconti of Milan in 1426.

[26] Francesco Bragadin (1458–1530) was a highborn Venetian whose physical disability (kyphosis) did not prevent him from becoming a highly respected figure in the political and cultural life of the republic. Marino Becichemo, *Centuria epistolicarum quaestionum* 31 (Brescia, 1505), says of him: "... omnium doctrinarum peritia cedit nemini." He goes on to address him thus: "tu ... qui nihil in philosophiae studiis, nihil in reliquis liberalibus artibus operosum omisisti, quod non perscrutatus fueris; nihil in mansuetiorum musarum penetralibus intactum reliquisti. Denique ad rem publicam tam plenus sapientia et rerum omnium cognitione accessisti, ut in eius gubernatione Solon omnibus videaris." These fulsome tributes date from the period (late 1504 to early 1506) when Bragadin was *podestà* of Brescia; Becichemo's chaps. 31–38 are in fact dedicated to him and to his fellow-praetor Domenico Contarini. Similarly, Elia Capriolo's *Chronica de rebus brixianorum* ends with an acknowledgement of his help

theologus, sapiens et sanctus vir, praetor erat, decretum hoc facere, quo gliscentem nimium ambitionem funerum cohercerent, et sollicitudines curasque afflictorum atque etiam sumptus plerisque graves minuerent. Nec vos propterea tamen ulla misericordia tantarum calamitatum retardabat ab hauriendo et combibendo parum id sanguinis quod reliquum miseris erat. Sanguis enim tum erat illa pecunia quae vobis pro mercede impensae in funere operae tradebatur, unde panem empturi eoque vitam tracturi erant qui ipsum curabant, qua per vos aversa partim fame, partim dolore mortuorum, partim infesto sidere moriebantur. Vos vero tum, quamquam plena orrea frumento habebatis quod vendebatis insano precio, non pudebat de privatis tectis victum quaerere, et audetis praedicare libris ad omnes gentes missis Brixianos esse excommunicatos, quia compulsi tantis necessitatibus modum sumptibus funerum statuerunt, quam rem innumeris ante saeculis sapientissimus ille legumlator Solon fecerat,[27] a cuius legibus Romani atque Imperatores

Francesco Bragadin,[26] a wise and holy man — decided to pass this decree in order to curb the excessive growth of rivalry over funerals, and to reduce the worries and concerns of the suffering, as well as the expenses which were a burden to most. Yet no resultant compassion for such misfortunes slowed down your swallowing and gulping down what little life-blood the wretches had left. Their life-blood then was the money being handed to you as your fee for work performed at a funeral, money with which those who arranged the funeral were going to buy bread and thus prolong their lives, but after you grabbed it they were dying, due partly to starvation, partly to grief for their dead, partly to bad luck. But you, though you had granaries full of corn which you sold at an absurd price, were not ashamed to seek sustenance from private houses, and you dare to preach, in books sent to every nation, that the Brescians are excommunicate because under the pressure of such emergencies they set a limit to funeral expenses. That was what, countless centuries earlier,

---

and encouragement: see Introduction, n. 10, where similar compliments paid to him by the Venetian humanist Pietro Bembo are also mentioned. By mid-1506 Bragadin was a member of the Republic's Council of Ten, a position which he retained (in alternation with similar positions of authority) until his death: A. Ventura, *DBI*, 13: 672–74; Cosenza, *Biographical and Bibliographical Dictionary*, 1: 701.

[27] Pseudo-Demosthenes, *Orations* 43. 62, quotes a "law of Solon" which gives rules for the laying-out of the deceased, the conduct of the funeral procession, and the minimum age and degree of relationship for women allowed to follow the deceased to burial and enter the burial-chamber. Plutarch, *Solon* 21.5–6, says that Solon made a law regulating women's public appearances, their mourning, and their festivals; that he banned from funerals the practices of self-laceration, of singing set dirges, and of lamenting anyone at another person's funeral (i.e., as done by hired mourners); and that he also forbade graveside sacrifices, burial of the dead with more than three sets of clothes, and visits to non-family tombs except at the time of burial. Interestingly, Cicero refers to Solon's funerary regulations in his own *De legibus* (2. 59 and 2. 64); and the former passage contains two sentences which clearly influenced the writer's final sentence in this paragraph: "Haec laudabilia et locupletibus fere cum plebe communia. Quod quidem maxime e natura est, tolli fortunae discrimen in morte." For further references to this philosophical work of Cicero (widely available in Renaissance Italy), see Valgulio, *Statute*, n. 12 et seqq. Also see the transmission as summarized in R. H. Rouse, "[Cicero's] *De natura deorum, De divinatione, Timaeus, De fato, Topica, Paradoxa Stoicorum, Academica priora, De legibus*," in *Texts and Transmission: A Survey of the Latin Classics*, ed. L. D. Reynolds (Oxford: Clarendon Press, 1983), 124–28.

suas leges sanxerunt, divinusque Plato fecit,[28] cuius leges adeo sanctae existimantur ut potius in republica aliqua caelesti quam terrestri servari posse videantur. Nulla namque necessitate perpulsi ambo funerum et sepulchrorum sumptus — solam rationem naturamque secuti, quae origo legum omnium et iuris atque iusti esse debent — suis legibus comminuerunt. Nullumque discrimen locupletibus ac plebi esse voluit Solon, quod maxime e natura esse iudicavit tollere fortunae discrimen in morte.

Igitur cum modum, mensuram, mediocritatem — in qua sita est virtus — omnibus in rebus recta ratio iubeat teneri atque servari, divinaque lex illa summa, aeterna, perpetua, naturae quoque ipsius lex non scripta, imperatoriae item ac pontificiae leges scriptae — sive indulcta, decreta, privilegia et quicquid est huiusmodi scriptum — ratione recta constent, conditoresque ipsi dum ea condunt nihil aliud quam rectam rationem spectent nihilque aliud sibi proponant, per quam unam similitudinem cum Deo habemus, quis est nisi temerarius atque impudens et aversus a ratione, qui dicere audeat statutum nostrum esse contra leges imperatorias vel pontificias seu indulcta vel canones, quia modum mensuramque adhibet suis civibus popularibusque in rebus — quaecunque illae sint — [quae] humano[g] arbitrio administrantur? Nam divina quia immutabilia sunt et uno semper modo se habent nec variant nec vertunt,[29] ad arbitrii humani administrationem non pertinent. At hi Fratres indulcta illa et canones a recta ratione — hoc est a moderatione

[g] *correxi*: humanae *cod.*

the famously wise lawgiver Solon had done,[27] on the basis of whose laws the Romans and the emperors enacted their own; and it was what divine Plato did,[28] whose laws are thought so sacred as to seem more capable of being observed in some heavenly state than in an earthly one. For both of them by their laws reduced expenditure on funerals and tombs, not under the pressure of any emergency but simply by following reason and nature, which should be the source of all statutes and of law and justice. Solon wanted no distinction between the well-off and the common people, for he considered it most natural to abolish any distinction of fortune at death.

Since, then, right reason orders the holding and keeping of a check, a limit, and a mean — the basis of virtue — in everything, and since supreme, eternal, and unchanging divine law, nature's own unwritten law too, and likewise the written laws of emperors and popes (or their indults, decrees, prerogatives, and any other such writing), rest on right reason, and those who frame them have nothing else in view and in their minds when framing them than right reason, the only quality in which we resemble God: who but a headstrong, shameless, and irrational person would dare to say that our statute contravenes imperial or papal laws, indults, or canons, because it applies a check and a limit to its own citizens and inhabitants in any affairs whatever which are controlled by human judgment? For the things of God, since they are constant, and always conform to a single pattern, and never chop or change,[29] are irrelevant to control by human judgment. But these brothers are trying to

---

[28] Plato, *Laws* 4. 717d–718a, enjoins giving one's parents a modest burial — neither ostentatious nor niggardly — and, similarly, expending on the annual rites of remembrance for the deceased a fair share of one's money. Later (*Laws* 12. 958d–960a) he defines where interment may take place, limits the size of burial-mounds and memorial stones, specifies the maximum period of lying-in-state, declares that in view of the body's inferiority to the soul one should avoid extravagant expenditure on "a soulless altar of the dead" (the total cost of a burial must not exceed the amount which he deems appropriate for each of the four property classes), and prohibits loud public displays of weeping and lamentation for the departed. Again, Plato's funerary rules are commended by Cicero, *De legibus* 2. 67–68; and the anonymous author's coupling of Plato with Solon as his 'classical' authorities no doubt owes something to Cicero's example.

[29] Cf. James 1: 17.

atque mediocritate — ad tyrannicam libidinem atque licentiam conantur detorquere, ut suis cupiditatibus supparasitentur.

"Non poterunt testatores iubere ut tot paria Fratrum adhibeantur suo funeri, magis expedire animae suae eum elemosynae modum iudicantes, obstante statuto vestro."[30] Demonstratum iam est hoc genus dationis non esse elemosynam. Atque ut sit elemosyna error est iudicii testantis, si deterrimum et inquinatum suspicione ambitionis et inanis gloriae ostentatione infectum caeteris omnibus modis sinceris, puris, omni labe male concupiti honoris vacantibus, qui non ante oculos vulgi sed secreto administrantur modum praeoptet.[31] Atque item repeto prudentem esse Imperatorem, alioquin pro legislatore habendus non esset. Prudentia est recta ratio: haec modum mediocritatemque civilibus actionibus statuit. Igitur idem volunt indulcta imperatoria et statutum nostrum, modum videlicet et mediocritatem, et in eandem sententiam conveniunt.

Quaeso, si quis improbo aut dementi consilio aliquo aut odio liberorum dissimilium ipsius aut inanis alicuius et stultae gloriae cupidine aut vestris persuasionibus terroribusque vestris — quarum rerum egregii artifices estis — male persuasus bona sua omnia leget opulentis vobis aut diti alii monasterio, parvos vero cum pia matre inopes relinquat liberos, quid dicturum Imperatorem putemus si vivens adesset? Profecto nihil aliud quam sua indulcta suasque leges omnia velle cum modo, mensura rectaque ratione fieri, sed impossibile esse suas leges, quia universales sint, particulares casus omnis propter instabilitatem rerum humanarum infinitos variosque ac diversos — circunstantiis subinde versantibus eos — posse complecti; atque idcirco concedi primo a natura, deinde a se omnibus populis ut sibi quisque condat particulares leges, quae statuta vocantur, rebus particularibus accommodatas, sicuti temporum ratio et res eorum publicae postulant, quae leges universales ubi ratio circunstantiarum exposcit corrigant. Si praeterea Imperator prudens, causa cognita qua populus Brixianus ad hoc statutum faciendum sit commotus, hoc iudicium iudicaturus esset, quid

twist those indults and canons away from right reason — that is, from moderation and restraint — towards despotic depravity and dissipation, so that like parasites they may batten on their own lusts.

"Testators will not be able to order that so many pairs of brothers be brought to their funerals if they judge that type of alms more profitable for their souls, since your decree prevents it."[30] It has already been shown that this sort of gift is not alms. And a request that it be 'alms' is an error of the testator's judgment, if he prefers the worst type — one sullied by the suspicion of rivalry and polluted by vainglorious showing-off — above all the other types which are genuine, pure, free from all taint of wrongly coveted honor, and bestowed not in public view but in secret.[31] And again I repeat that the emperor is prudent, otherwise he should not be considered a lawgiver. Prudence is right reason, which checks and restrains civil conduct. Imperial indults and our statute therefore have the same aim — namely, to check and to restrain — and share the same opinion.

I ask anyone who, misled by some rascally or crazy advice, or by hatred of children who are unlike him, or by desire for some empty, silly kudos, or by your inducements and threats (arts in which you are supremely expert), bequeaths all his property to you wealthy people or to another rich monastery, while leaving his little children and their devoted mother destitute, what would we expect the emperor to say if he were here in person? Surely nothing else than that he wished all his indults and his laws to accord with restraint, temperateness, and right reason, but that it is impossible for his laws, being general, to cover all specific situations which, because of the inconstancy of human affairs, are innumerable, changeable, and unpredictable, as circumstances repeatedly toss them about; and that all peoples are therefore allowed, first by nature and secondly by him, each to establish for themselves specific laws (called statutes) adapted to specific factors, as demanded by the logic of the times and by their political affairs — laws which may correct the general laws when the logic of circumstances requires it. Furthermore, if the prudent emperor, discovering what moved the Brescian people to

---

[30] *Quaestio* (sig. biiv): "non enim poterit paterfamilias in testamento disponere quod pro anima sua accipiantur tot fratres in suis exequiis, quod ipse magis expedire iudicabit pro anima sua quam alias elemosinas."

[31] Cf. Matthew 6: 1–4.

aliud existimandum est quam recte prudenterque fuisse factum iudicaturum, moramque potius reprehensurum, dicturumque haud dubie credendum est non se id suis indulctis agere, ut effrenatas atque inexplebiles cupiditates alat ecclesiasticorum, quin potius ut moderetur eas. Haud igitur Brixiani adversus indulcta Imperatoris nec contra libertatem Ecclesiae tendunt. Sed vos, quia immodicae atque impotenti cupiditati vestrae velut frenos esse impositos[h] cernitis, ne omnes fortunas populi Brixiani praedae haberetis, tanquam lymphatici atque bachantes supera commiscentes cum inferis, voluntati atque consilio moderatissimi Imperatoris rationem suam cum naturae numinisque divini ratione conformantis cupide et avare interpretando illam obviam itis. Quam rem permanifesto agitis, quando quidem decretum Brixianum oppugnatis cavens populo ne exhaurire rem omnem familiarem possitis, cui semper tanquam aliqua Charybdis[32] inhiatis, substinentium grave onus utriusque sexus liberorum.

[III]

Finem iam huic secundo capiti faciamus, quod quoniam penitus eversum est, ad tertium expugnandum descendamus. Haec acies specie horribilior est, revera autem infirmissima. Continet enim magnum numerum doctorum quos omnes dominos,[33] hoc est, tyrannos appellant

---

[h] *correxi*: datos *cod.*

A defense of the Brescians' statute

enact this statute, were about to judge this case, what else must one suppose but that he would judge it a right and prudent measure, and would rather criticize the delay: he would say, one must surely believe, that he did not aim by his indults to foster the unbridled and insatiable lusts of churchmen, but rather to moderate them. The Brescians are not, therefore, striving against the emperor's indults or the Church's freedom. But *you*, because you see that your unrestrained and uncontrollable lust has been, as it were, bridled so as to prevent your getting the Brescian people's total assets as your booty, are mingling heaven with hell in a kind of drunken frenzy, and opposing the considered intention of a very moderate emperor — who models his own procedure on that of nature and divine power — by your lustful and greedy interpretation of it. You are quite plainly doing this, since you attack the Brescian decree which protects the people against your stripping them of all the family property — which you, like some Charybdis,[32] are always hungry for — owned by children of both sexes who are bearing a heavy burden.

[III]

Let us now make an end of this second point: as it has been annihilated, let us proceed to demolish the third. This attacking force looks more fearsome but is in fact very weak, containing as it does a large number of

---

[32] A whirlpool in a narrow sea-channel opposite the ravenous monster Scylla, Charybdis sucked in and expelled the water three times a day, and the shipwrecked Odysseus escapes from it only by clinging to an overhanging tree: Homer, *Odyssey* 12. 101ff. and 432ff. It later became a byword for any serious danger: Horace, *Odes* 1. 27. 19.

[33] The "masters" (*domini*) cited in *Quaestio* (sigs. bivr–dr) to prove that the statute infringes church freedom include Niccolò de' Tudeschis (Panormitanus), Antonio Corsetto "Siculus", Giovanni da Imola, Pierre de Palu, Fra Antonino Pierozzi (archbishop of Florence), Pietro de Monte (bishop of Brescia), Giovanni Bertachino, Ludovico Pontano, Felino Maria Sandeo, and Andreas Barbatia. The term *dominus* (an academic title) is of course used simply as a courtesy title; the anonymous author's assumption that it must imply despotism is flatly contradicted in *Quaestio* (sig. diiiv): "Nam dominium in civitate non est despoticum, quo videlicet domini regunt servos, sed politicum, videlicet, quo domini regunt cives liberos in multis super paene omnibus negociis suis."

territandi causa nos, quorum omnis sapientia atque doctrina et ingenium in hac quadam dimicatione est per mortuaria intelligi ceram, pecuniam et numerum clericorum, nihil omnino aliud.[34] Unde autem hoc sumant, quibusve rationibus id asserant, nemo est tam sagax ut arbitrari aut coniecturasse qui aut divinare possit: non historiam veterem nec recentem, non legem canonemve ullum, non grammaticorum auctoritatem auctorumve probatorum usum, non rationem a philosophis [sig. Aiv v] vel a natura petitam ullam afferunt qua suam interpretationem probare valeant. Ut si quis dicat mortuaria esse legata ecclesiis spectantia ad mortuos — id quod profecto est, quodque permanifesto Summus Pontifex intelligit in eo canone ubi queritur de impietate atque temeritate laicorum qui bona ecclesiis addicta nullo respectu tanquam profana sibi vindicant illisque pro suis utuntur[35] — adversariorum causam nullam, debellatumque esse, eorum conatus cassos, arma, acies istorum doctorum irritas, et nequicquam instructas, et tanquam fumum et levem umbram dissipatas necesse est.[36] Nefas profecto videtur existimare Sanctitatem Pontificiam et Maiestatem Concilii tam levi tamque frivola de causa ad tantam indignationem — ne dicam furorem atque immanitatem — prorupisse ut a consortione Christianorum et a sacris interdicerent eos qui modum statuerent consumendae cerae circa cadavera, et temperarent flammulis in lumine et radio solis, et parvum numerum Fratrum sacerdotumque excirent a suis sanctis tectis ad evagandum per vias comitando cadavera, quodque paucis crucibus gravissimi ponderis non frangerent humeros gestantium eas pauperum. Illud vero consentaneum est, animadvertere in eos qui mortuaria — hoc est, iam ab aliquo dicata Ecclesiae et consecrata bona — usurpant et Ecclesiam impie atque nefarie fraudant. Sed quoniam indulcta quaedam sive canones sive decreta pontificum intentant ut nos in trepidationem coniiciant,

A defense of the Brescians' statute

"doctors" all of whom, in order to frighten us, they term "masters" (*domini*),[33] that is, despots. These men's whole wisdom, learning, and talent are involved in this particular contention: that by "death disbursements" (*mortuaria*) are meant candle-wax, cash, and a group of clergy — nothing else at all.[34] But where they get this idea from, and what arguments their assertion is based on, no one is acute enough to imagine, hypothesize, or guess, for they cite no history, ancient or modern, no law or canon, no precedent from grammarians or usage of respected writers, no argument culled from philosophers or from nature, by which they could validate their interpretation. So if anyone said that "death disbursements" are bequests to churches in respect of the dead — as is indeed true, and as the supreme pontiff quite plainly means in the canon where he bemoans the impiety and audacity of laypeople who disrespectfully claim for themselves, and use for their own purposes, property assigned to churches as though it were secular[35] — it follows that our opponents have no case, the battle is over, their efforts are in vain, the armed ranks of those "doctors" are useless, marshaled in vain, and dispersed like smoke and flimsy shadow.[36] It certainly seems wrong to suppose that for so trifling and trivial a reason his holiness the pope and the great council gave vent to such anger, not to say rage and ferocity, as to debar from association with Christians and from worship those who limited the consumption of candle-wax around corpses, economized on tapers in bright sunlight, and summoned a small number of brothers and priests from their hallowed houses to wander along the streets escorting corpses, and because, with few heavy crosses, they failed to break the shoulders of the poor men carrying them. But it *is* fitting to punish those who appropriate "death disbursements" — meaning property that someone has already assigned and dedicated to the Church — and who impiously and immorally swindle the Church. But since our opponents threaten us with certain papal

---

[34] *Quaestio* (sig. biiiv): "Et communiter doctores intelligunt per mortuaria numerum clericorum, candelas, denarios, et alia ad exequias pertinentia." (The last phrase contradicts the anonymous author.)

[35] Canon 44 of the Fourth Lateran Council, called by Innocent III (1215). *Quaestio* (sig. aiir–v) quotes it in full: see below, 158–60.

[36] Psalm 101: 4, "defecerunt sicut fumus dies mei," was sung at funerals. There may also be an echo of Anchises' shade in Vergil, *Aeneid* 5. 740.

hanc partem caputque tertium latius et accuratius quam causa postulet tractare institui, ut omnibus sit perspicuum quanta libido sit horum Fratrum criminandi populum religiosissimum atque moderatissimum, qui nulla certe ratione alia Fratres sunt nisi quia eandem omnes avaritiam matrem habent.

Enimvero, si Imperator imperatoriaque indulcta moderatione atque ratione refercta sunt, quanto perfectiore ratione, sapientia atque moderatione maiore praeditos fuisse pontifices superiores et esse eum qui superest, eorumque indulcta, decreta, canones omnesque eorum voluntates, sive scriptas sive non scriptas, virtutem continere — in qua est mediocritas — censendum est, cum sint proximiores Deo qui summa ratio, summa sapientia, summa moderatio est, quique ratione quadam rata et mediocritate harmonica cuncta moderatur et regit,[37] quam potissimum qui eius vicem tenent imitari omni opere ac studio debent. Nemo autem me putet dicere, cum expugnaturum me hoc tertium caput dico, adversus voluntatem pontificum tendere velle aut eorum canones oppugnare, quibus censeo super omnia mortalia omni cultu et reverentia parendum esse; sed demonstraturum nihil omnino nostrum statutum violare nec minima quidem in re ipsos laedere, remotaque esse et aliena et nihil ad causam pertinentia quae ab adversariis hoc loco afferuntur.

"Animae defunctorum quatuor modis solvuntur," Papam dicere adversarii aiunt: aut oblationibus sacerdotum, aut precibus sanctorum, aut elemosynis carorum, aut ieiunio cognatorum.[38] Cuinam parti huius

A defense of the Brescians' statute

indults, canons, or decrees in order to throw us into a state of terror, I have decided to treat this section and third point in greater breadth and detail than the case might demand, so as to make it perfectly plain to everyone how great is the desire of these brothers to denounce a most scrupulous and moderate people; they are surely brothers only in the sense that they all have the same mother: greed.

For indeed, if the emperor and imperial indults are replete with moderation and reason, how much more perfect must one suppose the reason and wisdom, how much greater the moderation, with which earlier popes were, and the present one is, endowed — their indults, decrees, canons, and all their other expressed wishes, whether written or unwritten, embracing virtue which includes temperateness — since they are closer to God who is supreme reason, wisdom, and moderation, and who moderates and controls everything in a certain fixed proportion and harmonious temperament![37] Those who represent him should especially emulate this quality with all their diligence and devotion. But let no one think that in promising to demolish this third argument I am saying that I wish to go against the will of the popes or to oppose their canons, for I believe that those canons, more than anything on earth, should be obeyed with all respect and deference. Rather, he should realize, I will show that in no way at all does our statute break or even minimally harm them, and that the things our opponents allege on this topic are far-fetched, out of place, and quite irrelevant to the case.

"The souls of the departed are released in four ways," our opponents report the pope as saying, "by the offerings of priests, by the prayers of

---

[37] This seems to be a clear reference to Plato's *Timaeus* which, in the fourth-century Latin version of Calcidius, was widely read in medieval Europe. In describing the creation of the world (33b–47d) Plato links the fixed ratios (identical with those of the musical scale) which determine the spacing of the world soul's material (i. e., the universe) with the proper balance attainable by the world soul's microcosmic reflection (i. e., the human soul) if humans model their mental revolutions on the intelligent revolutions of the heavens. Valgulio draws heavily on this part of the *Timaeus* in his *Contra vituperatorem musicae*: see sections (14)–(32) in the edition of this treatise cited below in Valgulio, *Statute*, n. 31.

[38] Released from purgatory, that is. The quotation — also used in *Quaestio* (sig. biiir) — is from the chapter "Animae defunctorum" (for which see Introduction, n.

disiuncti repugnat statutum nostrum modum sumptibus ponens funerum? Num vetat oblationes fieri? Num avertit a precibus sanctorum bonam mentem? An a ieiuniis deterret cognatos? "Elemosynas," nimirum dicent, "prohibet carorum." Hoc volunt intelligi prohiberi, propterea quod vetantur agmina religiosorum ad funera vocare.[39] Quisnam hoc statuto prohibetur quominus queat quocunque tempore cuicunque (vel religioso vel non religioso) et quotocunque numero quantumcunque rerum suarum elemosynae nomine conferre, tametsi — ut saepe dictum est — tollitur pars sumptuum et molestiarum populo manibus atque opere maxima ex parte victum quaerenti atque paranti? Missum faciam locum hunc iam supra amplissime tractatum atque conclusum, ubi planissime demonstratum est quod datur prosequentibus funus elemosynam non esse, sed mercedem praemiumque impensi officii, tum etiam quia non calamitosis nec egenis praebetur, tum quia non est gratuitum, quando quidem quasi ex pacto repensa opera exposcitur, et vicissim impensa opera mercedem flagitat. Dicamne maioris momenti rem, quae fortasse absurda auribus aliquorum videbitur? Ab invitis quoque ea merces tradebatur, sed verecundia quadam consuetudinis

saints, by the alms of loved ones, or by the fasting of relatives."[38] With which item in this list of options does our statute limiting funeral expenses clash? Does it forbid making offerings? Does it turn a virtuous mind away from the prayers of saints? Does it discourage relatives from fasting? "It does ban almsgiving by loved ones," they will no doubt say. They claim that this is understood as banned because inviting squads of religious to funerals is forbidden.[39] Who, pray, is banned by this statute from bestowing at any time on anybody (whether a religious or not), and on any number of people, any amount of his goods as "alms" although, as has often been stated, some of the expense and trouble is removed from ordinary people who largely seek and earn their living by manual labor? I will leave aside this topic as it has already been very fully treated and concluded above, where it was quite clearly shown that what is given to a funeral escort is not alms, but a fee and reward for a service performed. Other reasons are that it is not presented to the afflicted or the needy, and that it is not free, since by an unwritten agreement work that has been purchased is demanded and, conversely, work expended insists on a fee. Shall I mention something of greater importance, which will perhaps sound ridiculous to some? That fee was handed over even

---

56) of the *Decretum Gratiani*: C. 13 q. 2 c. 22; CIC 1: 728. The Council of Florence (1439) defined purgatory, noted that the souls of the penitent were "cleansed after death by cleansing pains; and the suffrages of the living faithful avail them in giving relief from such pains, that is, sacrifices of masses (*missarum scilicet sacrificia*), prayers (*orationes*), almsgiving and other acts of devotion (*elemosinae et alia pietatis officia*) which have been customarily performed by some of the faithful for others of the faithful in accordance with the Church's ordinance." (See *Decrees*, ed. Tanner, 1: 527, ll. 30–42.) On the origins of purgatory, see J. Le Goff, *The Birth of Purgatory*, trans. A. Goldhammer (Aldershot: Scolar Press, 1984).

[39] *Quaestio* (sigs. diiiv–divr): "respondetur quod imo facultas Ecclesiae tollitur, ne possit recipere liberas elemosinas, nec [non] hoc sequitur ad statutum, sed quod plus est directe est materia statuti, cum dicatur non possint habere nisi clericos vigintiquatuor, et non possint eis dari nisi duo solidi pro quolibet." *Quaestio* (sigs. divv–er) also quotes the opinion of an anonymous notary: that, of the four possible ways to release souls, "tria consequuntur ipsae animae per invitationem multorum religiosorum, qui rogant Deum in processione funebri, et demum, etiam dum celebrant pro elemosinis datis, elemosina quoque ipsa subvenit defunctis, tam ex parte operis operati quam etiam operantis, ut dicunt theologi."

nemo princeps tollendae eius volebat auctor videri, aut potius, ne cedere honori dignitatique alterius cui se parem aut superiorem esse existimabat videretur, nemo sibi consulebat, in diesque ambitio simul cum sumptibus adeo crescebat ut a multis grande aes alienum funerum ergo conflaretur. Id ita esse gaudia et approbationes omnium ordinum promulgatione decreti accepta declarant.

"Ergo statutum," inferunt, "est contra libertatem Ecclesiae, et qui ipsum fecerunt quique illi parent digni sunt qui a sacris et a communione hominum pellantur."[40] O praeclaram dialecticam, qua se tamen praecellere arrogantes homines cunctis mortalibus arbitrantur: ab alienis remotissimisque antecedentibus conclusionem se necessariam intulisse putant! Si quolibet uno quadripartiti disiuncti modo solvi animae defunctorum possunt, adhibito uno quocunque reliqui vacabunt. Nam si ligatum corpus solutis nexibus solvatur, nequicquam solvendi iam solutum gratia funes incidentur. Si carcere per ostium apertum clavi exemere detentum licet, quid ultra opus est perfractis claustris aut ruptis muris cuniculisve fossis aut aperto tecto ad eundem iam eductum eximendum? Quid in disiuncto pontificio sequatur latissime patet. Addunt importuni, cum innumerabiles quasi sint elemosynas faciendi modi, diversisque diversa placeant, velle limitare modos et quae secuntur est libertatem Ecclesiae violare.[41] An vobis pulchrum videtur oblectatque vos, ut opima ac satura armenta per florentia et mollia latissima pascua modo has, modo illas per lasciviam libant herbas, sic vos rem omnem familiarem bonaque omnia saecularium per quoslibet modos depascere ac populari? Non enim contenti estis una nec quatuor nec decem incisis venis haurire sanguinem, sed apertis universis absorbere uno suctu

A defense of the Brescians' statute

by unwilling donors, but owing to a sort of respect for the custom no one wanted to be seen as the prime mover in abolishing it — or rather, no one looked to his own interests, lest he seem less honorable or respectable than someone else to whom he considered himself equal or superior, and day by day rivalry, coupled with expenditure, grew so great that many people ran up a huge debt because of funerals. That this is so is proved by the joy and acclamation with which all orders greeted the decree's proclamation.

"So," they argue, "the statute goes against the Church's freedom, and those who made it and those who obey it deserve to be banished from the sacraments and from human society."[40] What fine logic, in which the presumptuous fellows nonetheless imagine they outdo the whole of humanity — they think that from incompatible and far-fetched premises they have drawn a necessary conclusion! If the souls of the dead can be released by any one of the four various methods, whichever one is used will make the rest redundant. For if a tied-up body is released by relaxing its bonds, it will be pointless to cut the ropes in order to release something already released. If one may remove a prisoner from his dungeon through an open door with a key, why bother to saw through the bars, break down the walls, dig tunnels, or open up the roof in order to remove someone already rescued? The pope's list of options has an utterly obvious consequence. The perverse fellows add that since there are almost countless ways of giving alms, and different things appeal to different people, the desire to restrict those ways — and so on — infringes the Church's freedom.[41] Does it seem to you noble, does it please you, that like plump and well-fed flocks wantonly nibbling now these, now those plants in flowery, gentle pastures stretching afar, so *you* are devouring and despoiling all the private property and goods of laypeople in any way you fancy? You are not satisfied with draining away their blood by

---

[40] *Quaestio* (sigs. aiiv–aiiir) quotes in full another chapter, beginning "Noverit fraternitas tua", from the *Decretal* of Gregory IX, *On the sentence of excommunication*, where Honorius III excommunicates those who make statutes against church freedom, those who write them down, those in authority who observe them, and those who make or publish judgements based on them: X 5. 39. 49; *CIC* 2: 910.

[41] *Quaestio* (sig. biiir): see n. 11 above.

vitam hominum placet. Sanguis enim est quod sanguinem facit, et vita quod est vitale. Tantaque immanitas atque saevitia[i] vestra est, adeo vilis, adeo contemptui vobis est Brixianus populus, ut, quia non occlusa sed restricta unica modo via innumeris aliis patentibus magnis compellentibus causis ire obviam aviditati vestrae ausus est, tanquam irritatae ferae falsis criminibus Apostolicam Sedem Christianumque omne nomen in ipsum concitare tanto studio tantoque conatu pergitis. Quare, si Summi Pontifices vicem Christi gerunt Sedemque Petri tenent et imitatores ipsorum sunt, si Ecclesia est contio congregatioque fidelium, si omnes modestiam, humilitatem, [sig. Avr] humanitatem charitatemque et in omnibus rebus moderationem et honestatem, in qua decorum situm est, instituunt et colunt, utri tandem contra iura pontificia facimus: nosne qui cavimus ne modus atque mensura et mediocritas in nostra civitate praeterirentur, an vos qui illam abhominamini et abhorretis et oppugnatis, quique ad eandem immodicitatem pontificia iura indulctaque ecclesiastica, refercta — ut diximus — ratione recta atque moderatione, pertrahere conamini?

Cum igitur apertissime demonstratum sit nostrum decretum nihil adversari indulctis sive decretis pontificiis, quin potius congruere in eandem voluntatem atque sententiam moderationis, non nos adversus libertatem Ecclesiae facimus sed vos, qui tantis conatibus ipsam moderationem evertere molimini, quique armis Ecclesiae comparatis ad continendum Christianos in officio virtutum et praeceptorum Christi, pietatis videlicet, misericordiae, humilitatis, modestiae abutimini ad explendas impotentes cupiditates vestras, territantes populum purae et simplicis fidei timentem Deum atque Ecclesiam terriculis omnibus diritatis excommunicationum, ut formidine consternatus se suaque omnia proiiciat ad pedes vestros avidissimorum et superbissimorum hominum,[42] qui tantos spiritus geritis nomine quodam Inquisitionis, gravi quidem per se et recte quondam a maioribus instituto, nunc autem per vos levi atque inani, quin potius fructuoso, nam ipsum — ut sermonibus hominum fertur — quaestui habetis. Quod officium, ut vestra vanitas et superbia est, pro quodam regno habetis, quodque ne vacet stolidas aliquas et stupore quodam ingenii rigentes anus de Valle

---

[i] *correxi:* scaevitia *cod.*

cutting one vein, or four, or ten, but choose to open the whole lot, and to draw the life out of people with one suck. Blood is what makes blood, and life is what gives life. Such is your brutality and cruelty, so cheap and contemptible are the people of Brescia in your eyes, that because they have for serious and pressing reasons narrowed (not blocked) just one road, with countless others still open, and have dared to confront your greed, like frustrated wild beasts you proceed with such zeal and such effort to rouse the apostolic see and all Christendom against them with false accusations! If, therefore, the supreme pontiffs represent Christ, occupy Peter's see, and emulate them both, if the Church is the assembly and congregation of the faithful, if all its members teach and observe modesty, meekness, humanity, and charity, and in all things moderation and integrity (the source of propriety), which of us, I ask you, are acting against papal laws: we who have taken care to counter the neglect of control, restraint, and temperateness in our city, or you who loathe, detest, and attack that city, and who try to drag into the same immoderateness papal laws and church indults which, as we said, are replete with right reason and moderation?

Since, then, our decree has been very plainly shown not to conflict at all with papal indults or decrees, but rather to share with them the same intention and opinion — one of moderation — it is not we who oppose the Church's freedom but *you*, who with such strenuous efforts contrive to upset this moderation, and who misuse the Church's weapons which were provided for keeping Christians faithful to the virtues and principles of Christ — that is, piety, compassion, meekness, and modesty — in order to satisfy your uncontrollable lusts, frightening a people of pure and simple faith, who fear God and the Church, with all the dreadful bogies of excommunication. Your aim is that this terror may shock them into casting themselves and everything they own at the feet of you greedy and haughty people,[42] who give yourselves such airs by using a certain title of the Inquisition — a title weighty in itself, and rightly established by our forebears long ago, but now weak and hollow thanks to you — or rather, lucrative, for according to popular gossip you use it for profit. You use the office (such is your vanity and pride)

---

[42] An allusion to Acts 4: 34–37.

Camonica ad vos rapitis, easque de fide, de Trinitate aliisque huiusmodi rebus anquiritis,[43] adhibitis notariis longos processus facitis, quaestiones tormentis habetis, ut excruciando et excarnificando eas — vix certe a brutis animalibus differentes — fidem Christianam tueri videamini. Cum tamen hi tam scrupulosi religiosi non vereantur in contionibus propalam, in templis, ubicunque locorum sine ullo respectu docere Virginem Mariam, matrem Domini Nostri Iesu Christi, nexibus atque periculis peccati originalis involutam et labe mixtionis polutam fuisse, non secus quam Longinus, quam Pilatus fuerint,[44] ac magnis contentionibus

almost as a kingdom and, lest it lie idle, you seize from the Valcamonica certain old women who are stupid and frozen in a kind of mental daze, and you interrogate them about their faith, the Trinity, and other such topics.[43] You bring in scribes and drag out the proceedings; you conduct examinations under torture so that, by inflicting pain and torment on women who are admittedly little different from brutish beasts, you may appear as guardians of the Christian faith. Since, however, these *so meticulous religious* are not afraid to teach openly — and quite irreverently — in assemblies, in churches, and anywhere whatsoever, that the Virgin Mary, mother of our Lord Jesus Christ, was caught up in the toils and snares of original sin and sullied by the taint of impurity just as

---

[43] The Valcamonica, situated to the northeast of Brescia and about ninety kilometers long, is the largest valley in Italy. Capriolo, *Chronicorum*, Book 13, col. 131, says more about this valley, and its association with witchcraft and other strange customs: "His praeterea temporibus aliud memoria dignum contigisse accepimus. Est locus in agri nostri finibus, id est in Vallis Monicae summitate, qui ineptis hominibus lamiisque semper abundavit, cuius incolarum multos nunc uxores invicem permutavisse relatum est: et qui hebetiorem dabat, addebat et capram, ut non minoris capra ab accipiente, quam alteri nobilior traditae uxoris conditio aestimari videretur. Quod tamen nefandum fertur amotum, ibi fundata divi *Francisci* sacra religione." On Dominicans' denunciation of witches, and their tendency to concentrate on witches' denial of the Christian faith rather than on their alleged *maleficium*, see P. Burke, "Witchcraft and Magic in Renaissance Italy: Gianfrancesco Pico and his *Strix*," in *The Damned Art: Essays in the Literature of Witchcraft*, ed. S. Anglo (London, Henley, and Boston: Routledge & Kegan Paul, 1977), 32–52, esp. 39–40. See also Introduction, n. 62.

[44] The belief that the Virgin Mary was free of original sin from the moment of her conception was opposed by the Dominican authorities St. Albert and St. Thomas Aquinas who argued that the stain of original sin was transmitted in every natural conception, and since Mary was conceived in this way, she could not be exempted from the law. However, the Franciscans opposed this view and in 1439 the Council of Basel affirmed the belief as a pious opinion in agreement with Catholic faith, reason, and scripture. In 1476 Sixtus IV approved the feast of the Immaculate Conception. See W. Sebastian, "The Controversy over the Immaculate Conception from after Scotus to the End of the Eighteenth Century," in *The Dogma of the Immaculate Conception*, ed. E. D. O'Connor (Notre Dame: University of Notre Dame Press, 1958), 213–39. Longinus (probably from Greek *longke*, 'lance') is the traditional name both of the soldier who pierced Christ's side with his spear (John 19: 34), and of the centurion in charge of the crucifixion who acknowledged Christ's divinity (Matthew 27:

id disputando tueri, Sanctum quoque Ioseph — propatrem Iesu Christi sponsumque Perpetuae Virginis et ipsum in connubio perpetuo virginem — celebrari et coli in terris dolent, nec dissimulare dolorem coram universo populo queunt.[45] Qualis fidei signa sint haec, nemini obscurum esse puto.

"At non sunt de essentia isthaec fidei." Fateor. Sed plerunque naturae occultae rerum per accidentia indagantur, et abditae hominum mentes atque ingenia deprehenduntur atque nudantur. O Fratres Minores, huic civitati semper venerandos, semper colendos et optandos! Vos veram, puram sinceramque fidem geritis, uti vera atque aperta sunt vulnera stigmatum vestri ducis Seraphici Francisci;[46] vos vestris prudentissimis praedicationibus, vita sponte paupere, mente sancta, exemplis omnium verarum virtutum vere Christi fidem tuemini et amplificatis. Vos vestris cohortationibus hospitalia pauperibus condidistis; vos ut Mons Pietatis[47] constitueretur auctores fuistis. Vos orationes ab ardente voluntate proficiscentes et veras preces pro vivis, pro mortuis ad Deum funditis, non empti, nec ulla spe terrenae mercedis contaminati.

Longinus and Pilate were,[44] and to maintain that view most emphatically in debate, they are also sorry that St. Joseph — Jesus Christ's foster-father and the lifelong Virgin's husband, and himself a virgin in his lifelong marriage — is praised and honored on earth, and are unable to conceal their sorrow in front of all the people.[45] No one, I think, is in any doubt as to what kind of faith *these* views indicate.

"But the views you mention do not affect the substance of faith." I admit that. But the hidden natures of things are often ascertained through their attributes, and so are men's secret thoughts and characters detected and exposed. How greatly should this city always revere, always honor and want to have you, Friars Minor! *You* carry with you the true, pure, and genuine faith in the same way that the wounds of the stigmata of your founder, Seraphic Francis, are true and visible.[46] By your most prudent sermons, your voluntary life of poverty, your holiness of mind, and the proofs you give of all true virtues you truly preserve and enhance the Christian faith. By your exhortations you founded hospitals for the poor; you were instrumental in the establishment of the *monte di pietà*.[47] You pour forth to God petitions stemming from fervent conviction, and true

---

54); he was later viewed as a Christian martyr (see *Jacobi a Voragine Legenda Aurea*, ed. Graesse, 202–3; *Jacobus de Voragine: The Golden Legend*, trans. Stace, 102). Even Pontius Pilate, the Roman procurator of Judaea who authorized the crucifixion, appears in a favorable light in certain apocryphal writings; it is usually stated that in the Coptic Church he too is revered as a martyr: see P. Luisier, "De Pilate chez les Coptes," *Orientalia Christiana Periodica* 62 (1996): 411–25.

[45] The cult of St. Joseph was promoted by the Franciscan reformer San Bernardino of Siena (1380–1444) and by the French churchman and spiritual writer Jean Gerson (1363–1429): their appreciation of his function as foster-father of Jesus led to the introduction of his feast into the Roman calendar in 1479. The Dominicans' alleged antipathy to the cult of St. Joseph, which spread quite widely in northern Italy between ca. 1480 and ca. 1520, may be related to its close association with the Franciscans (although a feast of Joseph was instituted for the Dominican order in its general chapter of 1508), and with Galeazzo Maria Sforza (1444–1476) of Milan. A church named after St. Joseph was founded in Brescia in 1515, probably as a form of appeal for the saint's intercession against warfare and plague. See C. C. Wilson, *St Joseph in Italian Renaissance Society and Art: New Directions and Interpretations* (Philadelphia: St Joseph's University Press, 2001), part 1.

[46] See n. 23 above.

[47] See notes 20 and 21 above.

Quod hi criminatores nostri cum faciant, nullum locum cum Christo sanctisque, ideo adeptis caelestes sedes quia terrena atque mortalia contempsere, habere possunt — qua re significatur pietatem esse gratam Deo, divitias ac sumptus a rebus divinis et a sacris esse reiiciendos. Nam istae vestrae preces et orationes locupletes Plutoni et fortunae diis gentilium sunt accommodatae,[48] non Deo Christo. Et indignantur hi Fratres quod civitas prudentissima veraeque pietatis amans et Sanctae Religionis cultrix eiusmodi preces decreto sustulerit, quamquam id non fecit, nec eius consilium fuit ut preces aut orationes tolleret, sed — quod totiens est ante memoratum — ut modus sumptibus adhiberetur. At utinam penitus sustulisset eas! Magnopere enim verendum est ne, ut adeo se captos cupidine funerum ob emolumentum inde ad eos proveniens ostendunt, crebra funera mortesque nostras orent atque precentur et magicis aliquibus precibus vi eas expugnent. Et praedicare audent fecisse nos adversus ecclesiasticam libertatem, quia operam dedimus ne pariter et rem omnem et vitam nostram adversis contrariisque precibus haurire possent!

Afferunt deinde canonem quendam de rebus Ecclesiae non alienandis, contra quem nostrum decretum esse contendunt.[49] Hoc introducendo loco duo supposita faciunt, quorum primum est auctoritatem Summi Pontificis et Concilii circa spiritualia et annexa spiritualibus non esse negandam.[50] Tantum absum ut huic supposito quicquam detrahere velim, ut ultro ipsum etiam augeam, nullius hominis, nullius magistratus, nullius officii, nullius denique rei veram et iustam auctoritatem contendens esse negandam. Alterum est de significatione vocis huius mortuaria,

prayers for the living and the dead, since you are not hired, nor corrupted by any hope of earthly wages. But since the latter *is* the case with these accusers of ours, they can have no place with Christ and his saints, who have reached the heavenly abodes precisely by scorning earthly, perishable things — a fact which shows that piety pleases God, whereas wealth and expenditure should be excluded from religious practices and from worship. Those money-laden prayers and petitions of yours [sc. the Dominicans] are suited to Pluto and the pagan gods of fortune,[48] not to God who is Christ! And these brothers are annoyed because a most prudent city which loves true piety and observes holy religion has, so they say, abolished such prayers by decree, though in fact it has not done so, nor did it intend to abolish prayers or petitions but, as so often stated before, to have a limit imposed on expenditure. Yet would that it *had* abolished them altogether, for it is greatly to be feared that, as these brothers show themselves to be gripped by *such* a lust for funerals because of the profit they get from them, they may plead and pray for frequent funerals and our deaths, and may achieve them forcibly by means of certain magical prayers! And they dare to preach that *we* attacked Church freedom because we took steps to prevent them from draining away both all our property and our lives with their hostile and harmful prayers!

Next, they cite a certain canon *On not alienating the Church's property* which, they assert, our decree contravenes.[49] In introducing this point they make two assumptions, the first of which is that the authority of the supreme pontiff and council in spiritual matters and their adjuncts must not be denied.[50] So far am I from wishing to subtract anything from this assumption that I am even happy to add to it: I assert that the valid and rightful authority of no man, no magistracy, no office, in a word nothing, should be denied. The second assumption concerns the meaning of

---

[48] Originally a divinity in his own right, in the fifth century B. C. Pluto became synonymous with Hades, god of the underworld, but his name ('The rich one') also connects him with Plutus ('Wealth'), and this connection is prominent here.

[49] *Quaestio* (sig. biiir) refers back to Canon 44 of the Fourth Lateran Council, which was quoted earlier: see below 158–60, 178–81.

[50] *Quaestio* (sig. biiir–v): "praesuppono primo quod nemo summi pontificis auctoritatem neget aut concilii circa spiritualia vel annexa spiritualibus et circa eorum declarationem."

quod nemo hominum dat nullaque omnino ratio concedit — mortuaria videlicet funera sive exequias significare[51] — praeter insanam et amentem cupiditatem vestram, quae vos a vero detorquet, quae mentes vestras praecipites agit fallitque ac decipit. Mortuaria enim id significat quod supra demonstravimus: legata ecclesiis mortuorum causa. Quod cum sit verum, vestra causa haeret in harena, nulla est et tota corruit. Fundamenta in aquam iecistis, praeterquam quod detexistis vestras voluntates antea non omnibus manifestas sine ullo operae precio vestro. Verum enimvero ut vobis hoc suppositum concedatur — mortuaria videlicet esse funera — doctoresque quos testes[52] citatis vera dicere atque interpretari fateamur, lumine solis clarius demonstrabo nihil decretum nostrum contra canonem nec contra interpretationem sententiamque doctorum vestrorum decernere.

"Est apertissime prohibitum," inquiunt, "quod saeculares non disponant circa mortuaria per Summum Pontificem et Concilium, et esse contra libertatem Ecclesiae." Addunt per nomen mortuaria doctores intelligere candelas, denarios et numerum clericorum.[53] Hunc locum existimant adversarii esse robur totius accusationis validissimum, invictum et inexpugnabile, si in forum contentiosum haec causa trahatur, cum omnino nullarum sit virium vel si illis concedatur quod ipsi sibi finxerunt de significatione dictionis mortuaria. Nego statutum nostrum quicquam decernere contra canonem hunc pontificium contraque sententiam istorum doctorum interpretantium canonem. Hocque apertissime demonstrabo, in quacunque significatione mortuaria capiatur, si aliqua prius de hisce doctoribus — quorum ingentem catervam percensent, ut consumere tempus isti religiosi in huiusmodi molibus volvendis librorum videantur — aliqua verba fecero.

A defense of the Brescians' statute

this term "death disbursements", an assumption which no human being grants and absolutely no logic allows: that "death disbursements" means funerals or obsequies.[51] Only your crazy and mindless lust makes you think so, twisting you away from the truth, driving your minds headlong, cheating and deceiving you. For, as we showed above, "death disbursements" means bequests to churches for the sake of the dead, and since that is true your case is bogged down, done for, and completely ruined. You have laid your foundations on water, as well as revealing your intentions — which were not clear to everyone before — without getting any of your pay for the job. But now, to grant you this assumption (that "death disbursements" *are* funerals) and admit that the "doctors" you cite as witnesses[52] speak and explain the truth, I will show more clearly than daylight that our decree determines nothing contrary to the canon or to the explanation and opinion of your "doctors".

"It is very plainly forbidden by the supreme pontiff and council," they say, "for laypeople to deal with 'death disbursements', and it contravenes the Church's freedom." They add that "doctors" understand by the term "death disbursements" candles, coins, and a group of clergy.[53] Our opponents think this point the strongest plank of their whole accusation, invincible and impregnable if this case is dragged into the fray of the lawcourt, though it carries absolutely no weight even if the fictitious meaning they have attached to the expression "death disbursements" is granted. I deny that our statute determines anything contrary to this papal canon or to the opinion of those "doctors" of yours who explain the canon. I will show this very plainly, whatever meaning "death disbursements" is taken to have, if I first say a few words about these "doctors". There is a large crowd of them whose writings those religious peruse, so that they seem to spend their time leafing through massive tomes of this kind.

---

[51] *Quaestio* (sig. biiiv): see below 158–60, 178–81.

[52] In this specific connection *Quaestio* (sig. biiiv) names Henricus de Segusio (1190/1200–1271), Giovanni d'Andrea (ca. 1270–1348), Pietro da Ancharano (ca. 1330/3–1416), Niccolò de' Tudeschis (Panormitanus) (1386–1445), and Giovanni da Imola (ca. 1367/72–1436). (Cf. the writers cited later as more generally opposed to the Brescian statute, and listed in n. 33 above.)

[53] Canon 44 mentions laypeople's "unlawful presumption" regarding "death disbursements" and "adjuncts of spiritual authority", but defines neither of these terms — it was the "doctors" who did that.

Horum pars aliqua nostro tempore fuit, pars haud procul a nostra memoria, hoc est, temporibus quibus ad honores immodicos divitiasque nullis metis circumscriptas prolapsi homines sunt, qui religionem Ecclesiamque sectantur. Ex hoc numero magna pars dignitates cum divitiis in Ecclesia sunt consecuti, quibus autem artibus ipsi viderint, minime certe illis laeti aviditate maiorum. Eorum omnis scientia, praeter admodum duum vel trium, in calliditate quadam atque solertia iuris quod in contentioni-[sig. Avv] bus ac litibus utriusque fori versatur sita est,[54] hoc est, circa meum et tuum. Atque ideo in magna sunt existimatione atque auctoritate apud vulgus hominum et apud hos Fratres, quoniam nihil magis admirantur quam divitias et meum. Videre licet unde auxilia, argumenta, fides, testimonia ad suam causam comprobandam petant. Ab Evangeliisne doctrinaque Christi clamantis, "Si duas tunicas habes, da unam pauperibus"[55] (hi plures habent quam scutum Aiacis versicolores,[56] laneas atque pelliceas); "nolite cogitare de crastino"[57] iubentis (hi conditam in annos annonam habent)? A Paulone? A Iacobo? Petro? Doctoribusne ullis Ecclesiae?[58] Verbum ab his nullum. A doctoribus et magistris cumulandae rei omnia praesidia suae causae mutuant. Ne a suo quidem Sancto Thoma, praeclaro theologo,[59] fidem ullam petunt, aut quia eius doctrina omnis sancta et virtutis morum atque Christianae plena adversus eorum cupiditates est, aut quia ex eo Doctore nihil accurate et studiose discunt quam fallaces conclusiunculas, quos elenchos et sophismata vocant, ut orbos et locupletes circumscribere, captare et

A defense of the Brescians' statute

Some of them lived in our time, others not far from our memory: that is, at those times when followers of religion and the Church fell for the temptation of excessive privileges and of wealth quite unlimited. Of this number a large part gained distinctions plus wealth in the Church. What their methods were, they themselves will have seen, but certainly they were not at all happy with their gains, through greed for greater ones. Except for a mere two or three of them, all their knowledge centered on a certain cunning and cleverness in the law concerning quarrels and disputes in both types of court:[54] that is, the law about what is mine and what is yours. And they were highly regarded and respected among the common people and among these brothers, for the very reason that they admire nothing more than wealth, and what is mine. One can see where they get the help, proof, confirmation, and evidence to bolster their case. Is it from the Gospels? From the teaching of Christ, who proclaims: "If you have two coats, give one to the poor"?[55] These men have more coats than Ajax's shield has,[56] multicolored and made of wool and leather. From Christ, who commands: "Take no thought for the morrow"?[57] These men have grain stocked up for years ahead. From Paul, from James or Peter? From any doctors of the Church?[58] No comment from these: they borrow all the ammunition for their case from "doctors" and teachers of property-gathering. They do not even seek any confirmation from their own St. Thomas, the renowned theologian,[59] either because his teaching, all-holy and full of moral and Christian virtue as it is, goes against their lusts, or because from that "doctor" they carefully and keenly learn nothing but misleading conclusions (which they term critical inquiries and sophistries), in order to cheat and cajole

---

[54] Ecclesiastical and civil courts, that is.

[55] Cf. Luke 3: 11: "Qui habet duas tunicas, det non habenti."

[56] Ajax (in Greek Aias), son of Telamon, was a leading Greek warrior at Troy, renowned for his enormous size and for his huge tower-like shield, which had seven layers of ox-hide overlaid with an eighth layer of bronze: Homer, *Iliad* 7. 206–223.

[57] Cf. Matthew 6: 34: "Nolite ergo solliciti esse in crastinum."

[58] Traditionally, the four most respected theologians of the Church in the west: Sts. Gregory the Great, Ambrose, Augustine, and Jerome.

[59] See n. 1 above. Canonized in 1323 by John XXII, Aquinas was made a doctor of the Church in 1567 by Pius V, who also ordered the first complete printed edition of his works.

ad sua vota ambiguos, restitantes, tergiversantes ac paene invitos pertrahere possint.

Maximam partem accusatorum libri sententiae horum doctorum obtinent super verbum mortuaria, in quibus insignis unius sententia est, quam propter absurditatem ipsius silentio praetereundam esse non putavi. Censet is praeclarus doctor, si equi, arma, insignia militaria honorandi causa militis alicuius cadaver sequantur funus, illos equos, illa arma, illa insignia addicta Ecclesiae esse oportere.[60] Atque ita in templis

A defense of the Brescians' statute

the bereaved and the well-off, and force them — ditherers, dawdlers, evaders, and near-recalcitrants — to do their wishes.

Our accusers' book is mainly occupied by the opinions of these "doctors" about the term "death disbursements", and among them one man's opinion stands out which is so ridiculous that I thought it should not be passed over in silence. The renowned "doctor" thinks that if, to honor some soldier's corpse, his horses, weapons, and military badges accompany the funeral, those horses, weapons, and badges ought to be assigned to the Church.[60] So, for nobody's benefit, those badges are

---

[60] *Quaestio* (sig. cv) identifies the writer as Baldus de Ubaldis (ca. 1327–1400), and quotes his opinion (reported by Fra Angelo Carletti in his *Summa angelica*, and based on the final paragraph of a law in Justinian's *Digest*, *On bequests of gold and silver*): "quod equi et arma ducti ad sepulturam militis, et cerei, debent remanere apud clericos vel fratres sepelientes, quasi sint sequela cadaveris," below, 191–93. Cf. *Digest*, 34.2.40.1; *CICv* 1: 527. (A similar reference to Baldus by Andreas Barbatia occurs later in *Quaestio* [sigs. ciiii–civr], below 198–201.)

The mention of weapons would have particular resonance for natives of Brescia, at this time Italy's main center for assembling and finishing hand-held military firearms. On the *trecento* habit of dedicating such items to religious causes, see Cohn, *The Cult of Remembrance*, 21, 134 (describing how in 1348 an Aretine condottiere bequeathed to the confraternity of the Misericordia all his armor except his helmet and other insignia, which were to be kept over his tomb in the city's Servite church), and M. Wackernagel, *The World of the Florentine Renaissance Artist: Projects and Patrons, Workshop and Art Market*, trans. A. Luchs (Princeton: Princeton University Press, 1981), 243: "In the precinct of his family altar, his chapel, the proprietor . . . considered himself so completely at home that all manner of trophies and personal memorabilia of famous ancestors were freely hung there on the family tombs: armor and other military apparatus, festive clothes, coats of arms, banners and the like. Although this custom gradually died out in the course of the Quattrocento, its effects were not removed from the church interiors until much later." Cf. Thomas More: "Mych have many of us bestowyd uppon rych men in gold rynges and blak gownys: mych in many tapers & torchys: mych in worldly pomp and hygh solempne ceremonyes about our funerallys wherof the brotle glory standeth us here god wot in very little stede but hath on the tother syde done us great dyspleasure. For albe yt yt the kynde solycytude & lovyng dylygence of the quyk used about the beryeng of the dede is well allowed and approvyd afore the face of god: yet mych superfluouse charge used for boste and ostentacyon namely devysed by the dede before hys dethe ys of god greatly myslyked: and moste especially that kynde & fassyon therof wherin some of us have fallen and many

insignia illa ad nullius utilitatem corrumpenda figuntur, quasi templa Christi et martyrum, mitissimorum sanctorum virginumque sanctarum a templis Bellonae ac Martis,[61] crudelis ac sanguinarii daemonis, differre aequum non sit. Cur non et vestes sequentium funus Ecclesiae sint? Cur non et ipsa humana corpora, quia sequantur funus, in servitium et ipsa religiosorum trahantur? Recens a Christo discipulisque ipsius Sancta illa prima Ecclesia vix Christum crucifixum pingi signumve ipsius in templis dedicari permiserunt, seu significantes puritate atque candore templorum divinam essentiam sequestratam esse ab omni mixtione et contagione cuiuscunque materiae, seu ne oculi occupati legendis picturis averterent orantium mentem a Deo, seu ne tardiores ac simpliciores in idololatriam illaberentur.[62] Nunc autem, nedum caetera, militaria quoque signa, cataphracti equi, et arma indicantia mutuas caedes Christianorum, crudelitates cladesque rerum omnium, quas bellum amat facere, in tectis divinis conspiciuntur. Quae cum monumenta decorum, gloriae, honorum et laudis bello partae alicuius hominis militaris sint, spectantes ea qui ad templum oratum veniunt Christiani multi — ut est proclivum genus humanum ad deteriora exempla capescenda[63] — studio eiusdem gloriae commoventur et ad similia facinora perpetranda concitantur, rati ab Ecclesia virisque sacris ea probari quorum instrumen-

hung up in churches to corrode, as though it were wrong for the churches of Christ and the martyrs, of the gentlest saints and of saintly virgins, to be any different from temples of Bellona and Mars,[61] that brutal and bloody spirit. Why should not the clothes of the funeral escort also belong to the Church? Why should not their actual human bodies too — those of religious even — themselves be dragged into slavery? When newly founded by Christ and his disciples, the early holy Church hardly allowed the painting of Christ's crucifixion or the consecration of a statue of him in churches, either indicating, by the cleanness and whiteness of churches, that the divine nature is separated from all dilution and pollution of any sort of matter; or fearing that eyes engrossed in picture-gazing might distract the minds of suppliants from God, or that duller and simpler people might lapse into idolatry.[62] But now — not to mention the rest — one may see in sacred buildings even military standards, mail-clad horses, and weapons which reveal Christians' slaughter of each other, their atrocities, and the wholesale destruction which war is wont to cause. Since these things are memorials of some military man's exploits, glory, distinctions, and praise won in war, when those many Christians who come to the church to pray look at them, such is mankind's tendency to follow inferior examples[63] that they are moved by a desire for the same glory and stirred to commit similar crimes, thinking that the Church and holy men approve of things whose implements and

---

besydys us now lye damnyd in hell. For some hathe there of us whyle we were in helthe not so mych studyed how we myght dye penytent and in good crysten plyght as how we myght be solempnely borne owte to beryeng have gay & goodly funerallys wyth herawdys at our hersys and ofrynge up oure helmettys settyng up our skouchyn and cote armours on the wall though never cam harneyse on our bakkys nor never auncestour of ours ever bare armis byfore": *The supplycacyon of soulys* (London, 1529), sig. L1r.

[61] Bellona was the Roman goddess of war, and hence came to be identified with Nerio, the cult-partner or wife of Mars.

[62] St. Paul stated that the truly faithful had no need of "signa": 1 Corinthians 1: 22, 14: 22. Between 726 and 843 the Church prohibited any representation of Christ except the Chi-Rho and the Alpha and Omega symbols. However, the Roman Catholic church accepted that images were *adiaphora* or dispensable aids to piety for those unable to read scripture but warned against their veneration, which could lead to idolatry.

[63] Probably an allusion to Ovid, *Metamorphoses* 7. 20–21: "Video meliora proboque, / deteriora sequor."

ta et simulachra in suis templis habere exoptent et laetentur. Ad rem nunc redeo. Sic itaque inquiunt.

"Est apertissime prohibitum quod saeculares non disponant circa mortuaria, et omnes doctores per mortuaria intelligunt candelas, pecuniam, numerum religiosorum."[64] Si saeculares de funeribus non disponant, quis ergo disponet? Ecclesiastici igitur et religiosi et vos Fratres disponetis aut nemo, quod quidem ferarum est. Cum itaque saecularis aliquis functus vita fuerit, curandumque funus erit, vosne Fratres candelas, pecuniam et numerum religiosorum procurabitis? Vestramne pecuniam vestramque ceram proponetis? An ad tabernas cerearias ibitis et accipietis quantumcunque numerum candelarum cuiuscunque ponderis vestra libido feret a mercatore impensis cognatorum defuncti inconsultis ipsis? An imperabitis propinquis — parenti, fratri, avunculo — ipsius humandi ut tantam vim pecuniae totque cereos et tanti ponderis et tot ordines Fratrum et numerum eorum parent, quantum libebit vobis? Hoc nimirum est disponere de funere et circa mortuaria. O impudentia capita![i] Non[j] cernitis ad quas insanias vos trahat vestra cupiditas et quaedam arrogantia seu ambitio ostentandi doctrinam et ingenium quasi supra fidem saecularium praecellens, ut quia vos taedet habitus suscepti et voti nuncupati et quasi desperati estis — non tamen de omnibus loquor — hac inani gloria consolari vestram inquietam et perturbatam mentem putastis, sive potius sollicitando ac perturbando quietos voluptatem aliquam vestris miseriis quaerere. Si haec curatio ad religiosos non pertinet, ad quosnam igitur spectabit? Profecto ad saeculares et propinquos, non ad alienum genus, ni forte quis careat propinquis, aut gravioribus causis[k] aut necessitate aliqua impediti eo munere fungi non possint. Tunc id officium elemosynae et misericordiae et humanitatis primo ad religiosos, absolute ad omnes pertinebit: nullam utique curam sepulturae habere ferarum est. Quid ad hoc respondebitis, Fratres? Quid aliud quam id quod verum est: Pontificem et doctores intelligere de funere quod actu iam est

---

[i] *correxi*: capitainon *cod.*

[k] *correxi*: ausis *cod.*

A defense of the Brescians' statute

images they are eager and happy to have in their churches. Now I return to the subject. This, then, is what they say.

"It is very plainly forbidden for laypeople to deal with 'death disbursements', and all the doctors understand by 'death disbursements' candles, cash, and a number of religious."[64] If laypeople are not to deal with them, who *will* then? Churchmen, religious, and you brothers will, or nobody will, as is the way of wild beasts. So when a layperson dies, and his funeral has to be arranged, will you brothers provide candles, cash, and a number of religious? Will you offer your cash and your candle-wax, or will you go to the chandlers' shops and take from the tradesman as large a number of candles — whatever their weight — as your whim dictates, at the expense of the deceased's relatives but without consulting them? Or will you order the kinsmen of the person who is to be buried — his parent, brother, uncle — to supply as much cash, as many tapers of such a weight, and as many ranks of brothers to such a number, as will please you? This, presumably, is what dealing with a funeral and "death disbursements" means! You shameless people! You do not see to what madness your lust is dragging you, as is a certain conceit or cockiness in parading your learning and intellect as if superior to laypeople's faith, so that, because you are bored with the habit you assumed and the vow you uttered, and are well-nigh desperate (though I am not speaking of everyone), you thought to comfort your troubled and disturbed minds with this vainglory, or rather to seek some pleasure in your wretchedness by harassing and disturbing peaceful people. If arranging a funeral does *not* devolve on religious, whom will it concern? Surely laypeople and relatives, not an outside body — unless a person has no relatives, or they are hindered from performing that duty by weightier matters or by some emergency. That service of alms, compassion, and humanity will then devolve primarily on religious, but quite simply on *everyone*: certainly, to have no burial arrangement is the way of wild beasts. What will be your answer to this, brothers? Surely, nothing but the truth: that regarding a funeral which actually exists now — granting your assumption — and regarding candles, cash, and everything else already attached and assigned to a funeral, the pope and the "doctors" mean

---

[64] *Quaestio* (sig. biiiv) has exactly the same wording as here in the first clause of this sentence, but differs slightly in the second: see below, 178–81.

(vestro supposito concesso), et de candelis, pecunia caeterisque omnibus rebus iam funeri annexis et dicatis — de his interdictum esse saecularibus ne quicquam decernant nec disponant, quia iam sacrata sunt. Nonne etiam ante hoc factum statutum saeculares pro arbitrio quisque suo de funeribus statuebat, nec quisquam tamen unquam dixit comminuere eos libertatem Ecclesiae, nec contra canonem illum pontificium facere, quamquam disponerent circa mortuaria, ut vos quidem intelligi vultis? Quid ita? Quid aliud nisi quia (ut dictum est) funera non sunt nec annexa funeri — cera, pecunia et caetera — id genus, cum saeculares de ipsis decernunt et statuunt quantum numerum quantumque pondus eorum adhiberi funeribus suorum velint.

"At non debet intercedere publica cura, quae libertatem adimat civibus privatis et populo, quominus de rebus suis statuant ut velint."[65] Nimirum ut et vos dicere possitis, quod mensarii Florentini dicere solent ubi agunt de re pecuniaria cum aliquo simplici et temporum crassorum viro quem expilant imprudentem: "Utinam plurimi essent similes tui." Ille vero laetus abit, existimans a mensario sapiens haberi.[66] Sic vos postulatis rem periniquam — ut nullus sit senatus, nullum publicum consilium, nec publica cura ulla privatorum et plebis, quae errata et pravas imprudentesque actiones populi lege aut decreto coherceant — ut quasi gregem ovium pastore et praesidio canum[67] destitutum tondere et devorare pro vestra insatiabili cupiditate possitis.

A defense of the Brescians' statute

that laypeople are banned from determining or dealing with anything, as those things are already hallowed. Even before this statute was passed did not laypeople each use their own judgment in deciding about funerals, yet no one ever said that they were destroying the Church's freedom or contravening that papal canon, although they did deal with "death disbursements" in the meaning you want them to carry? Why so? Only because, as has been said, funerals and funeral adjuncts — candle-wax, cash, and the rest — do not fall into that category when laypeople determine them and decide what number and weight of them they want to be brought to their relatives' funerals.

"But the government should not intervene to deprive private citizens and ordinary people of the power to decide on their own affairs as they wish."[65] No doubt this is to enable you too to say what Florentine moneylenders usually say when they have financial dealings with some simple, thick-skulled fellow whom in his ignorance they fleece: "If only there were plenty like you!" He, however, goes away happy, thinking that the moneylender considers him wise.[66] Similarly, *you* are making a very unjust demand: that there should be no senate, no public council, no government made up of private persons and common people which may, by popular law or decree, keep errors and base, ignorant actions within bounds. This is to enable you, with your insatiable lust, to shear and devour a flock of sheep, as it were, left without its shepherd and its guard-dogs.[67]

---

[65] *Quaestio* (sig. diiir–v) calls it false to say that the community in general can do whatever private persons can: see below, 212–15.

[66] The international operations of banking families like the Bardi and the Peruzzi in the fourteenth century, and the Medici in the fifteenth, helped to give Florence a reputation for hardheaded financial dealing. In the early sixteenth century it was still Italy's (and Europe's) busiest and richest money-lending center, and therefore provided a ready example of avarice.

[67] As the anonymous author's prime target is the Dominican Order, his reference to "dogs" clearly plays on the popular derivation of *Dominicani* as *Domini canes* ('the Lord's dogs'). This in turn alludes to the prophetic dream of Dominic's mother before his birth, that she had in her womb a little dog holding a flaming torch with which, when born, it would set the whole world ablaze (see *Jacobi a Voragine Legenda Aurea*, ed. Graesse, 466; *Jacobus de Voragine: The Golden Legend*, trans. Stace, 191). The biblical allusion is of course to John 10: 12.

Instant absolute canonem prohibere saeculares ne disponant circa mortuaria.⁶⁸ De quibusnam mortuariis, obsecro vos, saeculares non disponant? De hisne quae sunt, an de iis quae non sunt, nec unquam fuere? "De his videlicet," dicent, "quae sunt: stultum enim esset dicere de iis quae non sunt." At hoc facit nostrum statutum quod canon iubet: nihil enim disponit de funeribus quae iam sint in natura rerum, nec de candelis pecuniave quae iam funeri sint annexae. Non enim dici potest quicquam earum rerum [sig. Avir] prohibere quae iam funeri sint adiuncta, dicata, annexa, sed de rebus propriis tantummodo saecularium, nihil omnino Ecclesiam pertingentibus, nec addictis nec annexis nec ulli sacro aut spiritualibus rebus ullis destinatis.

"At solebat largior esse nostra merces" sive (ut vos vultis) "elemosyna."⁶⁹ Rogo vos: cuiusnam debet esse ea existimatio quantum detur? Dantisne sua, an accipientis aliena? Opinor dantis aequum esse. Nam si accipientis foret, vacuae paucis funeribus privatae domus erunt. Si merces non placet illa, tu operamne impendes?¹ (Liberum enim hoc vobis est.) "Si elemosyna natura rerum permutabitur, ut egens sit dominus locupletis, et locuples minister et quaestor pauperis, si pro arbitrio et voluntate ipsius erogabit quotcunque illi collibuerit." At elemosyna libera est in voluntate sita miserentis, gratuita non mercenaria, alioquin — ut in principio demonstravimus — desinit esse elemosyna.

Ut clarius sit quod dico, respondete mihi, vos Fratres: cum adhuc intra penates parentum vestrorum vitam ducebatis, in quorumnam tum potestate et cuius iuris eratis? Profecto parentum et civilis iuris et legum saecularium, et de vobis rebusque vestris illae leges statuere poterant. Post, ubi vero habitum induistis religionis et initiati sacris fuistis, desiistis esse in potestate eorum in qua eratis prius, et in ius ecclesiasticum concessistis.

---

¹ *correxi*: impende *cod.*

A defense of the Brescians' statute

"The canon," they insist, "unreservedly bans laypeople from dealing with 'death disbursements'."[68] *What* "death disbursements", pray, are laypeople not to deal with? Those that exist, or those that do not, and never did, exist? "Those that exist, of course," they will say, "for it would be silly to speak of those that do not." But our statute does what the canon orders, not dealing at all with funerals which are already a reality, nor with candles or cash which are already attached to a funeral. For it cannot be said to ban any of those things that are already appended, dedicated, and attached to a funeral. It deals only with laypeople's private property which does not concern the Church at all: neither assigned nor attached to it, and not earmarked for any sacred cause or any spiritual purposes.

"But our fee" — or, as you would have it, "alms" — "used to be bigger."[69] *Who*, I ask you, should judge the amount to be given? The one who gives his own money, or the one who receives another's? By rights the giver, I think. If it should be the receiver, private houses will be emptied by a few funerals. If the fee does not suit you, will you make the effort? (You are free to do so.) "Yes, if almsgiving is turned on its head, so as to make the poor man master of the rich one, and the rich man servant and supplier of the poor one, spending at the latter's discretion and desire whatever amount pleases him." But alms depend on the free will of the one who shows pity: they are gratis, not paid for, otherwise (as we showed at the start) they cease to be alms.

To clarify what I am saying, brothers, answer me this: in whose power and in what jurisdiction were you when you were still living in your parents' homes? Surely in that of your parents, civil law, and secular statutes, and those statutes could decide about you and your property. But later, when you donned the habit of your vocation and were admitted to the religious life, you ceased to be in the power of your previous masters, and passed into church jurisdiction. Similarly, rather

---

[68] After quoting the views of numerous "doctors" (see n. 33 above), *Quaestio* (sig. civr) refers again to Canon 44 (cf. notes 35, 49, 53): "Quod capitulum omnes doctores allegant ad probandum statutum laicorum super mortuariis non valere, et ita intelligunt Innocentium voluisse, ut patet in responsionibus eorum."

[69] Not a quotation from the *Quaestio* but, presumably, a complaint publicly voiced by the Dominicans.

Sic ille testator,^m priusquam tam locupletem hereditatem magno ante animo a Fratribus Minoribus recusatam vobis legaret, utrum potestatem nulli ecclesiae, nulli sacro legandi eam habebat, liberumque illi erat de ea statuere pro sua voluntate? Ita prorsus reor. Quid ita? Quia erant ea bona civis et saecularis constituti cum ipsis bonis suis sub imperio saecularium legum. Simulatque vero ea Ecclesiae dicavit annexuitque sacris et spiritualibus consecravit, amisit de ipsis ultra quicquam statuendi potestatem, nec ipse modo, sed ipsa quoque saecularia iura et leges civiles ea facultate privatae sunt, et imperio ecclesiastico cessere. Eadem sane parique ratione, sicuti funus iam actu, ordinatum, compositum et ductum, omniaque funeri dicata, annexa, adiuncta atque attributa — ceram, inquam, pecuniam, arma (si vultis) et equos — concedimus et fatemur ecclesiastici iuris et consecrata esse, nec ullam in eas res saeculares habere potestatem: sic, ante omnino quam funus in rerum natura foret, moriturusque atque humandus adhuc viveret, nullaque dum res destinata funeri esset, quippe quod nullum extaret, nec forte cera cereive facti erant, res illas omnes iuris civilis et saecularis esse, posseque nos libere de illis pro libertate atque arbitrio nostro decernere, nulloque prorsus modo res illas ad sacra Ecclesiamve seu ecclesiasticos pertinere contendimus. De his itaque rebus nostrum statutum decernit atque disponit, non de vestris mortuariis nec ullis spiritualibus annexis. Quae quidem res si ratione aliqua postea consecrentur, deque illis saeculares decreverint, merito plectendi erunt.

"At cum statuitur," inquiunt, "de numero clericorum, de rebus sacris decernitur."[70] Nihil vobis imperatur, nihil vobis vetatur, nulla vis infertur, nulla poena mulctave in vos statuitur. Intacti omnino estis, tanquam crabrones aculeati; integra vestra libertas manet, nec ulla ex parte comminuitur. Sive omnes sive nulli ad funus cuiusvis hominum accedere velitis, seu vocati seu invocati, liberum integrumque est vobis, impuneque per nostrum statutum id vobis facere licet. Solis saecularibus, in quos

---

^m *correxi:* testa *cod.*

A defense of the Brescians' statute

than bequeathing to you so rich an inheritance (magnanimously rejected by the Friars Minor), did the testator have the power to bequeath it to *no* church, *no* sacred cause, and was he free to decide about it as he wished? Yes indeed, I think. Why so? Because those goods belonged to a citizen and layperson established, with the goods themselves, under the authority of secular laws. But as soon as he dedicated them to the Church, attached them to sacred causes, and consecrated them to spiritual purposes, he lost the power to make any further decision about them, and not only did he himself do so, but also the secular laws and civil statutes were themselves stripped of that ability, and gave way to church authority. Surely, by the same and similar reasoning, just as we grant and admit that a funeral which actually now is organized, arranged, and conducted, and all the things dedicated, attached, appended, and ascribed to it — I mean candle-wax, cash, weapons (if you wish), and horses — are within church jurisdiction and consecrated, with laypeople having no power over them: so, before ever a funeral could be a reality, and when the person about to die and need burial was still alive, and nothing was yet earmarked for the funeral because there was none, and candle-wax and candles had perhaps not been made, we maintain that all *those* things come within civil and secular jurisdiction, that we can freely decide about them using our freedom and our own judgment, and that they have absolutely nothing to do with religion, the Church, or churchmen. These, then, are the matters our statute decides about and deals with: not your "death disbursements", nor any spiritual adjuncts. If later they *are* somehow consecrated, any laypeople who decide about them will rightly be punishable.

"But," they say, "a statute about the number of clergy is a decision about religious matters."[70] You are not ordered or forbidden to do anything; no force is applied; no penalty or fine is laid down for you. You are quite unharmed, like stinging hornets; your freedom remains intact and is in no respect destroyed. Whether all or none of you wish to attend any person's funeral, either invited or not, the choice, free and unrestricted, is yours, and our statute lets you do it unscathed. Only for lay-

---

[70] *Quaestio* (sig. er) argues that funerary extravagance is not an excuse for laypeople to interfere in spiritual matters or to act as judges of the clergy.

ius nobis est, poena indicitur, illisque iubetur, et legibus decretisque civitatis ii parere coguntur. "At vetatis eos posse extra certum numerum advocare ad funera sacerdotes." Prohibentur saeculares, qui prohiberi possunt, ne extra numerum accersant; non prohibentur qui a nobis prohiberi nequeunt, sacerdotes clericive, quominus eo voluntario munere (non mercenario nec coempto) quae vera et legittima misericordia atque elemosyna est fungantur. Sumptus tantummodo immodici saecularium prohibentur, qui prohiberi possunt, et res saeculares nulli dum adiunctae funeri aut rei spirituali annexae, quae res adhuc sunt in manu atque potestate saecularium, ut ratio nostrae rei publicae administrandae postulat disponuntur. Imponuntur[n] frena ambitioni civium in rebus tristibus in quibus minime omnium ambitio et contentio honorum convenit, quae frena a vobis imprimis imponenda[o] fuerunt, si Praedicatores bonorum morum, virtutis et veritatis, ac proximi charitatis estis. Denique non prohibentur religiosi quominus capiant quantamcunque immodicam vim auri et argenti opesque immensas — quam rem dicitis vestra sanctissima atque moderatissima indulcta concedere[71] — si illis dentur. Cavetur praeterea, et — quoad fieri potest — providetur a civitate coacta a feris et durissimis animis vestris, ne inter luctus, planctus ac mortes civium vestras inter vos rixas, vestros impetus et vestras dimicationes cernamus, quas minimo quoque irritamento cietis cum tot tantaque agmina Fratrum ad unum funus convocantur.

"At cum statutum," aiunt, "mentionem facit funerum seu sacerdotum fratrumve sive clericorum atque omnino vocabuli alicuius significantis rem sacram, quoniam haec ad ius ecclesiasticum pertinent, quaecunque res simul cum ipsis associatae et quacunque de causa atque ratione pariter scriptae, sive saecularium ac profanae sive cuiuscunque alterius generis sint, illae quoque res omnes ecclesiastici iuris

---

[n] *correxi*: dantur *cod*.
[o] *correxi*: danda *cod*.

A defense of the Brescians' statute

people, against whom our law is aimed, is a penalty laid down; *they* are given orders and *they* are bound to obey the city's statutes and decrees. "But you forbid them the power to invite to funerals more than a fixed number of priests." Laypeople, who *can* be banned, *are* banned from summoning more than that number; priests or clergy, whom we cannot ban, are not banned from performing that voluntary duty (not paid for or purchased) which constitutes true and authentic compassion and almsgiving. Only excessive spending by laypeople, which *can* be banned, *is* banned, and only secular property not yet appended to any funeral or attached to a spiritual purpose — property still in the possession and power of laypeople — is dealt with as the logic of our public policy demands. A curb is placed on citizens' rivalry in sad matters where rivalry and striving for honors are least of all appropriate, a curb which should have been applied by you especially, if you are preachers of good conduct — of virtue and truth — and friends of charity. Finally, religious are not banned from taking any excessive amount whatever of gold and silver, and wealth unbounded (something you say your most holy and moderate indults allow),[71] if they are *given* to them. Furthermore, the city takes care and, so far as possible, takes precautions — pressurized as it is by your wild, harsh attitudes — to prevent us, amid grief, mourning, and the deaths of fellow-citizens, from seeing your internal disputes, fights, and brawls, which you stir up at the least provocation whenever so many sizeable squads of brothers assemble at one funeral.

"But," they say, "when the statute mentions funerals, or priests, or brothers, or clergy, or absolutely any word denoting a sacred matter, since these things fall within the scope of church law, whatever matters are joined with them, and for whatever motive and reason written down side by side with them — whether belonging to laypeople, and secular, or of whatever other sort — all these things too are deemed to have passed

---

[71] Shortly after the passage quoted in n. 6 above, *Quaestio* adds (sig. bv): "unum de privilegiis Ecclesiae est ipsam esse capacem ut possit ei donari in infinitum absque aliqua insinuatione." In support of this it cites the paragraph "Sinimus" in one of Justinian's *Novellae leges*, *On not alienating or exchanging the Church's property*: CICv 3: 53.

censentur esse factae."⁷² Praestantiorem naturam trahere ad se naturas inferiores si adhaerescant opinari eos existimo: sicuti chamaeleontem aiunt omnes colores propinquarum rerum ducere, sic voces res ecclesiasticas et sacras significantes ad suam conditionem per constructa secum vocabula caetera omnia cuiuscunque conditionis significata asciscere.ᵖ Quidnam non erit iuris horum, si quicquid rerum saecularium in omnibus ratis scriptis — legibus, decretis, pactis, commertiis — scriptum omnibusve sermonibus commemoratum fuerit cum nomine aliquo significante sacrum aliquid, id nomen sacrum propinqua omnia devorabit? Si inanimes huiusmodi sacrae dictiones tantam rapacitatem habent, quantam putemus ipsa earum animalia habere? Quid? Fabulamne credimus fuisse quod de Mida traditur, quicquid ab eo tactum foret fuisse in aurum commutatum?⁷³ Nonne hoc persimile est, quin etiam magis mirum, ab inanimis naturam rerum commutari?

Urgent et instant: "Quia cera, pecunia caeteraque profana aliquando annecti funeribus possunt, ad ius ecclesiasticum pertinere censentur, cuius rei libertas vestro statuto tollitur."⁷⁴ Macti virtute! Universus orbis vestri iuris erit: nihil nostrum, nihil liberae nostrae potestatis rerum nostrarum, nihil proprium civium, nihil agricolarum, nihil artificum nec mercatorum tantis laboribus comparatum, nullum scholarium aut militum peculium erit studiis sapientiae ac per vulnera et sanguine

---

ᵖ *correxi:* assiscere *cod.*

A defense of the Brescians' statute

into church jurisdiction."[72] I think that they believe a superior quality attracts inferior qualities if they are tacked onto it: just as a chameleon (so they say) absorbs all the colors of things nearby, so they believe that words denoting churchly and sacred matters transfer to their own status, through terms linked with themselves, all other things, whatever status the latter are denoted as having. What indeed will *not* be under these people's jurisdiction, if whatever secular matter has been written down in any authoritative texts — laws, decrees, agreements, or contracts — or recorded in any conversations together with some name denoting something sacred, that sacred name swallows up all its neighbors? If such inanimate sacred terms are *that* rapacious, how rapacious must we imagine their animate exponents are? Well? Do we believe that the story of Midas — that whatever he touched was changed into gold — was mere fiction?[73] Is this not a very similar situation? Yes, and it is even more miraculous that the natural order is changed by inanimate things!

They press on relentlessly: "Because candles, cash, and other secular items may sometimes be attached to funerals, they are deemed to fall within the scope of church law, whose freedom is abolished by your decree."[74] Well done! The whole world will be under your jurisdiction — nothing will be ours; none of our property will be in our free choice; nothing that was acquired with such pains will be owned by citizens, farmers, craftsmen, or merchants; scholars or soldiers will own no nest-egg gained by

---

[72] *Quaestio* (sig. diiv): ". . . ad cognoscendum statutum esse contra ecclesiasticam libertatem . . . deveniri potest . . . quando de clericis vel religiosis in statuto sit expressa mentio et specialis." This is backed up by a tendentious reference to the chapter "Eos" of a canon in the *Liber sextus*, *On the immunity of churches*: VI 3. 23. 5; CIC 2: 1064 (see n. 86 below). The assumption that the statute was intended to infringe the Church's freedom, and was motivated by hatred of it, could — says *Quaestio* (sig. diiir) — be avoided "by using only general terms" ("tantum verbis generalibus utendo").

[73] As related by Ovid (*Metamorphoses* 11. 90–145), it was his greed for riches that made Midas choose the golden touch as his reward for restoring Silenus to his pupil Bacchus. There is an obvious parallel with the greed which the anonymous author imputes to the Dominicans.

[74] This takes us back to the "doctors" cited in *Quaestio* (sigs. bivr–dr), who take the view that anything connected with the burial service is a spiritual matter, and that only items of no concern to the Church (e.g., mourning garments) are within the scope of civil statutes.

fuso partum, quia quandoque funeribus sive ecclesiis et rebus spiritualibus annecti, dicari et omnino consecrari possint. Ac si quis fortunas suas omnis in mare proiiciat, quam rem aliquando fecisse aliquem philosophum traditur,[75] is excommunicatus erit, et adversus ecclesiasticam libertatem egisse dicetur, quia perfecerit auctorque fuerit ne pars ulla mersarum illarum fortunarum ullo unquam tempore ad Ecclesiam pervenire et consecrari queat. Saecularis quoque vir eadem ratione in ius vocabit saecularem aliquem qui omnia bona sua obligaverit[q] vel aliquo alio modo corruperit, ut Cleopatra, quae uno haustu unionem ingentis precii aceto resolutum devoravit,[76] et is qui unionem omnibus suis fortunis coemptum maleo obtrivit, quia per ipsum effectum fue-[sig. Aviv] rit ne ipse ullusve suae stirpis potiri unquam posset illis bonis, cum fieri potuisset ut olim potiretur ni ab eo abolita corruptaque fuissent.[77] Quo

---

[q] *correxi:* obliguriverit *cod.*

A defense of the Brescians' statute

the pursuit of wisdom or by wounds and bloodshed — because *sometimes* those things could be attached, dedicated, and generally consecrated to funerals or churches and spiritual purposes. And if anyone throws all his wealth into the sea, as once some philosopher is related to have done,[75] he will be excommunicate and said to have contravened Church freedom by managing and scheming to prevent any part of his drowned wealth from ever, at any time, reaching the Church and being consecrated. A layperson, too, will for the same reason take another layperson to court because he has squandered all his property or otherwise spoiled it, like Cleopatra who in one gulp swallowed a single pearl of great price dissolved in vinegar,[76] and like the man who, using all his wealth to buy a single pearl, crushed it with a hammer, because he could thereby ensure that neither he nor any member of his family would ever be able to possess that property, as would have been possible had he not ruined and spoiled it.[77] The

---

[75] Diogenes Laertius, *Lives and Views of Eminent Philosophers* 6. 87, reports that according to Diocles of Magnesia (a historian of philosophy, writing in the late first century B. C.) the Cynic philosopher Crates of Thebes (ca. 368/365–288/285 B. C.) was persuaded by his teacher Diogenes to give up his fields to sheep-pasture and to throw into the sea any money he had. Through his most famous pupil Zeno of Citium (335–263 B. C.) Crates became the link between Cynicism and Stoicism. In Pinturicchio's *Allegory of the Mountain of Virtue* (the only marble pavement-panel in the nave of Siena Cathedral for which we have an artist's name and a date — he was paid for designing it in March 1505) Crates is given equal prominence with Socrates. Both figures are clearly labeled, and Crates is shown emptying his basket of valuables over the cliff-edge of an island: see B. Santi, *The Marble Pavement of the Cathedral of Siena* (Florence: Scala, 1982), 14–15.

[76] Cleopatra is a classic example of conspicuous greed and extravagance. The story of the bet she made with Antony (that she could spend ten million sesterces on a single meal), and of the scientifically unlikely method by which she won it, occurs in Pliny, *Natural History* 9. 58. 119–21, in Macrobius, *Saturnalia* 3. 17. 14–18, and in Boccaccio, *De mulieribus claris* 88. 15–19. The anonymous author of course also works in the allusion to Matthew 13: 46.

[77] St. John, apostle and evangelist, is said to have reproved the philosopher Crato for inducing two rich young brothers to sell all their goods in order to buy gems, which they then publicly smashed to pieces, but which — after Crato's change of heart — John miraculously made perfect again so they could be sold to benefit the poor: *Jacobi a Voragine Legenda Aurea*, ed. Graesse, 57; *Jacobus de Voragine: The Golden Legend*, trans. Stace, 33–34. The anonymous author, however, here alludes to a

fiet ut vita humana non discrepet a vita ferarum, si omnia confusa, indistincta atque incondita sint.

Unde mihi saepe admittenda ad fidem eorum sententia videtur, ut futurum aliquando ut ecclesiastici et religiosi qui vocantur potiantur rerum omnium, agri omnes, domus, fortunae reliquae omnes privatorum illorum sint, saeculares homines eorum mancipia. Huius sententiae ratio in promptu est et expedita. Iam usque nunc magna parte potiuntur. Indulctum praeterea habent — ut ipsi quidem moderati homines in hac accusatione gloriantur — quo illis conceditur ut de bonis saecularium infinite capere possint. Lege alia cautum dicunt ne quicquam ipsi alienent de suo.[78] Si hoc etiam pervincunt, ut eorum iuris sint res nostrae quia aliquando esse possint, quid est dubitandum quin illi vera et sentiant et loquantur, ut videlicet quae omnium hominum sunt unius religiosorum sint futura ditionis, id — opinor — mandante Christo, id virtutibus morum postulantibus? Verum enimvero existimandum credendumque est iura imperatoria, indulcta, leges atque etiam multo magis pontificia decreta nihil velle quod ab honestate et a recta ratione dissentiat et discrepet. Refercta enim sunt — ut diximus — prudentia, moderatione et honestate. Cum quibus omnibus virtutibus quoniam

A defense of the Brescians' statute

result will be that human life will be no different from the life of wild beasts, if everything is mixed up, blurred, and disordered.

Hence *their* view often seems to me credible: that there will come a day when those called churchmen and religious will possess everything, all land and houses and all other wealth of private citizens will belong to them, and laypeople will be their slaves. The reason for this view is self-evident and ready to hand: already, as of now, they possess a large proportion, and they also have an indult (as indeed the moderate fellows themselves boast in this accusation) allowing them unlimited acquisition of laypeople's property; another law, they say, guards against their alienating anything they own.[78] If they win this further point, that our property should be within their jurisdiction because sometime it *could* be, is there any reason to doubt that they think and speak the truth: namely, that what belongs to everybody will be under the sole control of religious, as (I suppose) Christ commands and virtuous conduct demands? But one must nevertheless hold and trust that imperial laws, indults, statutes — and, very much more, papal decrees — intend nothing that conflicts and clashes with integrity and right reason for, as we have said, they are replete with prudence, moderation, and integrity. Since

---

different version of this story — where Crato himself smashes the gems — which he may well have just read, as given by the Croatian writer Marko Marulic (1450–1524) in his *De institutione bene vivendi* (Venice, 1506), chap. 2 (*De eleemosynis faciendis*): "Neque enim immerito Cratonem philosophum dum Ephesi contemnendarum opum ederet spectaculum, gemmas immodicae aestimationis contundentem a Ioanne apostolo reprehensum ferunt. Nam si pietati magis quam gloriae studuisset, nunquam profecto illas contrivisset; sed potius venditarum pretio indigentibus succurrisset. Quam quidem sententiam et ipse postea est secutus. Lapillis quippe ab Apostolo pristinae integritati restitutis, miraculo ad fidem Christi conversus, quod ad suam ipse iactantiam instituerat, ad proximorum vertit usum: iam satis edoctus, sapientiam huius mundi stultitiam esse apud Deum." Both versions of the Crato story were represented by fourteenth-century Italian artists: Voragine's by Giovanni di Bartolomeo Cristiani (signed and dated 1370: see B. Berenson, *Italian Pictures of the Renaissance*, vol. 1 [London: Phaidon Press, 1963], fig. 326); Marulic's by Francescuccio di Cecco Ghissi (probably also dating from the 1370s: see F. R. Shapley, *Paintings from the Samuel H. Kress Collection: XIII — XV Century*, vol. 1 [London: Phaidon Press, 1966], fig. 209).

[78] See below, 170–73, 158–60.

statutum nostrum, decernens suis civibus et plebi moderationem, mensuram et mediocritatem in re quadam particulari, congruit et consentit, necessario concluditur Brixianos nihil adversus ecclesiasticam libertatem per illud decretum fuisse molitos, proinde nec esse excommunicatos, ut etiam concedamus adversariis mortuaria significare funera atque exequias, quod est falsum. Indignum enim et nefas est sanctissimos gravissimosque Pontifices Conciliumque et Conventum tanti numeri sapientissimorum Patrum existimare fudisse tam levi de causa susceptas querimonias, et in leges sive canones retulisse eas, quia saeculares statuant de candelis quot et cuius ponderis sint ab se emendae et quot paria religiosorum sint adhibenda funeri suorum.

Simulque concluditur ratione contraria ipsos accusatores — quia moderationem, modum et mediocritatem impugnant, quia divina atque humana confundunt et fanda ac nefanda miscent, quia pontificia indulcta et canones et voluntatem Sanctissimi Concilii ad pessimum exemplum efrenorum sumptuum et immodicitatis et levitatis interpretantur, quia seditionem in senatu et in populo serunt, quia odia Sedis Apostolicae et omnium Christianorum adversus optimum, devotissimum et Catholicum populum falsis criminibus concitant — dignos esse qui a sacris et a communione modestorum et proborum hominum pellantur, nec cum hominibus frugi et verae sinceraeque religionis cultoribus aetatem agant, cum ipsi efrenatis et impotentibus cupiditatibus ducantur et vivant.

Profligati et debellati omnibus rationibus, ad impudentiam atque importunitatem et ad odia sophistica confugiunt: indirecte aiunt statuto nostro Ecclesiam laedi.[79] Si indirecte intelligi volunt insidiose, dolo malo, fraude et maliciose et ex animi sententia nos illi nocuisse, conficta alia causa impudentissime mentiuntur. Latissime enim patet vera et prope necessaria causa. Sin per accidens illud indirecte capiunt, in nulla

A defense of the Brescians' statute

our statute agrees and accords with all those virtues in decreeing for its citizens and common people moderation, control, and temperateness in a certain specific matter, the necessary conclusion is that the Brescians have contrived nothing against church freedom through that decree, and are accordingly not excommunicate either — even granting our opponents' point that "death disbursements" mean funerals and obsequies, which is mistaken. For it is shameful and wrong to imagine that holy and august popes, and the council and assembly of so many very wise fathers, issued a stream of complaints based on such trivial grounds, and embodied them in laws or canons, just because laypeople regulate the number and weight of candles they themselves are to buy, and how many pairs of religious they are to bring to a family funeral. Moreover, the converse conclusion is that the accusers themselves — since they attack moderation, control, and temperateness; mix up things divine and human; confuse right and wrong; interpret papal indults and canons, and the will of the holy council, as the very worst blueprint for unbridled spending, immoderateness, and irresponsibility; sow revolt in senate and people; rouse the hatred of the apostolic see and of all Christians against an excellent, most devout, Catholic people by means of false charges — deserve to be expelled from the sacraments and from association with well-behaved, upright people, and not to spend their lives with honest people who practice true and genuine religion, since they themselves are governed and sustained by unbridled and uncontrollable lusts.

Worsted and vanquished on all counts, they resort to shameless, inconsiderate behavior and to sophistical hatred: they say the Church is *indirectly* harmed by our statute.[79] If by "indirectly" they mean that we injured it using stealth, subterfuge, and deceit, maliciously and intentionally, this is another fabricated case, and they are shamelessly lying, for the true and almost incontrovertible case is utterly obvious. But

---

[79] *Quaestio* (sig. diiiv): "cum Ecclesia possit recipere elemosinas in infinitum et habeat liberas oblationes, apparet quod statutum per quod talis facultas et libertas [tolluntur] — saltem per indirectum, per poenam appositam vocantibus plures clericos quam xxiiii — sit contra libertatem Ecclesiae." The anonymous author's response here is appropriately couched in legal terminology.

culpa sumus. Nam causas per accidens, quoniam praeter mentem ac voluntatem propositumque agentis eveniunt, et infinitae interminataeque sunt, nullus sapiens, nullus aequus et bonus vir cuiquam fraudi unquam esse voluit, multo minus Sancta Ecclesia, multo etiam minus Deus. Ut si quis miserit ad hos Fratres vinum Gavardicum[80] nomine elemosynae, ipsi vero plusculum invitati eo inter se, ut quondam Lapithae,[81] fictilibus poculis conserta pugna vulnera in caput acceperint, nonne iniquissimum sit insimulare eum qui vinum miserit Ecclesiae per indirectum, hoc [est,] per accidens laesae, cum ipse mente bona vinum miserit?

[Conclusio]

Satisfactum hactenus plenissime reor omnibus capitibus ac fundamentis accusationis, omniaque argumenta rationesque, quae vel minimum momentum ad eorum causam facere videantur, nulla omnino praetermissa eversae sunt. Sequuntur ordine locatae in libro accusatorio refutationes illius Albrici[82] rationum ab eo pro ipsius ingenio et captu collectarum. Hic egregius doctor,[83] si accurate et acriter advertatur, respondens sibi inferior fuit. Quod autem Episcopus Brixiensis, sive De Monte sive De Dominicis,[84] scribat auctoritate se sua effecisse ut Brixiani idem statutum

A defense of the Brescians' statute 83

if they take "indirectly" as "by accident", we are not at all to blame. For since accidents occur contrary to the purpose, will, and intention of the doer, and are boundless and limitless, no wise, fair, and good man — much less holy Church and much less still God — has ever wished them to incriminate anyone. So if anybody sent wine from Gavardo[80] to these brothers, calling it "alms", but they got rather too carried away by it and, like the Lapiths of old,[81] started fighting each other with earthenware cups and suffered head-wounds, would it not be very unfair to charge the sender of the wine with harming the Church indirectly (that is, by accident), since his own intention in sending it was good?

[Conclusion]

I think that so far justice has been amply done to all the headings and bases of the accusation; and all the proofs and arguments which may seem of even the slightest importance to their case have, without a single exception, been overturned. There follow, placed in order in the accusing book, refutations of the arguments which the famous Alberico[82] marshaled in a manner worthy of his flair and ability. If one pays careful, close attention to this excellent "doctor",[83] he has been under par in his responses. And the fact that the bishop of Brescia (whether De Monte or De Dominicis) writes that by his own influence he got the Brescians

---

[80] Gavardo is a small town twenty-two kilometers to the northwest of Brescia. Since (according to Dott. Ennio Ferraglio) the region's wine became famous only in the eighteenth century, this is a surprisingly early reference to its viticulture.

[81] The Lapiths were a Thessalian tribe whose king was Pirithous, and who successfully fought the Centaurs (*not* "each other") when the latter got drunk at Pirithous's wedding to Hippodamia: Homer, *Odyssey* 21. 295–304; Ovid, *Metamorphoses* 12. 210–535. Yet again the anonymous writer implies a link between his target, the Dominicans, and an ancient example of dissoluteness. This incident may be depicted by Michelangelo's marble relief of ca. 1492, *The Battle of the Centaurs*. It is certainly the subject of a painting by Piero di Cosimo, ca. 1505–1507?, now in the National Gallery, London.

[82] See n. 8 above.

[83] The author of *Quaestio*, where (sigs. diiv–divv) his responses to Alberico's ten points appear.

antiquarent, parum id momenti habet ad causam. Cesserunt — si forte id fuit verum quod commemorant — auctoritati praestantissimi Episcopi utilis populo in magnos usus, atque fortasse (id quod persimile vero est) promisisse Episcopum reor eadem auctoritate perfecturum sese ut quem modum datura sumptibus funerum civitas erat sponte sua religiosi acciperent, non minuendo quidem numero sequentium funus, verum ut minore consueta mercede contenti essent. Quo fiebat ut, sumptu quem voluntas statuti decernere videbatur ratione rata pensato cum quotocunque religiosorum numero, voluntati Brixianorum et honori atque dignitati ecclesiasticorum consuleretur.

Illud vero ridiculum: "Nunquam usi sunt hoc statuto nec ipsum servarunt, ergo non tenet nec valet."[85] Cur non potius: "Ergo non faciunt Brixienses contra libertatem Ecclesiae, nec sunt excommunicati"? Sed quid obstabat de integro facere quod tum fecerant, si primum non tenebat? Nec minus est ignorantiae plenum et tarditatis illud argumentum quod a minori ad maius esse dicunt: Montem Olympum minorem esse colle nostrae arcis asserunt.[86] Quisnam est ita plumbeus qui ignoret gravius

A defense of the Brescians' statute

to reject the same statute has little bearing on the case.[84] They yielded (assuming that what people say was true) to the influence of an outstanding bishop who brings great benefits to the people, and I think that perhaps (as is very likely) the bishop promised to use the same influence to ensure that religious would voluntarily accept the city's forthcoming limit on funeral expenses, not by reducing the number of funeral attendants, but by agreeing to be satisfied with less than the usual fee. The hoped-for result was that, with the expenditure supposedly determined by the statute's intention being weighed against whatever the number of religious might be, due account would be taken of the Brescians' intention and of the churchmen's honor and dignity.

But it is absurd to say: "They never implemented or observed this statute, so it has no force or power."[85] Why not rather say: "So the Brescians do not contravene the Church's freedom and are not excommunicate"? But what stopped them repeating what they did then if at first it had no force? No less riddled with ignorance and stupidity is the proof which, they say, goes "from lesser to greater": Mount Olympus, they contend, is smaller than the hill of our citadel![86] Who, pray, is so dense

---

[84] Pietro de Monte (bishop of Brescia, 1442–1457) was succeeded by Bartolomeo Malipiero (Maripetrus) (1457–1464) and by Domenico de Dominicis (1464–1478): see Konrad Eubel, ed., *Hierarchia catholica medii aevi*, 2nd ed. (Regensburg: Sumptibus et typis librariae Regensbergianae, 1914), 2: 111; see also n. 88 below. *Quaestio* (sig. ciir–v) states unequivocally that it was De Monte who wrote: "An valeat statutum laicorum quod pro exequiis mortuorum non expendatur nisi tantum, dico quod non, per capitulum finale, *De rebus Ecclesiae non alienandis*, per quem textum feci revocari Brixiae quoddam statutum." (This, of course, is yet another reference to the oft-cited Canon 44.)

[85] *Quaestio* (sig. civr–v): "dico quod istud statutum, ex quo factum est, nunquam servatum est; et sic per non usum et contrariam consuetudinem sublatum est, nec amplius valet. Nam sunt fere triginta quinque anni quod fuit institutum, et nemo est qui recordetur illud praticatum et observatum fuisse."

[86] The Dominicans, our author claims, are grossly overestimating the importance of the Brescian statute. *Quaestio* (sig. civr), citing the chapter "Eos" from the *Liber sextus* (see n. 72 above), which enjoins excommunication for those who decree that no one is to sell to, buy from, mill grain or bake bread for clergy, uses the argument *a minori ad maius*: if excommunication is the penalty for withholding food from clergy, there is even more reason for imposing it on those who legislate to limit the numbers and the perquisites of clergy who attend funerals.

longe incommodum longeque acerbius malum invehi clericis, si illis prohibeantur venditiones rerum necessariarum et quoqui panem — quae res ne Iudaeis quidem prohibentur, nihil enim hoc aliud est nisi vetare eos vivere — quam prohibere ne nisi tot clerici ad funus accersantur, nec nisi tot unciarum candela et duo soldi dentur.

Multa praeterea de diritate excommunicationis disserunt: et an nunquam absolvi ab ea Brixiani possint qui auctores statuti fuere, et a quo tamen absolvi, et an ea contagio ad posteros stirpe continuante genus trahenteque quasi per manus exitialem labem sit perventura.[87] Haec omnia praetermittenda esse putavi, cum planissime sit demonstratum Brixianos nec facere contra libertatem Ecclesiae nec esse excommunicatos. Precor autem vos, Brixiani, ut si Fratres de quibus sermo est cognito errore suo damnare falsam sententiam voluerint et in contrariam, veram videlicet partem recinere, in gratiam pristinam eos recipiatis. Hoc enim mandat Dominus Noster Iesus Christus; hoc Sancta Ecclesia iubet, quam si forte in hac oratione mea prolixiore quam oportebat opinione aliqua minus cauta offendi, aut verbo aliquo inconsultius elapso violavi, id omnes intelligant praeter mentem meam propositumque meum et voluntatem meam excidisse, nec me illi vel per me vel per alium cognito aut omnino non cognito errori assentiri.

DE MANDATO ET SUMPTU REI PUBLICAE
BRIXIANAE IMPRESSA.
ET PER REVERENDISSIMUM DOMINUM
ARCHIEPISCOPUM EPISCOPI BRIXIENSIS LOCUM
TENENTEM GENERALEM VISA ET PROBATA.[88]

A defense of the Brescians' statute

as not to know that clergy would suffer a far worse inconvenience and a far more painful misfortune if they were banned from sales of basic necessities and from having bread baked for them — things not even Jews are banned from, for that would be no different from forbidding them to live — than if one bans more than *so* many clergy from being summoned to a funeral, or from being given more than *so* many ounces of candle-wax and two *soldi*?

They also discuss many points about the curse of excommunication: both whether the Brescians, who enacted the statute, could never be released from that curse, and by whom they nevertheless *could* be; and whether that taint would reach their posterity, since the family keeps a race going and bears on its hands, as it were, the deadly stain.[87] I thought I should omit all these things, since it has been very clearly shown that the Brescians are neither contravening the Church's freedom, nor are they excommunicate. But I beg you, Brescians, if the Brothers we speak of, recognizing their error, agree to condemn their wrong opinion and change their tune to the opposite (namely, the true) one, *please* take them back into your former favor. For this is what our Lord Jesus Christ commands; this is what holy Church orders, whom if I have chanced to offend in this speech of mine — longer than it should have been — by some rather ill-advised opinion, or dishonored by some word rather rashly uttered, may everyone realize that it dropped out contrary to my will, purpose, and intention, nor do I countenance that error, whether noticed by me or by another, or completely unnoticed.

PRINTED AT THE COMMAND AND EXPENSE OF THE REPUBLIC OF BRESCIA, AND VIEWED AND APPROVED BY THE MOST REVEREND LORD ARCHBISHOP, ACTING AS VICAR-GENERAL FOR THE BISHOP OF BRESCIA.[88]

---

[87] *Quaestio* (sigs. dr–diir) discusses these points at some length, and (on the final point mentioned here, about possible transfer of guilt) includes (sig. dr–v) a comment by Niccolò de' Tudeschis (Panormitanus) on Canon 44: "Conclude ergo quod statutarii, et alii de quibus in textu, sunt excommunicati ipso facto, sed successores eorum non sunt excommunicati, nisi quamprimum sciverint, non fecerint statuta deleri de libris."

[88] Paolo Zane (bishop from 1480 to 1531): Eubel, *Hierarchia catholica*, 2: 111.

Carlo Valgulio

Statutum Brixianorum de sumptibus funerum optima ratione nullum facere discrimen fortunae inter cives, nec esse honores qui vulgo putantur.

That the Brescians' statute about funeral expenditure with perfect logic makes no distinction of rank among citizens, and that what are commonly regarded as honors are not so.

Carlo Valgulio

[SIG. Ar] Statutum Brixianorum de sumptibus funerum optima ratione nullum facere discrimen fortunae inter cives, nec esse honores qui vulgo putantur.

Caroli Valgulii.

[I]

Quoniam permagni interest nostrae civitatis — tum ad dignitatem atque auctoritatem conservandam, tum etiam ad utilitatem tam publicam quam privatam tuendam — ut decretum funerarium a senatu Brixiano conditum non modo non abrogetur, verum etiam ne ulla parte immutetur, ad quam rem efficiendam novas rationes repertas novasque faces[a] ad excitanda magna incendia in animis civium aliquorum a quibusdam video esse incensas ut propter aliqua insignia fortunae vivos et mortuos praestare se caeteris debere putent, ad hanc quoque secundam patriae dignitatis propugnationem tanquam fidus civis accedere constitui, et eo libentius quoniam, si haec pugna statuto defenso vincatur, utrique parti victoriam, sin victa sit decreto mutato, victoribus pariter et victis animadverto non modicam cladem esse allaturam. Nam adversarii pro stulta et falsa opinione honoris proeliantur, nos pro moderatione, honestate, virtute et aequabilitate — e quibus verus honor commodumque publicum et privatum existit et coniunctio atque societas civilis continetur — contendimus. Decretum enim statuit modum non tam sumptibus quam ambitioni funerum, qua civitas pessimo publico atque privato antea ardebat. Arduum profecto

---

[a] *correxi*: facies *cod*.

Carlo Valgulio

That the Brescians' statute about funeral expenditure with perfect logic makes no distinction of rank among citizens, and that what are commonly regarded as honors are not so.

By Carlo Valgulio.

[I]

It is very important for our city — in order to preserve its reputation and influence, and also to safeguard both public and private well-being — that the funerary decree passed by the Brescian senate should not only not be rescinded, but should not even be changed in any way. But *that* is the purpose for which, I see, certain people have concocted fresh arguments and struck fresh sparks in some citizens' minds, in order to kindle the belief that, in life and in death, they should be preferred to the rest because of certain badges of rank. As a loyal citizen, I have therefore decided to come and fight for my city's reputation a second time, all the more gladly as I perceive that if this fight results in the law's retention, it will bring victory to both sides, whereas if it results in its alteration, it will bring a terrible defeat to victors and vanquished alike. Our opponents are battling for a silly, false notion of honor; we are striving for moderation, integrity, virtue, and fairness — the sources of true honor and of public and private welfare, and the bonds of civil association and fellowship. For the decree curbs less the expense than the rivalry of funerals, which previously raged in the city, with dire public and private results.

atque difficile est hoc certamen, tum propter opinionem in vulgus probabilem, quod videlicet profusi sumptus funerum honorem pariant et vivis eos facientibus et mortuis quorum gratia administrentur, adversus quam certamus, tum propter eius forte opinionis suasores aliquos, qui habitu et nomine ac specie religionis auctoritatem suae causae tribuunt,[1] et multitudinem imperitam et aliquos simplices atque superstitiosos cives ad se deceptos trahunt. Sed quemadmodum priorem pugnam longe graviorem atque periculosiorem vicimus, ad quam oppugnandam ingentia auxilia — libertas ecclesiastica, sedes apostolica, Christianum omne nomen — libris ad omnes Christiani orbis partes contra nos ab adversariis emissis excita fuerant,[2] non dubitamus quin hanc quoque superaturi simus.[3] Este igitur omnes, precor, animis aequis et attentis quibus studium est cognoscendi quid in hac causa veri sit, quae quidem est huiusmodi.

Postquam pervinci non potuit ut hoc funerarium decretum ecclesiasticam libertatem violaret, perniciosum aliud ac detestandum a nonnullis facinus tentatum est, qui ambitionis atque superbiae patrocinium susceperunt: non esse aequandos ordines in sumptibus funerum quos statutum exaequet. "Equestrem," inquiunt, "cum plebeio, locupletem cum paupere, comites cum caeteris in eadem re non esse faciendos pares." Adeunt singulos ad quos haec res spectare videri possit et ambitiosos omnis; eorum animos irritant, concitant, inflamant quos possunt hanc ignominiam non esse ferendam, indignum facinus frementes ut cadavera nobiliorum et locupletiorum in eandem paremque conditionem cum tenuioribus atque pauperioribus trahantur ac simili aequabilitate atque moderatione sumptuum ad sepulturam ducantur. O praeclaros apostolos Christi et egregios contemptus mundi praedicatores,[4] ut omnes tollant crucem suam et sequantur Christum,[5] quam

That the Brescians' statute about funeral expenditure

This struggle is certainly a tough and difficult one, partly because of the popularly accepted notion — which we dispute — that lavish spending on funerals confers honor both on the living who do it and on the dead for whose sakes it is performed, partly perhaps because of certain advocates of that notion who give weight to their cause by a religious manner, title, and appearance,[1] deceitfully indoctrinating the ignorant crowd and some simple-minded, superstitious citizens. However, we won the earlier — far more serious and dangerous — fight, which our opponents pursued by attacking us in books disseminated throughout the Christian world, and by summoning up the huge reserves of church freedom, the apostolic see, and all Christendom.[2] We are therefore confident of winning this fight too.[3] So listen calmly and carefully, I beg, all of you who are keen to learn the truth of this matter, which is as follows.

After the failure of their plea that this funerary decree infringed church freedom, another deadly and detestable crime has been attempted by several people who took on the defense of rivalry and pride: they argue that those orders the law makes equal should not be equated in funeral expense. A knight, they say, should not be put on a par with a plebeian in the same situation, a rich man with a pauper, or the nobility with the rest. They approach any individuals whom this matter might seem to concern, and all the self-seeking ones; they rub up, stir up, and fire up whoever they can into thinking this ignominy intolerable, raving that it is a shameful crime for the corpses of nobler and richer people to be consigned to a state identical or similar to that of the humbler and poorer, and to be taken for burial at similarly fair and moderate expense. What glorious apostles of Christ, what excellent preachers of unworldliness,[4] that they should all take up their cross and follow Christ[5] — and they

---

[1] Valgulio's target is the same as that of his anonymous colleague, i.e., the Dominican Order, but (unlike him) he is careful *not* to name names.

[2] For details of this "fight", see Introduction, section II.

[3] Valgulio, writing after the rejection of the Dominicans' second appeal to the pope, now wishes to counteract a less publicized but more insidious attempt on their part to influence Brescia's 'social climbers'.

[4] Another dig at the Dominicans, the Order of Preachers (*Ordo Praedicatorum*); as below, 96–97 ("praedicatoribus ... praedicata").

[5] The allusion of course is to Matthew 16: 24; Mark 8: 34; Luke 9: 23.

rem ut pervincant nihil intentatum relinquunt! Quis autem furor hos homines ita praecipites agat — spesne pecuniae si causam vicerint, an quod se gloriam atque auctoritatem apud illud nobile genus hominum comparaturos arbitrentur, an quia eorum ingenium atque natura exultet in malo — mihi parum compertum est. Certe, quaecunque illa [sig. Av] sit, sive cunctae simul — quod magis creditur — pessimam esse necesse est, cum ambitionem, superbiam, intemperantiam civibus suadeant, foveant, augeant, et seditionem quaerant. Nam id indagare non est praesentis temporis res, sed demonstrare decretum hoc funerarium iustissimis de causis et optima ratione non fecisse discrimen fortunae in morte inter ordines civium. Contra autem isti censent: iniquum esse atque viciosum contendunt quia discrimen non facit, cadavera comitum, equitum, locupletiorum et huiusmodi generis hominum oportere sumptibus maioribus cum ad sepulturam efferuntur quam caeterorum hominum esse honoranda, tacentibus omnibus ad quos haec res spectare videtur, ni forte pudore causae ipsi deterriti perfricatissima fronte unius cuiusdam importune offerentis sese utantur,[6] et ipsi suas occulunt voluntates.

    Primum itaque dico ad societatem humani generis tuendam et civitates in concordia conservandas ius aequabile omnibus esse oportere, summosque cum infimis pari iure esse retinendos, et leges atque decreta sive statuta omnibus populis quibus quaeque data sunt una eademque voce loqui debere. Quae res magis patet et constat quam ab ullo sit demonstranda, propterea quod si secus fiat contentionibus et seditionibus humanam vitam refertam esse necesse est, et civilem societatem dissolvi. Deinde nego ullis vivis sumptuosa funera honori esse, quin potius dedecori ac levitati, si vulgi honoris captandi et aurae popularis aucupandae gratia eos sumptus faciant. Quam rem ipsimet apertissime profitentur, quandoquidem eam facultatem honestandi ordinis equestris, et huiusmodi insignibus sive familiae honoris adhibendi causa sibi concedendam esse postulant. Mortuis vero prorsus neque honori neque ignominiae esse posse. Hocque me omnibus modo non omnino ambitione perditis aut non nimium tardis hominibus probaturum profiteor,

leave nothing undone to prove their point! But I cannot discover what madness drives them to such haste: is it hope of money if they win their case, or that they expect to gain fame and power with that noble class of people, or that their natural inclination is to rejoice in evil? Certainly, whichever hope they have (more likely, they have all three at once), it is bound to be very wicked, since they urge, foment, and aggravate rivalry, pride, and extravagance among citizens, and seek to create discord. It is not our present concern to investigate that matter, but to show that for the soundest reasons and with perfect logic this funerary decree made no distinction of rank at death among classes of citizens. Our opponents think differently: they maintain that it is unfair and unsound *because* it makes no distinction. When the corpses of counts, knights, richer people, and those like them, are taken out for burial, they should — so they say — be honored by greater expenditure than those of other people. Meanwhile all those likely to have an interest in this matter keep quiet unless, themselves deterred by shame at their cause, they perhaps shelter behind the effrontery of a certain person who pushes himself forward relentlessly.[6] Thus they conceal their own wishes.

First, then, I say that in order to safeguard human society and keep cities harmonious there should be a legal code that is fair to all, the highest should remain on an equal footing with the lowest, and laws and decrees or statutes should speak with one and the same voice to all peoples to whom they have been severally given. This truth is too obvious and well-known to need proof from anyone, for if it were otherwise, human life would inevitably abound in strife and discord, and civil society would disintegrate. Next, I say that expensive funerals do not bring honor to any living people but rather disgrace and folly, if they spend that money in order to gain honor with the populace and win public favor. They themselves openly admit it, since they demand that this chance be given them so as to honor the knightly order, and bring honor to such badges or to their family. As for the dead, I say that such funerals simply *cannot* bring them either honor or ignominy. I promise to prove this to all those people who are not altogether ruined by rivalry or excessively stu-

---

[6] The identity of this person is not revealed, but he is clearly a religious (see note 30 below).

seu Christi seu naturae seu civilis facultatis voluntatem attendere velimus.

Quonam pacto profusi sumptus non necessarii nec caritatis misericordiaeve — quae eadem elemosyna dicitur[7] — sed inanis gloriae et mundani honoris gratia administrati apud Christum probari possunt? Qui non modo huiusmodi honores damnat, verum etiam ipsas divitias et terrenas omnis opes et comitatus istos et equestria ista caeteraque istiusmodi insignia[b] propter quae hos honores exposcitis contemni et tanquam adversa atque inimica verae virtuti et veris honoribus et aeternae gloriae abiici iubet?[8] Humilitatem, paupertatem, contemptum humanae laudis et gloriae, rerumque omnium mundanarum despicientiam commendans,[9] et amplexandam atque colendam praecipiens? Quae praecepta et instituta Christi universo generi humano nulla exceptione facta ullius personae et hominum conditionis a legitimis apostolis Christi et praedicatoribus veritatis eadem voce iisdemque verbis tradita atque praedicata sunt. Hic vero divitias, terrenas opes, aurum equestre et huiusce generis vana insignia, muneraque caecae et iniquissimae fortunae, pompasque et humanos honores extollit, laudat, suadet, admiratur et defendit. Hos sumptus dices elemosynam esse: nugae merae sunt![10] Nam elemosyna gratuita est, non mercenaria, ab animo maerente proficiscens ob alicuius hominis calamitates in quas non sua culpa inciderit.[11] Haec vero datio verius mercatura est et faeneratio quam elemosyna, cum maiora exposcat et expectet quam ipsa sit. Exposcit enim honorem ac laudem tanquam maiora. Semper enim maiora illa sunt quorum causa alia administrantur quam ea ipsa sint quae eorum gratia fiunt: fiunt autem

---

[b] correxi: insigna cod.

pid, whether we choose to examine the will of Christ, that of nature, or that of civil authority.

How can lavish spending, which is unnecessary, and inspired not by charity or compassion (*misericordia*) — also called almsgiving (*elemosyna*)[7] — but by vainglory and worldly honor, meet with Christ's approval? Surely he not only condemns such honors, but also orders that wealth itself and all earthly possessions — those countships, those knightly and similar badges which cause you to demand these honors — be despised and discarded as hostile and harmful to true virtue, true honors, and eternal glory?[8] Surely he preaches humility, poverty, contempt for human praise and glory, and disdain for all worldly things,[9] and commands that such qualities be welcomed and cherished? These commands and precepts of Christ have been passed on and preached to the whole human race — with no exception for any person or category of people — by Christ's genuine apostles and preachers of the truth, with the same voice and the same words. *This* fellow, though, exalts, praises, commends, admires, and defends wealth, earthly possessions, knightly gold, and similar worthless badges, the gifts of blind and unfair fortune, and processions and human honors. This spending, you will say, is almsgiving: it is mere trash![10] Alms are gratis, not paid for, and proceed from a mind which grieves at someone's undeserved troubles.[11] *This* gift, however, is more truly commerce and usury than alms, since it demands and expects things greater than itself: it demands honor and praise, as being greater. Always the things for whose sake other things are performed are greater than those done to gain them: and in fact —

---

[7] This Greek word (literally 'pity') is the actual source of English 'alms', in which sense it appears several times in the Vulgate: e.g., Matthew 6: 2, Luke 11: 41, and Acts 3: 2. (See also *Defense*, sig. A2v [above, 13].)

[8] Cf. Matthew 6: 19–21 and 24. These admonitions, and those referred to in the next note, form part of the summary of Christ's ethical teachings in the Sermon on the Mount.

[9] Cf. Matthew 6: 1–6.

[10] The tag *nugae merae* is from Plautus, *Poenulus* 348.

[11] Cf. Cicero, *Tusculanae disputationes* 4. 18: "Misericordia est aegritudo ex miseria alterius iniuria laborantis." (Cf. *Defense*, above, 13.)

sumptus propter — ut inquam — ipsum honorem. Neque porro eadem ratione liberalitas est, quoniam fructum quaerit. Nam et ipsa quoque liberalitas et liberalis officium non fructum sequuntur:[12] fructus enim et velut precium est honor a vulgo quaesitus. Haec pauca de voluntate [sig. A2r] Christi, quoniam omnibus Christianis notissima sunt, breviter dicta sufficiant. Nunc videamus quid velit natura.

Omnis homines pares ac similes natura sunt: dissimiles nostrae voluntates atque opiniones faciunt.[13] Quod autem natura gignat pares, diffinitio quae omnes homines complectitur declarat. Nam aeque omnes

as I say — the object of the expenditure is honor itself. For the same reason it is not generosity either, since it seeks profit. The aim both of generosity itself and of a generous person is obligation, not profit:[12] honor sought from the populace *is* profit, and a kind of reward. Let these few briefly stated facts about Christ's will suffice, familiar as they are to all Christians. Now let us see what nature's will is.

All men are by nature equal and alike: it is our wishes and beliefs that make us unlike.[13] The definition that embraces all mankind proves that nature creates us equal: we are all equally mortal and possessed of

---

[12] Cf. Cicero, *De legibus* 1. 48: "Quid liberalitas? Gratuitane est an mercenaria? Si sine praemio benignus est, gratuita; si cum mercede, conducta. Nec est dubium quin is qui liberalis benignusve dicitur, officium, non fructum sequatur. Ergo item iustitia nihil expetit praemii, nihil pretii: per se igitur expetitur, eademque omnium virtutum causa atque sententia est." This is the first of Valgulio's many 'allusions' in the present treatise to the *De legibus*, a work which he had every reason to know, following its discovery (together with several other philosophical writings of Cicero) by Poggio Bracciolini in Strasbourg (ca. 1417), and its subsequent copying in various (manuscript and printed) versions in Renaissance Italy: see Rouse, "[Cicero's] *De natura deorum, De divinatione, Timaeus, De fato, Topica, Paradoxa Stoicorum, Academica priora, De legibus*," in *Texts and Transmission*, ed. Reynolds, 124–28 (cf. above, 33 n. 27).

[13] The whole of this paragraph sets out the Stoic belief in 'natural law': what is just is based on 'nature', i.e., objective reality; all human beings are essentially equal, being endowed with reason, the senses, and the power of speech; therefore all can attain moral excellence by following nature. Valgulio's argument here is very similar to Cicero's in *De legibus* 1. 29–30: "Nihil est enim unum uni tam simile, tam par, quam omnes inter nosmet ipsos sumus. Quodsi depravatio consuetudinum, si opinionum varietas non inbecillitatem animorum torqueret et flecteret quocumque coepisset, sui nemo ipse tam similis esset quam omnes essent omnium. Itaque quaecumque est hominis definitio, una in omnis valet. Quod argumenti satis est nullam dissimilitudinem esse in genere. Quae si esset, non una omnis definitio contineret. Etenim ratio, qua una praestamus beluis, per quam coniectura valemus, argumentamur, refellimus, disserimus, conficimus aliquid, concludimus, certe est communis, doctrina differens, discendi quidem facultate par. Nam et sensibus eadem omnium conprehenduntur, et ea quae movent sensus, itidem movent omnium, quaeque in animis inprimuntur, de quibus ante dixi, inchoatae intelligentiae, similiter in omnibus inprimuntur, interpresque mentis oratio verbis discrepat, sententiis congruens. Nec est quisquam gentis ullius, qui ducem nactus [naturam] ad virtutem pervenire non possit."

mortales et rationis et orationis participes sumus. Per rationem communis omnibus est doctrina, scientia et virtus. Sensus omnium eadem comprehendunt, moventurque omnium ab rebus quae vim movendi eos habent. Oratio itidem omnibus est communis interpres mentis, tametsi verbis aliis aliae gentes utantur: sententiae tamen eaedem omnibus sunt. Corpora omnium eadem materia et iisdem elementis constant, et in eadem aeque omnia resolvuntur. Cum igitur pares natura simus, latissime patet per legem voluntatemque naturae nemini licere quod alii non liceat, nec alium alii praestare. Qui itaque vult sibi plus licere quam alii, is contra naturam facit et — quantum in ipso est — coniunctionem et societatem, quam natura inter homines conciliat, evertit et interimit.[14] Qui haec committunt non modo non sunt digni honore, sed summo dedecore afficiendi et suppliciis sunt coercendi, si alia ratione coerceri nequeant.

Ad leges et iura atque instituta civilia transeamus — de veris ac rectae rationi congruentibus loquor — et videamus an in republica bene constituta et recte administrata largiores sumptus quos civis aliquis sua causa et propter se tantummodo facit, ac non ea mente atque consilio ut aliis benefaciat, sive in funere illi administrentur sive in quacunque re alia fiant, honori cuiquam esse possint, an contra potius ignominiam ac dedecus apportent, et malo publico atque privato profundantur. Ac primum quidem quae causa impulerit homines ad condendum ius civile scribendasque leges perscrutemur.

Satis constat, cum plerique homines errore opinionum et illecebris voluptatis (omnium malorum matris) et facibus cupiditatum inflammati a natura, hoc est, a ratione desciscerent, quae propria est humanae naturae (semper enim id est maxime natura illi rei quod ei est optimum),[15] ac pauci ad virtutem venirent, quae quidem est absolutio atque perfectio

reason and speech. Through reason we all share in learning, knowledge, and virtue. Everyone's senses take in the same things, and everyone's are stirred by whatever is able to stir them. Similarly, the power of speech, the mind's interpreter, is shared by all, even though different races use different words: everyone has the same ways of thinking. The bodies of us all consist of the same substance and the same elements, and all equally are reduced to the same ones. Since, then, we are by nature equal, it is abundantly clear that by nature's law and will no one is allowed what another is not, and no one takes precedence over another. So the person who wants to be allowed more than another is acting against nature and — so far as lies in him — is upsetting and destroying that association and fellowship which nature fosters among mankind.[14] Those who perpetrate this are not only unworthy of honor, but should suffer utter disgrace and be restrained by penalties, if no other means of restraint is possible.

Let us pass on to civil laws, statutes, and ordinances — those, I mean, that are sound and consistent with right reason — and let us see if, in a well-ordered and rightly-governed state, more liberal spending done by some citizen purely for his own sake and on his own behalf, rather than with the idea and intention of benefitting others, and whether performed at a funeral or associated with any other event, can bring honor to anyone or if, on the contrary, it carries with it ignominy and disgrace, and the lavish outlay is socially and personally harmful. Let us first examine what motive drove people to establish civil law and draw up statutes.

It is fairly certain that most people were incited by erroneous beliefs, and by the enticements of pleasure (the mother of all evils) and the flames of lust, to rebel against nature — against reason, that is, which is specific to human nature. (Always, of course, what is most natural for something is what is best for it.)[15] Thus, few attained virtue, which is the absolute

---

[14] Cf. Cicero, *De legibus* 1. 49: "Quodsi amicitia per se colenda est, societas quoque hominum et aequalitas et iustitia per se expetenda. Quod ni ita est, omnino iustitia nulla est. Id enim iniustissimum ipsum est, iustitiae mercedem quaerere."

[15] Cf. Cicero, *De legibus* 1. 47: "Animis omnes tenduntur insidiae, vel ab iis quos modo enumeravi, qui teneros et rudes quom acceperunt, inficiunt et flectunt ut volunt, vel ab ea quae penitus in omni sensu inplicata insidet, imitatrix boni voluptas, malorum autem mater omnium; quoius blanditiis corrupti, quae natura bona sunt, quia dulcedine hac et scabie carent, non cernunt[ur] satis."

rationis, cum aeque omnes ad ipsam venire possent, perturbatissimaque vita hominum ac plena malorum foret, scribere leges et iura constituere necessarium fuit. Quae condita nunquam fuissent — a sapientibus videlicet ac bonis viris — si mortales secundum naturam et iura ipsius vixissent: neque enim oportuisset. Nam ipsam beatitudinem quae in hac vita esse potest sequentibus naturam ducem — hoc est, rationem a qua iustae, fortes, temperatae et liberales actiones proficiscuntur[16] — adepti fuissent, sicuti neque fuisset opus naturam humanam adiungi divinae ut una ex duabus naturis persona confecta — quae Christus nominata est — nova condita lege humano generi consuleret, si primus conditus homo in excellentia atque praestantia qua fuerat creatus permansisset.[17] Civiles itaque leges necessario perlatae fuere quae — tum imperando,

perfection of reason, though all were equally capable of attaining it. Human life was therefore very disturbed and full of evils, and this made it necessary to draw up statutes and create laws. These would never have been established — by wise and good men, I mean — if mortals had lived in accord with nature and her laws, for they would have been pointless. People would have gained the very bliss which is available in this life to those who follow nature as their leader — reason, that is, from which just, brave, controlled, and generous actions stem.[16] Similarly, there would have been no need for human and divine natures to be fused so that one person composed of them both — who was named Christ — might by making a new law show concern for the human race, if the first-made human being had remained in the state of excellence and superiority which he had been in at his creation.[17] Of necessity, therefore, civil laws were passed — some

---

[16] The four classical virtues. (See below, n. 23.) Cf. Cicero, *De legibus* 1. 33: "Sequitur igitur ad participandum alium [cum] alio communicandumque inter omnes ius nos natura esse factos. Atque hoc in omni hac disputatione sic intellegi volo, [ius] quod dicam natura esse, tantam autem esse corruptelam malae consuetudinis, ut ab ea tamquam igniculi exstinguantur a natura dati, exorianturque et confirmentur vitia contraria. Quodsi, quo modo est natura, sic iudicio homines humani — ut ait poeta — nihil a se alienum putarent, coleretur ius aeque ab omnibus. Quibus enim ratio a natura data est, isdem etiam recta ratio data est; ergo et lex, quae est recta ratio in iubendo et vetando; si lex, ius quoque. Et omnibus ratio: ius igitur datum est omnibus, recteque Socrates exsecrari eum solebat qui primus utilitatem a iure seiunxisset; id enim querebatur caput esse exitiorum omnium."

[17] The Council of Chalcedon (451) defined the Christian doctrine of incarnation and stated that Christ had been consubstantial with God in divinity and also consubstantial with man in humanity. While this indivisible union was basically undisputed in the later medieval period, there was some debate — alluded to here — as to whether the incarnation would have occurred without the Fall. Ironically, Valgulio seems to side with the Thomist position that the incarnation was contingent on man's first transgression. There was also some debate in Brescia in 1462 about the blood of Christ which was deemed by a Franciscan preacher as being separated from the body of Christ, thereby separated from his divinity, and consequently not entitled to adoration during Christ's entombment. A Dominican, James of Brescia, demanded a retraction and the pope presided over a disputation, ruling in 1464 that no further debate on this matter should take place. See Jaroslav Pelikan, *The Christian Tradition: A History of the Development of Doctrine*, vol. 1, *The Emergence of the Catholic Tradition (100–600)* (Chicago: University of Chicago Press, 1971), 256–77.

tum prohibendo — malos voluntate homines et perturbatores humanae societatis et naturalis coniunctionis poenis praemiisque propositis a vi, caede, superbia, fraude, iniuria alios metu suppliciorum deterritos coercerent, alios spe praemiorum illectos ad officium invitarent, omnes artibus institutisque civilibus in natura — quoad fieri posset — homines continerent. Perardui sane operis res, propterea quod homo callidissimum, astutissimum, vafrum ad simulandum atque dissimulandum, fallendum et decipiendum opportunissimum atque aptissimum est animal. Bonis viris et secundum naturam rationemque viventibus minime oportebat scribere leges, ut diximus.

Quare, cum propter homines iniustos, impios, crudeles, superbos, avaros conditae leges fuerint, et supplitia ipsis proposita et exilia et ignominiae propter vicia a legibus in-[sig. A2v]tentatae, praemia vero iustis et probis et virtute praeditis, latissime patet vim omnem bonam in rebus humanis — omnem dignitatem, honorem, decus et auctoritatem — in virtutibus animi voluntariis et naturalibus, sed potissimum voluntariis, esse positam, et contra vim omnem malam — ignominiam, infamiam, dedecus et contemptum — in viciis locatum. Corpora vero et quae externa sunt omnia — divitias, opes, equestre aurum, comitatus, regna — nihil suapte vi suapteque natura boni malive in se continere, instrumentaque tantum animorum esse in potestate atque imperio dominantis artificis animi sita. Quae si bono, iusto moderatoque domino serviant, utilia et bona dicantur, sin iniusto, superbo et improbo, inutilia ac mala. Quo fit ut nec honorem nec laudem, nec ignominiam nec vituperationem mereantur. Multo minus igitur ipsis possessoribus et dominis suis laudem vel vituperationem adhibere possint: nihil enim dat quod non habet.[18] Quare nec pauper nec imbecillo infirmoque utens corpore quisquam laude atque honore non dignus, si bonus et virtute praeditus, nec contra affluens divitiis valentique et pulcro corpore utens dedecore, ignominia, vituperatione atque contemptu, si malus.

Quam rem clare intelligemus, si quid sit honor, quid virtus, quid bonum nostrum quidque malum cognoscemus. Est autem honor quicquid adhibetur homini virtute ornato, sive in praemium sive in testimonium virtutis, aut — quod verius est — tacitum iudicium in mentibus

prescriptive, others proscriptive — using a system of punishments and rewards to restrain some ill-willed people, disturbers of human society and natural association, from violence, murder, pride, deceit, and misconduct by the deterrent of dreaded penalties, to encourage others to their duty by the enticement of hoped-for rewards, and, so far as possible, to keep *all* people within the bounds of nature by means of civil schemes and ordinances. This was indeed a formidable task, since man is a supremely clever, cunning, and crafty creature, very quick and ready to pretend and dissemble, to cheat and deceive. For good men living in accord with nature and reason it would, as we said, have been quite pointless to draw up laws.

Since, then, laws were made because of unjust, ungodly, cruel, proud, and greedy people, with penalties laid down for them, and the legal threat of exile and ignominy because of their vices, but with rewards for the just, the upright, and the virtuous, it is abundantly clear that all force for good in human affairs — all dignity, honor, distinction, and authority — rests in mental virtues which are willed and natural, but especially *willed* ones, whereas all force for evil — all ignominy, ill fame, disgrace, and contempt — lies in vices. But our bodies and all externals — wealth, possessions, knightly gold, countships, and kingdoms — by their own power and by their own nature contain no good or evil, and are merely mental implements dependent on the power and control of the ruling creative mind. They would therefore be called useful and good if the master they served were good, just, and moderate, but useless and bad if he were unjust, proud, and unprincipled. As a result, they do not deserve honor and praise, or ignominy and censure. Much less, then, can they confer praise or censure on their owners and masters: for nothing gives what it does not have.[18] Any poor or physically weak and feeble person, therefore, deserves praise and honor if he is good and virtuous, and, conversely, a wealthy and physically fit and handsome person deserves disgrace, ignominy, censure, and contempt if he is bad.

We shall understand this clearly if we learn what honor is, what virtue is, what is good or bad for us. Honor is whatever is conferred on a person graced with virtue, whether to reward it or to testify to it, or — more truly — it is a silent mental judgement by prudent men who agree

---

[18] "Nemo dat quod non habet" is a law maxim.

prudentium virorum de virtutibus alicuius consentientium, vel si nulla nota signumve eius prodeat foras. Aliena utique res et in aliena potestate sita est honor, non in eorum qui virtutem habent, quibus debetur sive persolvatur sive secus,[19] nam — ut diximus — virtus vera splendore suo et amplitudine sua contenta est.[20] Virtus autem est in se perfecta et ad summum perducta ratio, a qua semper iustae, fortes, temperatae et liberales actiones rectaque officia in Deum, in patriam, in parentes, in omne denique humanum genus (ordine ut convenit servato) et hercule erga semetipsos singulorum proficiscuntur.[21] "Semper," dico, si occasio

about someone's virtues even if no mark or sign of it emerge. Certainly honor belongs to other people and lies in their power, not in the power of those who possess virtue and who are owed honor, whether they be paid it or not,[19] for true virtue, as we have said, is satisfied by its own radiance and its own abundance.[20] Virtue is reason that is perfect in itself and taken to its peak; from it always flow each person's just, brave, controlled, and generous actions, due respect shown to God, to country, to parents, in short to all mankind (observing the proper priorities) and, of course, towards themselves.[21] I say "always", provided that an occasion

---

[19] Cf. Poliziano, *Epicteti Stoici Enchiridion* [sic], in *Omnia opera Angeli Politiani* (Venice: Aldus Manutius, 1498), fol. 296r, cap. xxix: "Hae te cogitationes ne cruciant, honore carebo, neque usquam ullus ero. Si enim carere honore in malis est (ut certe est), non potest in malo esse propter aliud, non magis quam in turpi." It should be noted that later editions of the *Encheiridion*, in its original Greek, are arranged differently, in fifty-three chapters instead of Poliziano's sixty-eight: the latter's cap. xxix corresponds to Greek chap. 24; in later references to this work the Roman number of Poliziano's chapter will be followed in parenthesis by the Arabic number of the Greek chapter as given in *Epictetus: Discourses, Fragments, and the Encheiridion*, trans. W. A. Oldfather, Loeb Classical Library (London and New York: W. Heinemann and G. P. Putnam's Sons, 1928), 2: 479–537. As Poliziano explains in a dedicatory letter to his patron Lorenzo de' Medici (*Omnia opera*, fol. 293r–v), in his 1479 Latin version of the *Encheiridion* he had to supplement the two inaccurate and incomplete manuscripts he had found in Lorenzo's collection by borrowing from Simplicius's sixth-century commentary (see now Simplicius, *On Epictetus's Handbook*, trans. Charles Brittain and Tad Brennan, 2 vols. [London: Duckworth, 2001–2002]).

[20] Valgulio's emphasis on virtue as desirable in itself again resembles Cicero's in *De legibus* 1. 48: see the quotation in n. 12 above.

[21] Cf. Cicero, *De legibus* 1. 45: "Est enim virtus perfecta ratio, quod certe in natura est: igitur omnis honestas eodem modo." (See also Cicero, *Tusculanae disputationes* 5. 1: "Placere enim tibi admodum sensi ... virtutem ad beate vivendum se ipsa esse contentam.") For the typically Stoic insistence on inner virtue, see Poliziano, *Epicteti Stoici Enchiridion*, fol. 300r, cap. lxiii (chap. 48): "Ineruditi status et formula est, nunquam a seipso expectare utilitatem aut nocumentum, sed ab externis. Philosophi status est et formula, omnem utilitatem ac nocumentum a seipso expectare." An earlier passage in the same work — fol. 298r, cap. xxxvi (chap. 31) — is relevant to Valgulio's mention of the obligations of *pietas*: "Libare autem et sacrificare secundum patrios mores ununquemque decet pure, absque lascivia, absque negligentia: non parce, non supra facultatem." His 'descending scale' of obligations (God — country — parents — others) may be influenced by Cicero, *De officiis* 1. 160: "In ipsa autem communitate sunt gradus officiorum, ex quibus quid cuique praestet intellegi possit, ut prima dis immortalibus, secunda patriae, tertia parentibus, deinceps gradatim reliquis debeantur."

opportunitasque agendi detur, nec actio extrinsecus impediatur. Quod etsi contingat, nihilominus perpetui virtutum actus in mente praediti virtute viri tanquam formae quaedam seu ideae actionum illarum externarum vigent, paratae praestoque semper — oblata materia et instrumentis suppeditatis — parere exteriores actiones quae morales civilesque nominantur.[22] Nec aliud quicquam spectat nec expetit praeter ipsam honestatem et officium, non honoris, non voluptatis, non utilitatis nec gratiae comparandae causa quicquam agens sed quia, ut dixi, quod honestum, rectum bonumque est, id per se expetendum et instituendum atque sumendum ducit.[23] Et contra vicium fugit non metu, non infamia, non dolore, nulla denique causa alia nisi quoniam est per se turpe et contra naturam.

Quibus ex rebus plane declaratur nostrum bonum malumque nostrum, cum illud sit virtus ac vitium, in nostro arbitrio nostraque potestate et omnino in nobis situm esse, caeteraque omnia non esse nostra nec in nobis, sed aliena.[24] Unde, cum nihil commereamur nisi ab iis rebus quae nostrae sunt potestatis, necessario concluditur ratio nihil nisi virtutem honore et laude dignum esse, nihil ignominia atque vituperatione et dedecore nisi vicium. Profecto Deus iniuria ab hominibus[c] poenas sumeret praemiaque illis daret, si bona et mala propter quae ea facit in nostra voluntate atque potestate non collocasset. Atque ideo nec Deus nec quidem legum voluntas actiones hominum in iudicando spectant, quoniam in potestate arbitrioque eorum non sunt, nec liberae sunt actiones ipsae hominum, sed servae rerum omnium quae extrinsecus impedire et prohibere eas queunt. Spectant autem solum

---

[c] *correxi*: abominibus *cod.*

and opportunity for action be given, and there be no outward obstacle to it. But even in that case, in the mind of a virtuous man the eternal virtuous actions nonetheless live on as what one might call 'forms' or 'ideas' of those outward actions, always ready and waiting — if the situation is right and the wherewithal is available — to produce the outward actions which are termed civil and moral.[22] Virtue neither expects nor desires anything except uprightness and obligation: doing nothing for the sake of winning honor, pleasure, advantage, or favor, but because — as I said — it thinks that what is upright, proper, and good should be desired, inculcated, and adopted for itself.[23] And, conversely, it flees from vice not because of fear, ill fame, pain, or anything at all apart from its intrinsic baseness and unnaturalness.

These facts make it absolutely clear that what is good or bad for us, since that means virtue or vice, lies in our choice, in our power, and wholly in *us*, and that everything else is not ours nor in us, but belongs to others.[24] Thus, since our deserts depend only on things within our power, the inevitable conclusion is that only virtue merits honor and praise, and only vice merits ignominy, censure, and disgrace. God would surely be wrong to punish and reward people unless he had put within our will and power the good and bad things which cause him to do so. That is why both God, and even the intention of laws, have no regard to people's actions when judging them, since the actions themselves are not in their power and choice, and are not free, but subject to all the external pressures which may hinder and prevent them. Rather, they

---

[22] A reference to Plato's theory of 'forms' or 'ideas', as developed in the *Republic*.

[23] Cf. Cicero, *De legibus* 1. 48 (the passage immediately preceding that quoted in n. 12 above): "Sequitur ... et ius et omne honestum sua sponte esse expetendum. Etenim omnes viri boni ipsam aequitatem et ius ipsum amant, nec est viri boni errare et diligere quod per se non sit diligendum: per se igitur ius est expetendum et colendum. Quod si ius, etiam iustitia; sin ea, reliquae quoque virtutes per se colendae sunt."

[24] Cf. Poliziano, *Epicteti Stoici Enchiridion*, fol. 293v, cap. i (chap. 1): "Eorum quae sunt, partim in nobis est, partim non est. In nobis est opinio, conatus, appetitus, declinatio, et ut uno dicam verbo quaecunque nostra sunt opera; non sunt in nobis corpus, possessio, gloria, principatus, et uno verbo quaecunque nostra opera non sunt. Quae igitur in nobis sunt, natura sunt libera, nec quae prohiberi impedirive possit. Quae in nobis non sunt, ea imbecilla, serva, et quae prohiberi possint, atque aliena."

qua mente, quo consilio, qua voluntate aliquid faciendum vel non faciendum susce-[sig. Aiiir]perimus, vel si non fecerimus: id solum nobis vel acceptum vel expensum referunt. Administratores vero legum, quoniam hominum mentes ignorant, ab externis argumentis ac testibus probationibus sumptis sola facta iudicant. Solae namque optiones nostrae iudiciaque — deligendi, colendi, appetendi rem expetitam et optatam, aut aspernandi non placentem et invisam — in nostra sunt potestate et in nobis: in ipsisque solis nostrum bonum et malum situm est. Haud enim aequum erat ut Deus nostra bona nostraque mala, a quibus exigit vitae actae rationes a nobis, in aliena poneret voluntate et potestate. Honores igitur, divitiae, insignia, magistratus et caetera eiusdem generis — forma, valitudo, vires — in aliena, non in nostra potestate cum sint, nec bona nec mala nostra esse necesse est;[25] quin potius, ut supra est demonstratum, suapte natura omnino nec bona sunt nec mala. Verum solae virtutes quae voluntariae nominantur — pietas, fides, spes, caritas, iustitia, temperantia, misericordia,[26] et reliquae — bona nostra sunt, e quibus veri honores et verae laudes existunt. Certe saltem dignae illis

have regard only to our mind, purpose, and will when we conceived that something should or should not be done, even if we did nothing: that is all they credit or debit us with. Legal officers, however, not knowing people's thoughts, accept the evidence of external proofs and witnesses, and judge only the facts. Only our choices and our decisions — whether to prefer, cherish, and strive for something we desire and crave, or to spurn something we dislike and hate — are in our power and in *us*: in ourselves alone lies what is good or bad for us. It would have been unfair of God to place in others' will and power those things, whether good or bad for us, which he insists that we account for at the end of our life. So, since honors, wealth, badges, magistracies, and things of that kind — physique, health, and strength — are in others' power, not in ours, they must be neither good nor bad for us.[25] Further, as was shown above, by their own nature they simply *are* neither good nor bad. Only the virtues called 'voluntary' — loyalty, faith, hope, charity, justice, temperance, compassion,[26] and the rest — are good for us, and sources of true honor and true praise. At the very least they are *worthy* of them, even

---

[25] For Stoic indifference to the externals of life, see Poliziano, *Epicteti Stoici Enchiridion*, fol. 295v, cap. xx (chap. 15): "Memento oportere te in convivio versari. In quo si fercula ad te perveniunt, extenta manu modeste carpe. Si transit, qui fert, ne eum detine; si nondum pervenit, ne procul appetitum extende, sed expecta, dum ad te veniat. Sic erga filios, sic erga uxorem, sic erga principatus, sic erga divitias; erisque aliquando dignus deorum convivio." See also the passage quoted in n. 24 above.

[26] Valgulio includes in his list all three theological virtues (faith, hope, and charity), but keeps only two (justice and temperance) of the four natural (or cardinal) virtues normally joined with them to make up the seven virtues, replacing prudence (*prudentia*) with loyalty (*pietas*), and fortitude (*fortitudo*) with compassion (*misericordia*). Perhaps Cicero's influence was again at work. In *De officiis* 1. 160 community obligations are set above all others, so that "considered action" is superior to "prudent reflection": "Quare hoc quidem effectum sit, in officiis deligendis hoc genus officiorum excellere quod teneatur hominum societate. Etenim cognitionem prudentiamque sequetur considerata actio; ita fit ut agere considerate pluris sit quam cogitare prudenter" (followed by the hierarchy of societal obligations — those of *pietas*, in effect — quoted in n. 21 above); and (1. 20) *beneficentia*, named as the companion of *iustitia* and equated with *benignitas* and *liberalitas*, closely resembles *misericordia* as Valgulio defines it (see n. 7 above), whereas (*De officiis* 1. 62) *fortitudo* is accepted as virtuous only if devoid of personal motives (see n. 55 below).

sunt, vel si ab hominibus non honorentur nec laudentur: neque enim id expetunt. Contraria vero mala sunt, a quibus meritae vituperationes atque ignominiae iustae demanant.

    Hoc sentiunt praecepta divina, hoc naturalia, hoc civilia; et ipse etiam consensus hominum id iudicat, omnisque ratio comprobat. Si dubitas id civilem facultatem praeceptaque politica et rerum publicarum administrandarum rationem sentire, nec tibi probantur quae a me sunt commemorata pluraque requiris, lege Aristotelis politicos libros novem et Platonis decem, eiusdemque duodecim voluminibus explicatas Leges, addito Epinomide tertio decimo.[27] Non dubito quin tibi, vel si pessimo tardissimove ingenio sis, tibi sint probaturi neminem videlicet esse honore afficiendum — nec quidem affici vere posse nisi fucato forte ac falso — praeter bonum ac iustum et virtute praeditum virum, nec contra dedecore nisi malum et viciis contaminatum, quoniam sola vitia solaeque virtutes in nostra voluntate sitae sunt.[28] Caetera omnia (ut saepe dixi) — nobilitas generis, divitiae, opes, potentia, equestre aurum, comitatus quos vocant, imperia, regna, vita, integra valitudo, pulchritudo et similia, et contra paupertas, repulsae, servitus, mors, infirma valitudo,

if they may not be honored or praised by people: they do not seek that. Conversely, those things are bad from which deserved censure and just ignominy derive.

This is the tenor of divine, of natural, and of civil principles; it is also the generally agreed judgment of humankind, and all philosophy confirms it. If you doubt that this is the tenor of civil authority and of political theory and philosophy, and if you disagree with my remarks and demand more, read Aristotle's nine books on politics and Plato's ten, plus the latter's *Laws*, unfolded in twelve books with an extra thirteenth, *Epinomis*.[27] Even if you are intellectually very weak or very slow, I am sure they will prove to you that no man should receive honor — nor indeed *can* he truly receive honor, except perhaps the sham and fake type — who is not good, just, and virtuous; and that, conversely, no one should suffer disgrace unless he is bad and corrupted by vices, since only vices and virtues rest on our will.[28] All other things (as I have often said) — noble birth, wealth, possessions, power, knightly gold, what they call "countships", empires, kingdoms, life, sound health, beauty, and the like, and on the other hand poverty, electoral failures, slavery, death, poor health,

---

[27] The *Epinomis* is concerned with wisdom, and describes how the members of the nocturnal council referred to in the final book of Plato's *Laws* are to attain the level of virtue and bliss demanded of them. It is therefore understandable that it should sometimes have been regarded as an appendix to the *Laws*, even though there remains some doubt about its authorship. Valgulio probably knew Aristotle's eight (not nine, as he states here) books of *Politics* through the Latin version by William of Moerbeke (ca. 1215–1286) or, more probably, the Greek *editio princeps* issued by Aldus Manutius in Venice in 1498. Italian humanists such as Leonardo Bruni (ca. 1370–1444) in Florence turned to the *Politics* for a frame of reference in their investigation (and often praise) of the constitutions of city-states and republics. See Jean Dunbabin, "The Reception and Interpretation of Aristotle's *Politics*," in *The Cambridge History of Later Medieval Philosophy: From the Rediscovery of Aristotle to the Disintegration of Scholasticism, 1100–1600*, ed. Norman Kretzmann, Antony Kenny, and Jan Pinborg, assoc. ed. Eleonore Stump (Cambridge: Cambridge University Press, 1982), 723–37; and Quentin Skinner, "Political Philosophy," in *The Cambridge History of Renaissance Philosophy*, gen. ed. Charles B. Schmitt, eds. Quentin Skinner and Eckhard Kessler, assoc. ed. Jill Kraye (Cambridge: Cambridge University Press, 1988), 389–452.

[28] Cf. Aristotle, *Politics* 1323a38: "It is not by means of external goods that men acquire and keep the virtues, but the other way round."

debilitas, deformitas — quia nostri arbitrii non sunt[d] nec in nostra optione delectus posita sed in aliena, et pro libidine fortunae temeritatis abeunt, accedunt, et innumerabiles varietates habent, et caduca atque infirma sunt, nulla in neutram partem merita obtinent, hoc est, nec laude nec vituperatione, nec honore nec ignominia sunt digna.

Et haec omnia praecepta — Christiana, naturae, et civilia — eundem finem spectant: ut homines videlicet beatitudinem consequantur. Verum naturae et civilia in hac vita felicitatem proponunt, quam per actiones atque officia naturae et rectae rationi congruentia adipiscamur, per quam civilem felicitatem ad praestantiorem quandam aliam felicitatem a negociis liberi contemplando et pura intelligentia res prospiciendo pervenire adhuc in vita manentes possimus. At Christi praecepta nullam in vita beatitudinem noverunt; aeternam, caelestem illam solam proponunt et docent, ad quam nisi spe, fide et caritate adire nequeamus — despectis prorsusque contemptis et pro nihilo habitis corporibus et caducis rebus omnibus, ac labe geniturae atque mixtionis per sacramentum regenerationis purgata.

Cum igitur constet ac late pateat per nullam legem nullamque rationem, sive divinam sive naturalem sive civilem et humanam, honori cuiquam esse posse rem ullam quae in alterius potestate ac voluntate posita, quaeque ipsa per se et sua vi bona non sit, quis nisi rationis expers dicet sumptum quem aliquis civis propter se facit — hoc est, ut laudetur et honore afficiatur — aestimatione ulla dignum esse, divitiasque et aurum equestre et comitatus caeteraque huiusmodi ornamenta donaque fortunae esse honoranda? Qui sumptus si quandoque apud prudentes aestimationem et laudem atque honorem habet, idcirco habet quia benefaciendi aliis gratia et sane indigentibus et quibus oportet erogatio [sig. Aiiiv] illa administrata fuerit, non propter fructum consequendum. Sic et quando illa insignia ob res aliquas praeclare gestas et per virtutem vitam actam sponte alicui collata sint et non ambita, aliqua aestimatione sunt digna. Sin homini cuiquam sint tributa propter divitias tantum quibus prodige vel avare utatur, vel propter generis nobilitatem, aliasve ob huiusmodi causas aliquas, atque omnino abhorrenti a virtute, nihil vir iste ab equo ignavo et degeneri differt quem dominus, spetie corporis eius delectatus, ornatissimis phaleris insignivit ut a vulgo cum admiratione spectetur.

---

[d] *correxi*: sint *cod.*

infirmity, ugliness — are not under our control, do not depend on our preferred choice but on other people's, come and go at the whim of random fortune, undergo countless changes, and are fleeting and fragile. They therefore earn no deserts either way: that is, they are worthy neither of praise nor of censure, neither of honor nor of ignominy.

All these Christian, natural, and civil principles have the same end in view: namely, that human beings may achieve bliss. But the natural and civil ones offer happiness in this life: we may attain it through actions and obligations consistent with nature and right reason; and through that civil happiness we who are free from business affairs may be able, by meditating and by applying pure thought to the study of reality, to reach some other, superior, happiness while still alive. Christ's principles, however, recognize no bliss during life; they offer and teach only the bliss that is eternal and heavenly, which we can approach only by hope, faith, and charity — by scorning, utterly despising, and holding valueless our bodies and all that is fleeting, and by purging away the stain of our procreation and impurity through the sacrament of new birth [sc. baptism].

Since, therefore, it is certain and perfectly clear that by no law or logic, whether divine, or natural, or civil and human, can anything which lies in another's power and will, and is not in itself and in its own right good, bring honor to anyone, who but a simpleton will say that the spending some citizen does for his own purposes — that is, to win praise and honor for himself — is worthy of any esteem, or that wealth, knightly gold, countships, and other such baubles and gifts of fortune should be honored? If such expenditure does sometimes meet with esteem, praise, and honor among prudent people, it is because that outlay has been employed for the benefit of others — the needy, certainly, and those one ought to help — and not in order to gain profit. So also when, for certain outstanding achievements and a life virtuously lived, those badges have been spontaneously granted to someone who did not solicit them, they are worthy of some esteem. But if they have been awarded to any person merely because of wealth which he uses wastefully or stingily, because of noble birth, or for some other similar reasons, and he is a total stranger to virtue, that man is no different from a lazy and lowbred horse whom his master, pleased by his physical appearance, has decorated with resplendent brasses so that the populace may gaze admiringly at him.

Quapropter statutum nostrum, minuens sumptus funerum immoderatos — non omnes tollens, sed modum tantum illis adhibens — ambitionemque civium et insanas stultorum honorum contentiones in rebus luctuosis ac tristibus, quae solae vel arrogantissimos et superbissimos et insanos quoque homines admonent suae imbecillitatis et infirmitatis et miseriarum humanarum, si quis damnat et accusat, quia caeteris exaequet locupletiores et equites et huiusmodi insignibus praeditos homines et in eandem moderationem cogat, aequabilitatem hanc existimans ignominiae atque dedecori illis esse, contra vero honori ac dignitati maiores sumptus facere, in turpissimo et perniciosissimo errore versatur ac, si alios in eundem errorem cohortando pergat trahere, de civitate pellendum censeo tanquam bonorum morum atque institutorum corruptorem.[29]

Postquam in universum atque in genere, quoad brevissime fieri per me potuit, est demonstratum solam animi virtutem — quae est ad summum perfectionis perducta ratio — esse honorandam, propterea quod in ea sola nostrum bonum est, et ipsa in nostra voluntate est posita, a qua una voluntate omnia merita nostra existunt, vitium vero — quod quidem est naturae et rationis absoluta depravatio — inhonorandum et probro ac odio persequendum, quoniam in eo solo situm est nostrum malum, eiusque fuga in nostra voluntate atque potestate est locata, et haec omnia omnibus generibus legum (divinis, naturalibus, et civilibus) sunt comprobata, nunc privatim videamus quam sit absurdum, quam stultum, quantum a ratione aversum, existimare affici honore mortuos si eorum cadavera magnis sumptibus ad sepulturam efferantur.

[II]

Cedo tu mihi, devotissime et contemptor mundi vir,[30] quidnam tandem credis honorari in mortuo? Totumne hominem, hoc est, anima et corpore constantem? At sero id facis, dissolutus enim iam est, nec amplius

That the Brescians' statute about funeral expenditure 117

Our statute, therefore, reduces excessive spending on funerals — not stopping it altogether, just moderating it — and also reduces rivalry among citizens, and mad scrambling for silly honors, at those times of grief and gloom which alone remind even the proudest and haughtiest people — and mad ones too — of their own vulnerability and fragility, and of human wretchedness. So anyone who condemns and criticizes this statute for making richer people, knights, and those with similar badges equal with the rest, and for forcing on them the same moderation, and considers that this fairness brings them ignominy and disgrace, whereas greater expenditure gives them honor and dignity — such a person is making a foul and fatal mistake, and if his advice causes others to be drawn into making the same mistake, I think he should be driven out of the city as a corrupter of morals and manners.[29]

In broad and general terms it has been shown, so far as I could very briefly show, that only mental virtue — reason taken to the peak of perfection — should be honored, since what is good for us rests in it alone, and since it lies in our will, which is the sole source of all our deserts; whereas vice — the complete distortion of nature and reason — should be dishonored, and pursued with reproach and hatred, since what is bad for us rests in it alone, and escape from it lies in our will and power. All this has also been confirmed by all types of law (divine, natural, and civil). Now let us consider separately how ridiculous, how stupid, and how unreasonable it is to imagine that the dead receive honor if their corpses are carried out for burial at great expense.

[II]

Come now, devout scorner of the world,[30] what exactly do you suppose *is* honored in the case of a dead man? Is it the whole person, meaning its combination of soul and body? But your action is too late, for the person has already been broken up and no longer exists. Surely you do

---

[29] For a similar suggestion of exile for the offending party, see the *Defense* above, 25.

[30] See n. 6 above: presumably Valgulio is now addressing the same person directly.

est homo. Num animam censes?[31] Partemne illam quae vacat ratione, quae blandas sensibus voluptates hauriens, cum est in corpore, plausibus vulgi et populari aura falsisque exultat honoribus? At ea nulla est, et cum corpore est extincta. An illam immortalem et divinam rationis participem? At ea exempta vinculis atque impedimentis et carcere et sepulchro corporis, et soluta cupiditatibus pessimis degendae vitae consultoribus hostibusque praecipuis suis, verum iam tandem sentit et aperte cognoscit et vere iudicat.[32] Quae si angore conscientiae male cum corpore actae vitae fraudumque cruciatu aeternas luit poenas,[33] nihil ei profusi sumptus isti in eius honorem celebrati prosunt, quandoquidem ne ipsae quidem elemosynae nec preces sanctorum hominum iuvare illas queunt.[34]

Sin constanti puritate vitae per virtutem et praecepta Christi actae ad beatas atque aeternas sedes velis passis pervecta divinis bonis atque honoribus et sempiterna fruitur gloria, nihil indiget flammulis istis in modica cera excitatis, cum ipsa splendore solis sit fulgentior;

not think it is the soul?[31] Do you mean that irrational part which, when inside the body, drinks in seductive pleasures through the senses, reveling in the applause of the populace, in public favor and fake honors? But that is no longer there, and was snuffed out with the body. Is it, then, the immortal and divine rational part? But once that is freed from its chains and shackles, and from the body's jail and tomb, once it is released from lusts which are its worst advisers on how to live, and its chief foes, now at last it perceives, clearly discerns, and truly judges the truth.[32] And if it suffers eternal punishment through anguished awareness of a life lived badly in the flesh, and through torture for its offences,[33] then the lavish spending *you* want, performed in its honor, is no use to it, since not even alms, nor the prayers of saints, can alleviate the punishment.[34]

But if, through the steadfast purity of a life guided by virtue and Christ's principles, it speeds with sails outspread to the blest eternal abodes, and there enjoys divine benefits and honors and everlasting glory, it has no need of *your* tiny flames, kindled with ordinary candle-wax, for it is itself brighter than the sun's radiance; nor indeed is it delighted

---

[31] In this paragraph, as in his *Contra vituperatorem musicae* (see Aegidius Carlerius, Johannes Tinctoris and Carlo Valgulio: *"That liberal and virtuous art": Three Humanist Treatises on Music*, ed. and trans. Cullington and Strohm, 92, n. 12), Valgulio follows Plato (e.g., *Republic* 434d–441c) and Aristotle (e.g., *Politics* 1333a17) in adopting a broad division of the soul or mind into intellectual and physically-directed components, whereas in his earlier *Proem on Plutarch's* Musica *to Titus Pyrrhinus* he opts for an 'ascending tetrachord' of *sensus, imaginatio, ratio,* and *intellectus*: see Palisca, "Carlo Valgulio: The Proem," 31 and n. 3. This was a common medieval classification from Boethius onwards: see C. S. Lewis, *The Discarded Image* (Cambridge: Cambridge University Press, 1964), 88, 156–65.

[32] Valgulio is no doubt alluding to the Myth of Er which ends Plato's *Republic*, and to the Dream of Scipio which ends Cicero's *De republica*. Indeed this whole passage recalls Macrobius, *Commentary on the Dream of Scipio* 1. 11 (and 1. 9).

[33] Cf. Cicero, *De legibus* 1. 40: "At vero scelerum in homines atque in d[eos inp]ietatum nulla expiatio est. Itaque poenas luunt, non tam iudiciis . . . , at eos agitant insectanturque furiae, non ardentibus taedis sicut in fabulis, sed angore conscientiae fraudisque cruciatu."

[34] An allusion to the chapter "Animae defunctorum" of the *Decretum Gratiani*, as cited by the Dominicans: see the *Defense* above, n. 38, and Introduction, n. 56.

neque vero caterva illa comitantium corpus acerrimum hostem quondam suum laetatur, cum quo quamdiu cum ipso vixit perpetua atque periculosa bella gessit, quodque felicitati eius verae et immortali semper fuerat adversatum, quandoquidem animis caelestes sedes [Aiiiir] tenentibus universa tellus cum aqua simul et cunctis animalibus ne instar quidem speciesque magnitudinis grani milii est! Sin labe obstante aliqua impeditum iter offenderit, quo minus purissima atque aeterna illa regna divinaque consortia tanquam portum recto cursu reflantibus ventis tenere potuerit, certam tamen diluta atque purgata labe potiundi aliquando caelestes honores et sempiterna fruendi gloria, inanes sumptus istos ambitionem spirantes et umbras istas honorum leves circa putridam terram — quorum forte similium insulsa nimis dulcedine capta contraxerat labem, dum illa circundata humo erat quae cursum rectum in avitam patriam est rememorata — non modo contemnere, verum etiam invisum habere, doloresque ac poenas maiores propter illos excipere credibile est, praesertim cum sciat per speciem honorandi vita functos sibi fructum a vulgo — pessimo rerum iudice — inanem gloriam ac laudem viventes quaerere, quarum oblectatione et scabie[35] deliniti maculam ipsi quoque ac labem animis suis contrahant, ad quam purgandam et diluendam pares aut forte maiores poenas sint persoluturi.

Quod autem vivi celebritates istas et pompas funerum honoris ac laudis suae apud populum aucupandae causa instituant, perspicuum postulationis genus facit, verum hoc quoque argumento declaratur, quod si ii qui sumptum faciunt in funere ducendo vel populum ignoraturum vel in maiore se auctoritate ac laude propter sumptum apud vulgus non futuros existimarent, satis constat apud omnes ab illo sumptu fuisse temperaturos, aut, si facerent, eo modo facerent qui gratus est Deo et virtuti consentaneus et probis viris. Secreto namque egentibus administrarent, non eo uterentur qui ab omnibus damnaretur nec ullum operae precium faceret apud ullum genus hominum, multo minus apud Deum

by that throng of people escorting the body, once its fiercest foe, with which it waged perpetual and perilous wars as long as it lived with it, and which had always been opposed to its true and immortal happiness, since for the souls who occupy the heavenly abodes the whole earth, including the sea and all living things, does not even match or mimic the size of a grain of millet! If, however, it has found its route blocked by the obstacle of some stain, so that it has been unable to reach the haven of those pure, eternal realms and divine companies by steering a straight course against headwinds, *sometime* it is nonetheless sure — when its stain is dissolved and purged away — to attain heavenly honors and enjoy everlasting glory. So, one may believe, it not only despises the vain expense *you* want, reeking of rivalry, and *your* flimsy, shadowy honors concerned with rotting earth — for it was perhaps through addiction to the cloying sweetness of similar honors that it had incurred the stain, hemmed in as it was by that soil which impeded a straight course back to its ancestral homeland — but also hates them, and sustains greater pains and penalties because of them. This is especially likely since it knows that, on the pretext of honoring the dead, the living seek as their reward from the populace — the worst judge of facts — vainglory and praise, and that, cajoled by a liking and itch[35] for these things, they too incur in their own souls a taint and a stain which they will have to pay equal or perhaps greater penalties to purge away and dissolve.

That the living establish *your* funeral solemnities and processions in order to snatch honor and praise for themselves with the people is obvious from the type of demand they make, but this piece of evidence also proves it: it is universally agreed that if those who spend money on a funeral service thought either that the people would be unaware of this, or that the money would not bring them greater influence and praise with the populace, they would have refrained from spending it, or else, if they spent it, they would do so by the method that is acceptable to God and agreeable to virtue and honest men. They would bestow it on the needy in secret, and would not adopt the method that was universally condemned, and that achieved no worthwhile result with any type of people, much less

---

[35] The word *scabies* is rarely used in this metaphorical sense but, significantly, Cicero does so use it in a very similar context in *De legibus* 1. 47: see n. 15 above.

et sapientes viros. Taceo multos qui sumptum magnum in funere aliquorum faciunt, quos vivos et oderunt et contemptui habuerunt, nec mortuos postea cessarunt omnibus probris lacerare. Sed haec notissima sunt.

"Nonne ergo preces et elemosynae," dicet aliquis, "purgandis animis defunctorum prosunt?" Mea quidem sententia ut mortuis non prosint, quam rem vir sanctissimus et princeps theologorum Dionysius Areopagita sentire videtur.[36] Profecto caritas illa et misericordia vivis prodest,

with God and wise men. I omit to mention many who go to great expense for the funerals of certain people whom, when alive, they hated and despised and whom later, even when dead, they did not cease to lambaste with all sorts of reproaches. These things, however, are well known.

"Well then," someone will say, "are prayers and alms no good for purging the souls of the deceased?" In my opinion they are no good for the dead — which is what Dionysius the Areopagite, most holy man and prince of theologians, seems to think.[36] Certainly such charity and

---

[36] Dionysius the Areopagite, whose conversion by Paul is recorded in Acts 17: 34, was traditionally considered the author of several theological writings now thought to date from the late fifth century. The final section of *The Ecclesiastical Hierarchy* is largely devoted to funerals, and includes a discussion of the purpose of "sacred prayer over the deceased" : though it might seem pointless to offer it — since divine justice determines that each person will receive what his deeds on earth deserve, and scripture tells us that the prayers of the just are useful only to those worthy of them, and only in this life, not after death — nevertheless such "prayers of the saints" are very helpful in this life for anyone who longs for "the sacred gifts", has a devout disposition to receive them, and humbly approaches some holy man for his help and intercession; this holy man will not offer prayer for "the unholy dead" — which God would in any case reject — but simply for the fulfillment of scriptural promises to those who have lived holy (if not perfect) lives, and therefore for what pleases God and will be freely given by him. (See PG 3: 559–64; *Über die Kirchliche Hierarchie*, trans. G. Heil [Stuttgart: Hiersemann, 1986]; *Corpus Dionysiacum* 2, ed. G. Heil and A. M. Ritter, Patristiche Texte und Studien 36 [Berlin: de Gruyter, 1991]; *Pseudo-Dionysius: Complete Works*, trans. C. Luibheid [London: SPCK, 1987], 254–56.) It is worth noting that in 1436–1437 the Camaldolese General Ambrogio Traversari completed elegant and influential translations of all four Pseudo-Dionysian treatises (*The Divine Names*, *The Mystical Theology*, *The Celestial Hierarchy* and *The Ecclesiastical Hierarchy*), that in 1482 Marsilio Ficino — ignoring doubts about the authenticity of these writings raised by Lorenzo Valla in 1457 — drew on 'Dionysius' for his *Platonic Theology*, and that in 1492 he followed Traversari's example by undertaking a new translation (with commentary) of *The Divine Names* and *The Mystical Theology*: see D. F. Lackner, "The Camaldolese Academy: Ambrogio Traversari, Marsilio Ficino and the Christian Platonic Tradition," in *Marsilio Ficino: His Theology, his Philosophy, his Legacy*, ed. M. J. B. Allen and V. Rees with M. Davies (Leiden, Boston, and Köln: Brill, 2002), 21–22; and K. Froehlich, "Introduction III: Pseudo-Dionysius and the Reformation of the Sixteenth Century," in *Pseudo-Dionysius: Complete Works*, trans. Luibheid, 34–39. Valgulio's respectful reference here to the views of "Dionysius the Areopagite" on prayers for the dead shows that he shared his friend Ficino's unbounded admiration for this author.

et maxime Deo est grata. Verum enim vero magnopere cavendum est ne et nosmetipsos atque alios fallamus, ut quod ad pompam et inanem gloriam et laudem apud imperitam multitudinem venandam facimus, id liberalitatem atque elemosynam esse arbitremur, aut aliis videri velimus. Certe preces sacerdotum quos pecunia publice emimus ut in conspectu populi eas decantent — ore ac verbis tenus tantum fusae — mortuis utiles non sunt. Vivis vero qui illas emerunt et sacerdotibus qui vendiderunt perniciosas apud Deum — verum iudicem et cognitorem voluntatum, quas solas iudicat — et dedecori apud prudentes viros esse arbitror. Nam utraeque elemosyna et preces, ut saepe iam dictum est, gratuitae sunt, non mercenariae, nec fructum expetunt. Si secus sint et expetant fructum, mercatura est invisa Deo ac bonis viris: in arcano et pura mente ac tacita sunt administrandae.[37] "Fratresne igitur et religiosi, rerum omnium necessariarum egentes, nulli[e] alii rei quam rebus divinis et precibus pro vivis, pro mortuis vacantes, destituentur, et fame ipsos conflictari et contabefieri sinemus?" Minime omnium: debent enim saeculares et ipsi quoque fratres locupletes et omnes qui possunt sponte sua non modo illis, sed quibuscunque indigentibus opem ferre — sive ad comitanda cadavera ad sepulturam veniant sive non veniant — iustitiae divinae, naturali atque civili obtemperantes, quibus parere omni ope debemus. Cui generi sumptuum nul-[sig. Aiiiiv]la lege nulloque statuto ullus est cuiquam praescriptus et terminatus modus.

Quanam igitur caecitate mentis, aut potius scelere, quisquam agitatus censebit cadavera alia aliis praestare, et oportere defuncta cadavera vita, quia — dum spirabant et aura vescebantur — equestre aurum gestaverant aut alia aliqua maiore fortuna insignita erant, maiore sumptu et comitatu sacerdotum humari, cum plane constet (ut est demonstratum) nec aurum nec ulla regna — propter quae honorari vultis — nec quidem ipsos animos, si boni non sint, honore dignos esse? O miseros

---

[e] *correxi:* nullum *cod.*

compassion is good for the living, and very pleasing to God. But all the same we must take great care not to fool ourselves and others, so that we believe — or wish others to think — that what we do in pursuit of ostentation, vainglory, and praise from the ignorant crowd is generosity and almsgiving. Surely the prayers of priests whom we have hired with public money to recite them in full view of the people — prayers poured forth by means of lips and words alone — are no use to the dead. But for the living who bought and the priests who sold them they are, I consider, disastrous in the eyes of God — the true judge and knower of desires which alone he judges — and disgraceful in the eyes of prudent men. For, as often stated already, both alms and prayers are gratis, not paid for, and do not seek profit. If they *were* otherwise and *did* seek profit, such commerce is hateful to God and to good men, for those activities ought to be performed in secret and with a pure, quiet mind.[37]

"So will brothers and religious, who lack all life's necessities and spend their time wholly in divine rites and prayers for the living and the dead, be abandoned? Shall we allow them to be racked and ravaged by hunger?" Not at all: laypeople, prosperous brothers themselves too, and all who can — whether or not they come to escort corpses to burial — should voluntarily assist not only them, but whoever are in need, thus complying with divine, natural, and civil justice, which we should make every effort to obey. Regarding *that* type of spending, no law or statute sets or defines any limit for anyone.

What mental blindness, therefore, or rather villainy, will provoke anyone to believe that some corpses are superior to others, and that lifeless corpses should be buried at greater expense and with a bigger escort of priests, because, when they breathed and took air in, they had worn knightly gold or borne the badge of some other bigger stroke of luck, although (as has been shown) it is quite certain that neither gold nor any domains — things which prompt your wish to be honored — nor even souls themselves, unless they be good, are worthy of honor? Poor folk!

---

[37] Cf. Matthew 6: 3–4 and 6: "Te autem faciente eleemosynam, nesciat sinistra tua quid faciat dextera tua: ut sit eleemosyna tua in abscondito, et Pater tuus, qui videt in abscondito, reddet tibi." "Tu autem cum oraveris, intra in cubiculum tuum, et clauso ostio, ora Patrem tuum in abscondito: et Pater tuus, qui videt in abscondito, reddet tibi." (Also alluded to by the author of the *Defense*, above, 37.)

homines! Vultis vestra corpora, sensu et spiritu destituta, honoratiora esse quam aliorum? At natura, potentior vobis, non vult: putrefacit enim ilico aeque omnia et corrumpit, et similes ea depascunt vermes. Hyrcani quondam viam discriminis invenerant. Nam qui potentiores erant grandiores et praestantiores domi alebant canes, a quibus corpora eorum vorabantur: plebs autem[f] publicis ignobilioribus canibus tanquam sepulchris utebatur.[38] Persae et Aegiptii odoratioribus et conservantioribus rebus nobiliorum hominum corpora oblita[g] in aedibus servabant, caeteri pro facultate.[39] At vos insani et miserandi mortales, qui funera vestra comitatiora et sumptuosiora esse oportere censetis quam aliorum, quonam illa brevissima et momentanea quadam pompa associata fertis? In Capitoliumne tanquam quadrigis triumphalibus invecta?[40] An

[f] *correxi*: a *cod.*
[g] *correxi*: obita *cod.*

Do you want your bodies, bereft of sense and spirit, to be more honored than other people's? But nature, whose power is greater than yours, does *not* want it: she at once causes all bodies equally to rot and decay, and similar worms eat them up. The Hyrcanians had in ancient times found a way to distinguish them. More powerful people bred at their homes larger and superior dogs by which their bodies were devoured: ordinary people used as their tombs less well-bred communal dogs.[38] The Persians and the Egyptians smeared nobler people's bodies with more fragrant and more effective preservatives and kept them in their houses, while others did according to their means.[39] But *you* mad and miserable mortals who believe that your funerals should be better-attended and better-financed than other people's, where do you take those corpses in the very brief and short-lived procession associated with them? To the Capitol, as though riding in triumphal four-horse chariots?[40] Or do you lead them, joyful and exultant, with merriment, laughter, and a nuptial or

---

[38] Hyrcania, the ancient region southeast of the Caspian Sea, formed part of the Median, Achaemenian, Seleucid, and Parthian empires. Herodotus barely mentions its inhabitants (*Histories* 3. 117 and 7. 62), and it is to the Persian priestly caste, the Magi, that he attributes the custom of burying male Persians only after their corpses have been torn by a bird or a dog — in contrast to the normal Persian practice of covering a body with wax before burying it (*Histories* 1. 140). Valgulio, however, gets all his data from Cicero's examples (drawn from the Stoic philosopher Chrysippus) of various peoples' false ideas about the dead in *Tusculanae disputationes* 1. 108: "Condiunt Aegyptii mortuos et eos servant domi, Persae etiam cera circumlitos condunt, ut quam maxime permaneant diuturna corpora; Magorum mos est non humare corpora suorum, nisi a feris sint ante laniata; in Hyrcania plebs publicos alit canes, optimates domesticos: nobile autem genus canum illud scimus esse, sed pro sua quisque facultate parat a quibus lanietur, eamque optimam illi esse censent sepulturam."

[39] For the Egyptians Valgulio's likely main source was Herodotus (one of several major Greek authors given first editions by Aldus Manutius in 1502–1504): in *Histories* 2. 86–88 the three methods — most expensive, next best, and cheapest — used by their professional embalmers are detailed. In lumping the Persians and the Egyptians together here, however, he ignores what both Herodotus and Cicero say about the different treatment the former normally gave their dead (see previous note). See A. B. Lloyd, "Egypt," in *Brill's Companion to Herodotus*, ed. E. J. Baker et al. (Leiden: Brill, 2002), 415–36.

[40] In traditional Roman triumphs the victorious general rode in a four-horse chariot (*quadriga*) to the temple of Jupiter on the Capitol.

ad dapes et voluptates Sardanapalli, cum iocis et risibus et carmine nuptiali vel triumphali, ducitis laetantia atque exultantia?[41] Ad obruendum nimirum ea atque calcandum multa terra cum ululatibus et ploratibus atque gemitibus fertis, et molibus saxorum concluditis et oneratis ut,[h] si forte (quod aliquando usu venit) mortua vere non fuissent, exire ad vitam nequeant![i] Atque ita illa ea hora ibi conditis ut nunquam amplius postea revisatis: quin formidantur a plerisque ut a transitu etiam eius loci ubi humata sunt abstineant — quis honor iste sit, vos qui sapitis reputate! Nec pudet istum religiosum virum,[42] cum sola mors summos cum infimis, reges cum servis exaequet, et sola superbos et inflatos favore contemptibili stultissimae fortunae homines — Capaneosque ipsos et Pharaones et Nabuchdonosores[43] impiissimosque tyrannos — vel modo cogitata ad sensum verum sui et cognitionem suae eorum infirmitatis atque caducitatis et aequabilitatis cum caeteris, humanae conditionis gnaros[j] facit, ut nihil se ab ignobilissimo et contemptissimo et pauperrimo homine, in eo quod homines sunt, differre intelligant — non pudet, inquam, id postulare quod neque Deus neque natura neque humana ulla ratio patitur: ut cadavera alia aliis excellant et honore magis digna sint. Qui honor nec ad animas illorum cadaverum quondam incolas potest pertinere, ut supra est demonstratum. Et fortassis illae animae, quarum corpora (propter divitias quas ante possederant et propter insignia quibus tanquam equi phaleris exultaverant) honoratiora esse vultis, absque illis divitiis atque insignibus sed in paupertate atque ignobilitate vixisse

---

[h] *correxi*: ne *cod.*
[i] *correxi*: nequeunt *cod.*
[j] *correxi*: gnaro *cod.*

triumphal song, to the feasts and pleasures of Sardanapalus?[41] Naturally, you take them to be covered and crushed by much earth, with repeated wailing, weeping, and groaning; you shut them in and weigh them down with massive rocks so that, if (as may sometimes happen) they prove not to have been really dead, they cannot get out and back to life! You also hide them there so well at that time that you never afterwards pay them another visit: indeed, most people are afraid that they may not even refrain from haunting the place where they were buried — just think, you wise ones, what honor *you* give the dead! And yet *your* "religious"[42] man is not ashamed, although death alone equates highest with lowest, kings with slaves; it alone makes the proud, those puffed up by foolish fortune's despicable favor — even the Capaneuses, the Pharaohs, the Nebuchadnezzars,[43] and the most godless tyrants — conscious of their human nature, even if their thoughts about death are limited to a true sense of themselves and an awareness of their own frailty, transience, and equality with the rest, so that they realize they are no different from the lowest-born, the most despised, and the poorest human being, in that they *are* human — *he*, I say, is not ashamed to demand what neither God nor nature nor any human philosophy permits: that some corpses should outshine others and be more worthy of honor. Nor can this honor belong to the souls which formerly dwelt in those corpses, as was shown above. Perhaps, too, those souls whose bodies you wish to be more honored (owing to the wealth they had possessed before and the badges they had rejoiced in, like horses with their brasses) would have preferred to have lived without such wealth and badges but in poverty

---

[41] Sardanapalus is the Greek name of the Assyrian king Assurbanipal, who probably lived in the seventh century B. C., and was famed for his wealth and luxurious life-style: see Cicero, *Tusculanae disputationes* 5. 101; Cicero, *De finibus* 2.106; and Juvenal 10. 362.

[42] See n. 6 above.

[43] Capaneus, one of the 'Seven against Thebes', boasted that he could sack the city whatever Zeus did, and was struck down by a thunderbolt: Aeschylus, *Seven against Thebes* 423ff.; Euripides, *The Phoenician Women* 1172ff. Nebuchadnezzar, king of Babylon, was punished for his sins by losing his kingdom and having to live like an animal: Daniel 4: 28–30. "Pharaoh" here is probably the Pharaoh of the Exodus, drowned in the Red Sea.

maluissent. "Quam vellent aethere in alto nunc et pauperiem et duros perferre labores,"[44] scientes tum propter ministras voluptatum divitias, tum propter inanem gloriam ab eiusmodi insignibus haustam non modo in extremum contemptum inferni loci detrusas, verum etiam in poenas atque supplicia sempiterna fuisse coniectas, in quas non fuissent si in paupertate atque humilitate libentes aetatem duxissent.

Quare vos locupletes et equites et comites et id genus omnis homines, pro studio quo teneor veritatis et caritatis, hortor atque etiam rogo ne consultoribus talibus praebere aures velitis, sive habitu exteriore religionis tanquam cortice quodam sint contecti sive non sint qui consulunt. Nam qui intus re-[sig. Avr]ligionis habitum in mente gerunt, qui verus et optimus habitus est, certo scio nunquam esse eiusmodi consulturos; qui nanque vos ad haec cohortantur nihil aliud agunt quam quod discordias et seditiones malosque mores in civitate serunt. Satis superque[45] videri vobis debet, si propter istas divitias et potentiam et istud aurum equestre et propter eiusmodi fortunae ludibria, non propter vestram virtutem — de iis loquor qui tales sunt et de quibus id vere dici potest (ego eos ignoro: ipsi sciunt, et qui eos cum vero iudicio experiuntur) — in maiore honore apud imperitam multitudinem esse videmini, exterioribus signis credentes. Ac potius, si me auditis, istos quoque honores tanquam falsos testes vestrorum meritorum repudiabitis, et adhiberi vobis tanquam mendaces et irrisores vestros dolebitis.

Profecto, si verum reputare velimus, et intimos hominum sensus[k] cogitando rimari, non vos sed ea quae vos circunstant a vulgo quoque honorari comperiemus, aut potius, per speciem vestrae agendae rei (hoc est, vos honorandi). Ea enim vestra tum res est, quia eam in primis cupitis de vulgo: homines rem propriam agere sese arbitrari. Argumento hoc id probatur, quod si illis alicuius a vobis potiundi commodi spes dematur, et incommodi patiendi metus, in tanto vos honore habebunt in quanto ignobilissimum quenque et pauperrimum habeant — atque etiam

---

[k] *correxi*: sensns *cod*.

and obscurity. "How they would like to endure penury and hard toils now in the air above!",[44] knowing that it was partly wealth, the minion of pleasure, partly vainglory, the product of such badges, that caused them not only to be thrust into the utter humiliation of the nether regions, but also to be cast into everlasting pain and punishment, which would not have happened if they had gladly lived poor and humble lives.

So, you rich people, knights, counts, and suchlike, my zeal for truth and charity leads me to urge and beg all of you not to lend a willing ear to advisers of *this* kind, whether or not those who so advise are encased in the shell of religion's outer clothing. For I am sure that those who mentally wear religion's *inner* clothing, which is the true and the best sort, will never give such advice; those who urge you on to *these* actions do nothing but sow strife, discord, and wicked ways in the city. You ought to regard it as enough, and more,[45] if through that wealth and power of yours, that knightly gold, and similar playthings of fortune, not through your virtue — I speak of those who *are* like that, and of whom this can truly be said (I do not know who they are, but *they* know, and so do those who use true judgment in testing them) — if you, with your belief in outward signs, appear to be more highly honored by the ignorant crowd. And, if you listen to me, you will prefer to reject even the honors *you* want, as being false witnesses to your deserts, and you will resent their lying and mocking attachment to you.

Indeed, if we wish to ponder the truth, and by reflection probe people's deepest feelings, we shall find that it is not you but your circumstances that are honored, even by the populace; or rather, they do so on the pretext of acting in your interest (to honor you, that is). That *is* your interest then, since it is what you particularly desire from the populace: that people should think they are acting in their own interest. This is the evidence that clinches it: if they lose the hope of gaining some advantage from you, and the fear of suffering some disadvantage, they will give you the same amount of honor as they would give any of the meanest and poorest

---

[44] Vergil, *Aeneid* 6.436–37, describing those in Hades who had killed themselves merely because they hated life.

[45] "Satis superque" is a tag from Catullus 7. 2.

in minore! Quin potius contemptui habituros et odio persecuturos vos puto si, quoniam iniquitas et temeritas caecae fortunae immerito vobis illuxit, praestare illis velitis qui se, propter industriam et artes quas exercent utiles hominum generi, praestare vobis debere arbitrentur, vestros luxus, vestram superbiam, ignaviam, ventrem, libidines et insolentiam arguentes,[46] eos vero qui pares cum caeteris esse velint honore atque amore prosecuturos.

Quibus ex rebus latissime patet solas virtutes non modo a Deo et a natura et a prudentibus viris honorandas, colendas atque expetendas esse propter se iudicari, verum etiam ab ipso vulgo et ab infima plebe idem censeri si illi sint cognitae, vel si in pauperrimo et infimae plebis homine habitent — tametsi spem ac metum plerunque id genus hominum secutum secus facere videatur. Et contra vitium in quocunque homine sit — sive equite seu comite seu rege — esse contemnendum, inhonorandum et odio prosequendum, eodemque pacto afficiendos esse homines qui virtutes et qui vitia colunt. Quisnam per Deum immortalem non amat et veneratur et colit hominem pium, iustum, temperatum, misericordem et doctum,[47] vel si Iro et Cricca sit pauperior et ignobilior?[48] Quis ex adverso non odit, et in sede intima iudicii non contemnit et

people — and even less! Indeed, I expect them to despise you and pursue you with hatred if, just because the unfair and random light of blind fortune has undeservedly shone on you, you wish for precedence over those who think their diligence, and the socially useful skills they practice, entitle them to precedence over you, and who criticize your over-indulgence, your pride, sloth, gluttony, lusts, and arrogance.[46] But I expect them to lavish honor and love on those who wish to be on a par with the rest.

These facts make it abundantly clear, not just that God, nature, and prudent men consider that virtues alone should be honored, cherished, and desired for their own sakes, but also that even the populace and the lowliest folk share this opinion if they recognize such virtues, even if they reside in the poorest and lowliest person — although hope or fear usually seems to prompt that class of people to act differently. On the other hand, it is clear that vice should be despised, dishonored, and hated wherever it occurs — whether in knight, in count, or in king — and that those who cherish virtues or vices should in either case be treated similarly. Who, for God's sake, does not love, revere, and cherish a loyal, just, temperate, merciful, and learned person,[47] even if he be poorer and lowlier than Irus and Cricca?[48] Conversely, who does not hate, and in the depths of his conscience despise and abhor, a disloyal, unjust, proud,

---

[46] As with the list of seven virtues (see n. 26 above), Valgulio modifies the normal list of seven deadly sins: he includes pride, sloth, gluttony, and lust, but replaces covetousness/greed and anger with over-indulgence (*luxus*) and arrogance (*insolentia*), and omits envy altogether.

[47] Here Valgulio omits the three theological virtues, but retains his amended version of the four natural virtues (see again n. 26 above), and atones for his earlier omission of prudence (*prudentia*) by making this virtuous person learned (*doctus*).

[48] Irus is the beggar who in Homer's *Odyssey* 18. 1–7 aggressively confronts Odysseus on his return to Ithaca, and who is soundly thrashed in the subsequent boxing match. References to him by Latin authors as the embodiment of poverty include Propertius (3. 5. 17), Ovid (*Tristia* 3. 7. 42), and Martial (5. 39. 9); and in Erasmus's *Adages* — a work which Valgulio is likely to have known, perhaps in the enlarged edition printed by Aldus Manutius (Venice, 1508) — he and Codrus are cited (I. vi. 76) as proverbial opposites (*Iro, Codro pauperior*) of the plutocrats Croesus and Crassus (*Croeso, Crasso ditior*) just mentioned (I. vi. 74): see Erasmus, *Adages*, ed. and trans. R. A. B. Mynors, *The Collected Works of Erasmus* 32 (Toronto, Buffalo, and London: University of Toronto Press, 1989), 50–52. Cricca is not an identifiable name in this connection. We would

execratur, impium, iniustum, superbum, rapacem, avarum, crudelem, arrogantem et ignorantem[49] — sive ille sit eques, sive comes, sive etiam rex — tametsi contemptum illum odiumque illud vel spe vel metu commoti contegimus atque dissimulamus?

An non perspicitis et cogitatione reputatis vos, qui equestre istud aurum et comitatum tanti facitis, a quibus et quibus hominibus et quas ob causas insignia ista tradantur? Novi equidem multos privatos cives et — si diis placet! — simplices presbyteros aliquos (neque enim hoc dictum sit contemptus causa istorum civium, sed potius honoris: haud enim in praesentia hoc agitur), qui conferendi huiusmodi insignia facultatem habent — quin etiam faciendi quod neque Deus neque natura potuit: ut indocti sint doctores et vulgo procreati sint legitimi.[50] Quibus autem conferantur, quis ignorat? Nonne publicanis? Nonne testium dentiumque vulsoribus? Nonne tubicinibus et tibicinibus? Nonne etiam proditoribus? Nonne quibuscunque modo volentibus? Et nimirum rogatis et paene invitis aliquibus? Sed prudentes contemnunt vulgare munus: multi propter sumptum et servitutem famulorum comitantium quae requiritur illi muneri, ut non potius decora quam dedecora recte

grasping, greedy, cruel, insolent, and ignorant person[49] — whether he be knight, or count, or even king — although either hope or fear moves us to cover and cloak that contempt and hatred?

You who set so much store by that knightly gold and countship, do you not notice, and thoughtfully consider, by whom, on whom, and for what reasons those badges are conferred? I myself know many private citizens and — if you please! — some guileless priests (may this statement not convey contempt of those citizens, but rather honor: that is not the point at issue now), who have the power of awarding such badges — or rather, of doing what neither God nor nature has been able to do: making the unlearned learned, and bastards legitimate.[50] But who does *not* know what people they are awarded to? Is it not to tax farmers? Is it not to castrators and dentists? Is it not to trumpeters and flautists? Is it not to traitors too? Is it not to whoever are merely willing? And indeed to some who, when asked, are almost reluctant? But prudent people despise the vulgar gift: many because of the expense, and the slavery of attendant lackeys which that gift demands. Consequently, people of sound

---

expect Erasmus's Codrus who, poor but respectable, appears in Juvenal (3. 203–11). Another name for a typical pauper, however, is the Cinna who appears in Martial 8. 19. 1 (*Pauper videri Cinna vult, et est pauper*) and is coupled with Codrus in Ravisius Textor, *Officina* (Paris, 1532), fol. 283v, as examples 9–10 of "Pauperes" (Irus appears as example 1, fol. 283r). A third name — again found in Erasmus's *Adages* (II. ii. 78) — is Cinclus, referring primarily to a 'wagtail' which laid its eggs in other birds' nests because it was too poor to have its own, but secondarily (according to Erasmus) to a beggar or vagabond: see Erasmus, *Collected Works*, 33: 116. Perhaps Valgulio, relying on memory, mixed up all three names (Codrus, Cinna, and Cinclus) and 'invented' a fourth: Cricca.

[49] In his biggest rhetorical salvo of epithets — directed at Brescia's 'social climbers' and, by implication, at the clergy who tacitly encourage their aspirations — Valgulio includes four opposites of virtues he has just listed (see n. 47 above): *pius* changes to *impius*, *iustus* to *iniustus*, *misericors* to *crudelis*, and *doctus* to *ignorans*. To them he adds *superbus* and *arrogans* from his amended list of deadly sins (see n. 46 above), and *rapax* and *avarus* — epithets which between them remedy his previous omission of covetousness/greed.

[50] In other Italian city-states making bastards legitimate had been an important strategy for the ruling succession. See Jane Fair Bestor, "Marriage and Succession in the House of Este: A Literary Perspective," in *Phaeton's Children: The Este Court and its Culture in Early Modern Ferrara*, ed. D. Looney and D. Shemek, MRTS 286 (Tempe, ACMRS, 2005), 49–85.

iudicantibus insignia [sig. Avv] ista videri possint. Si cui vero doctrina, virtute et genere spectato viro conferantur (quales nonnulli in civitate nostra sunt), et qui contulit laudem meretur propter rectum iudicium et voluntatem honestandi honore dignos viros — non propter facultatem hanc conferendi insignia, sed quoniam cum habeat recte utatur ea — et is cui collata merito sunt, quasi praedicantibus et vere demonstrantibus insignibus virtutem viri, iure commendatur et honoratur — haud quidem propter insignia, sed quia ipse insignibus est dignus et honorem meretur. Et mea quidem sententia si quis insignia illa quaesiverit atque ambiverit, ac non potius oblata magno animo contempserit et modeste animo et verbis reiecerit, quamvis civili causa aliqua commotus tandem cesserit, vera in eo viro virtus esse putanda non est, propterea quod vera et solida virtus splendore et amplitudine sua contenta huiuscemodi exteriora signa contemnit. Quid vero sit de iis existimandum qui insigne virtutis propositum sine virtute habent, omnes nisi prorsus expertes rationis intelligunt. Perspicuum enim est nihil aliud eos agere quam quod decipiunt homines, haud aliter quam peregrinantes fallantur si quando, itinere diurno confecto, insigne diversoriae tabernae intuiti ad ipsam diverterunt atque ibi nihil pro se, nihil pro equo ad vescendum bibendumque repererunt. Nonne execrari et signum et eos qui ipsum adhibuere ad decipiendos[l] homines credibile est? Quas autem ob causas insignia ista conferantur, clarius notiusque est quam ut a me sit demonstrandum.

Quae cum ita sint, cognoscere potestis quanta insania sit et quam stolida superbia postulare atque expetere, ut vestra corpora pluris sint aestimanda quam aliorum et maioribus sumptibus funerum honoranda, et honorem ac laudem inde petere unde potius vituperationem et odium paretis. Nam nolle aequo iure et iisdem decretis atque institutis civitatis cuius partes ac membra estis cum caeteris vivere,[51] quid est aliud quam civilem congregationem dissolvere, et partes a suo toto et membra a suo corpore divellere, et ritu ferarum viribus et potentia fretos caeteris[m] velle dominari? Non vobis hoc statuto funerario tollitur potestas libertasve quantum vobis libet vestrarum divitiarum — veris

---

[l] *correxi*: decipiendas *cod.*
[m] *correxi*: caereris *cod.*

judgement may regard those badges of yours not as graces, but as disgraces. But if they were awarded to a man respected for his learning, virtue, and birth (there are plenty like this in our city), then the awarder deserves praise for his sound judgement and his desire to honor men worthy of honor — not for this power of awarding badges, but because he uses it properly when he has it — and the deserving awardee, since the badges proclaim and truly represent a man's virtue, is rightly praised and honored, not indeed by virtue of the badges, but because he himself is worthy of them and deserves honor. And, in my opinion, if anyone has sought and solicited those badges, rather than magnanimously despising them and modestly refusing the offer of them mentally and verbally, that man, even though some civic reason has finally moved him to give them up, must not be thought to have virtue, since true, sterling virtue is satisfied by its own radiance and abundance, and despises such outward symbols. Surely everyone who is not utterly irrational knows what to think of those who have virtue's sign on display but lack virtue. Obviously they do nothing but mislead people, just as travellers would be fooled if ever, at the end of a day's journey, they saw an inn-sign, stayed at the inn, and found there nothing for themselves or their horse to eat and drink. Is it not likely that they would curse both the symbol and those who used it to mislead people? As for the reasons why those badges are awarded, *that* is too clear and well-known to need any explanation from me.

These being the facts, you can gather what madness, what stubborn pride it is to demand and desire that your bodies should be more highly valued than other people's, and be honored by greater funeral expenditure, and to look for honor and praise from something which may bring you censure and hatred instead. For what is an unwillingness to live on equal terms with the rest, and according to the same decrees and ordinances of the city whose parts and members you are[51] — what else is it but a rupturing of civic association, a rending of parts from their whole, and of members from their body, and a desire to lord it over others as wild beasts do, relying on brute strength? This funerary law does not remove your power or your freedom to bestow as much of your wealth

---

[51] A shift of the Christian discourse (alluding to 1 Corinthians 12: 12–28) to the sphere of the city-state.

elemosynis et vera liberalitate pro anima vestra atque vestrorum — conferendi quibuscunque et quotienscunque, et innumeris aliis rationibus famam atque gloriam parandi, seu pro anima seu pro corpore, seu privatim seu publice sumptum facere libeat. Qui sumptus nulla lege nulloque statuto prohibetur, nec odium sed gratiam parat.

Nonne cernitis, cum operam datis stimulante devotissimo et humillimo et religioso viro isto[52] ut corpora vestra sensu et vita destituta omnique anima carentia caeteris humanis corporibus similibus vestris honore ac dignitate praestent (quae res est auditu monstrum horrendum ingens!),[53] vos plebem a qua honores ambitis a vobis alienam facere, et ad indignationem atque odium in vos concitare, ut ne viventibus quidem postea debitos honores sit exhibitura, aut — si sit — indignanti et execranti animo cum animadvertit tanta vos superbia inflatos, usque adeo se vilem et contemptam haberi a vobis, sub pedibusque vestris teneri, ut quod Deus, quod natura, quod ratio civilis, quod omnium hominum consensus et ipsorum sensuum veritas volunt — ut corpora videlicet humana paria et aequalia sint — vos, cum Deo et cum omnibus veritatibus pugnantes, imparia esse vultis? Nonne reputatis quae portenta misceatis, ut cadavera cadaveribus dignitate atque honore praestent quia, dum animata erant, insignita fallacissimis et mendacibus insignibus fortunae temerariae, caecae, instabilis et a nullo unquam sapiente viro cultae sed contemptae fuerant? At cum est quis functus vita, nec dives est nec comes nec eques, sed inops omnium rerum eius corpus est praeterquam ponderis et foetoris, atque etiam cum sol cuncta animata atque inanima et sordida quaeque intueatur et lustret,[54] vos vestra cadavera sub terram conditis, ut a sole cerni nequeant quo-[sig. Avir]rum honorem tantopere cupere videri vultis!

Si vestra cadavera usque adeo colenda esse putatis, atque aliis cadaveribus honoratiora esse oportere censetis, cur ea in aedibus vestris consuetis non retinetis? Cur exemplo effertis, et hora vobis annus videtur

as you wish on any people any number of times — in true almsgiving and true generosity for the benefit of your own souls and those of your loved ones — and to acquire fame and glory by countless other methods, whether you wish to spend money for the benefit of soul or body, whether in private or in public. Such expenditure is prevented by no law or statute, and brings favor, not hatred.

Do you not see that when, spurred on by *your* most devout, humble, and religious man,[52] you attempt to make your senseless, lifeless, and totally soulless bodies superior in honor and dignity to the rest of human bodies like yours (a gross aberration, terrible to hear of!),[53] you are alienating the common folk from whom you solicit honors, and inciting them to resent and hate you? Afterwards, as a result, they will not render due honors even to the living, or, if they do, it will be with resentment and abhorrence when they notice you puffed up with such pride, while they themselves are held so mean and despicable by you, and are so trampled under your feet, that you ignore the will of God, nature, social doctrine, universal opinion, and the truth of the very senses — that is, for human bodies to be of equal and uniform status — and, in opposition to God and all kinds of truth, wish them to be unequal. Do you not consider what weird ideas you are stirring up? That some corpses should be superior in dignity and honor to others because, while they lived, they had been marked by the lying and deceitful tokens of random, blind, and fickle fortune, which no wise man ever cherished but, rather, despised? When anyone has died, his body is neither rich, nor a count, nor a knight, but devoid of everything except its weight and stench, and even though the sun observes and surveys all living things *and* all lifeless and dirty ones,[54] you hide your bodies underground, making those for whose honor you wish to seem so eager invisible to the sun!

If you deem your corpses so worthy of respect, and think they should be more honored than others, why do you not keep them in your ordinary houses? Why do you take them for burial immediately, and an hour seems like a year to you in your impatience to have them removed from

---

[52] See n. 6 above.
[53] "monstrum horrendum ingens" is a tag from Vergil, *Aeneid* 4. 181.
[54] An allusion to Matthew 5: 45.

ut ex oculis vestris ablata sub terra opprimantur pastum futura vermibus, nec ea amplius unquam (ut dixi) invisitis, sed formidatis? Cur non, per Deum immortalem, indignamini inferiorum et pauperiorum civium corpora in eodem elemento humari quo vestra humantur? At nullum terra vilius est! Date igitur vos vestra reliquis elementis nobilioribus: nemo impediet honores vestros, nec ullum decretum vetabit eos; et si ab ipsis recipientur, universus tum orbis nihil cunctabitur veros adhibere honores et tanquam augustiora venerabitur et vere imparia existimabit. Date aquae: at ea repudiabit, ad littusque ac terram fluctibus reiiciet. Date aeri, si potestis: at multo ocius quam aqua ad terram deiiciet. Date igni: at quasi indignatus ac furens ea in cinerem conflabit humique restituet quod terrae erat.

Quare, obsecro vos, abiicite ex animo portentosas hiuiusmodi opiniones honorum ineptas ac falsas — sive sua sponte ortas in mentibus vestris sive a pseudo-fratribus aliquibus immissas — Deo, naturae hominibusque invisas; nec quaerite ubi esse non potest discrimen. Quod etsi pro vestra sententia atque postulatione daretur, orietur nihilominus quae nunc vos sollicitat eadem contentio — et forte acrior et scelestior. Nam et eques genere et maiorum nobilitate clarus indignabitur publicanum aut sordidi generis et instituti contemptibilis equitem exaequari sibi, et comites cum equitibus et inter se conditionibus variantibus differentias in sumptibus funerum aegre ferent comparari. Magnae enim et variae differentiae et distantiae atque discrimina in hoc hominum genere — auctoritatis, divitiarum, virtutis, rerum gestarum, vetustatis, et mille aliarum rerum — esse possunt: ut omnibus rationibus praestet iustissimo et aequissimo atque moderatissimo statuto obtemperare, tum ad famam et ad opinionem moderationis, tum ad crimen superbiae deprecandum, quod Deus super omnia crimina invisum habet et omnes homines a natura tanquam omnium scelerum nefandissimum summo odio persequuntur, tum etiam quoniam nihil aliud a vobis quaeri optarique manifestissime constat quam umbram et fumum honorum.

Existimabunt homines multos ex vobis magnis sumptibus fuisse funera celebraturos si statutum non obstitisset, qui tamen tenues et inopes fecissent vel si nihil offecisset et liberi sumptus fuissent. Sed, quaeso, an vobis parvus numerus sacerdotum videtur quattuor et viginti, quem

your sight and concealed underground as food for worms, nor (as I said) do you ever visit them again, but dread them? Why, for God's sake, do you not resent the burial of lowlier and poorer citizens' bodies in the same element as yours? None is meaner than earth! Give your bodies to the other, nobler elements: no one will obstruct your "honors", nor will any decree forbid them; and if your bodies are recovered from those elements, the whole world will lose no time in according them *true* honors, and will revere them as being more glorious, and consider them *truly* unequal. Give them to water: it will reject them, and with its waves cast them back to shore and earth. Give them to air, if you can: it will cast them back to earth faster than water will. Give them to fire: as if resentful and angry, it will reduce them to ash, and on the ground restore what belonged to earth.

So cast out of your heads, I beg you, such weird, silly, and mistaken ideas about honors, whether they have arisen spontaneously in your minds or been put there by certain false brothers, for they are hateful to God, nature, and mankind; and do not seek for a distinction where it cannot exist. Even if, as you desire and demand, it were allowed, the same competitiveness that now plagues you will be no less rampant: perhaps it will be fiercer and more villainous. A knight famed for his birth and noble ancestry will resent having a tax farmer, or a knight of low birth and vulgar manners, equated with himself, and counts will be vexed at being grouped with knights and with each other, as circumstances create changing differentials in funeral expenditure. Many and various are the differences, diversities, and distinctions that can exist within our human race, involving influence, wealth, virtue, achievements, age, and a thousand other things. It is therefore on all grounds preferable to obey an absolutely just, fair, and moderate law, in order both to win the name and cachet of moderation, and to try and avoid the sin of pride, which God hates above all sins, and which all people naturally pursue with utter hatred, as being the most heinous of all offences. A further reason is the perfectly plain truth that what you seek and desire is merely the shadow and semblance of honors.

People will think that many of you would have spent a great deal of money on funeral ceremonies if the law had not prevented it, though in fact their expenditure would have been small and scanty even if no obstacle to free spending had existed. But, I ask, does twenty-four seem to

numerum adhibere quisque ad comitandum funus potest concedente statuto? Numerusque quotuscunque signorum crucis conceditur: magnitudo tollitur, ne humeri multorum gestantium frangantur. Equidem existimo, si ulla in re decretum hoc peccat, in eo peccat quod numerum sacerdotum et signorum crucis concedit, propterea quod unus sacerdos unaque crux vicem et instar multorum obtinent. Nam verba quae ecclesia dicenda in humationibus praecipit, sive unus sacerdos sive plures ea dicant, tantundem valent, ut qui sacramentum regenerationis (hoc est, baptismi) atque alia sacramenta tradit: unus qui ea rite tradit perinde satisfacit atque si mille, quoniam momentum non est in numero, sed in mysterio. Et iussa ab uno praecone populo pronunciata aeque valent atque si ab innumeris pronunciarentur; et unus procurator sive patronus pro cliente opportuna in iudicio dicens tantundem in eo munere satisfacit atque si centum eodem nomine eadem et pro eodem in eademque causa dicerent. Supervacuus enim numerus est. Omne autem supervacuum viciosum esse constat, tam in moribus quam in natura — et hercule omnibus in re-[sig. Aviv]bus! Eadem ratio est de signis crucis. Nolimus igitur in huiusmodi sanctissimis, gravissimis divinisque mysteriis superbos et inanes et vanos honores sectari, ne Deum ac sanctos ad iram ultionemque provocemus. Dabuntur innumeris aliis modis temporibusque aptioribus opportunitates atque occasiones ostentandi magnitudinem animi vestri veram, si magnanimi estis — nam istaec omnino adversa contrariaque sunt huic admirandae virtuti,[55] quae tanto studio duce religiosi nominis et vestitus viro persequimini — et honores ac gloriam comparandi sine offensione Dei et absque fastidio hominum reliquorum.

Finis.

you a small number of priests, this being the maximum number the statute permits each person to bring as a funeral escort? And however small the number of ornamental crosses allowed, a large quantity is excluded in order to prevent the fracture of many bearers' shoulders. To my mind, if the decree errs in anything, it errs in permitting *a number* of priests and ornamental crosses: *one* priest and *one* cross represent and symbolize many. For whether the words prescribed by the Church to be said at burials are said by one priest or by several, they have the same force, just as with the person who mediates the sacrament of new birth (baptism, that is) and other sacraments: one person mediating them correctly gives as much satisfaction as if a thousand did so, for what matters is *numen*, not number. One preacher's public exhortations, too, are just as valid as if countless preachers made them; and one attorney or advocate pleading his client's case appropriately in court gives the same satisfaction in that role as if a hundred people with the same title were making the same plea for the same client in the same trial. *A number* of them is superfluous. But it is agreed that all superfluity is unhealthy, in morals as in nature — and indeed in everything! The same argument applies to ornamental crosses.

Let us not, therefore, in such sacred, solemn, and holy mysteries chase after proud, vain, and empty honors, lest we provoke God and the saints to wrath and retribution. In countless other ways, and at more suitable times, you will be given opportunities and occasions to display your true magnanimity if you *are* magnanimous — for *your* aims, which you pursue so eagerly at the behest of a man whose name and garb are religious, are diametrically opposed to this admirable virtue[55] — and to acquire honors and glory without offending God and disgusting the rest of mankind.

The End.

---

[55] The four virtues listed as components of "the honorable" (*honestum*) in Cicero's *De officiis* 1. 15–92 are wisdom (*sapientia / prudentia*), justice (*iustitia*), beneficence (*beneficentia*), and magnanimity (*magnitudo animi*). The last of these is equated with *fortitudo*, but only in the special Stoic sense of 'fighting for fairness': "Itaque probe definitur a Stoicis fortitudo cum eam virtutem esse dicunt propugnantem pro aequitate" (*De officiis* 1. 62). (See also n. 26 above.)

Appendix 1

Generalis rubrica de funeribus mortuorum.

General regulation for funerals of the dead.

Appendix I[1]

[sig. aviir] Generalis rubrica de funeribus mortuorum.

Ad evitandas damnosas expensas et inutiles consuetudines in exequiis mortuorum, aliqua persona non induatur vestibus lugubribus[2a] longis sive brevibus incapironatis in domo nec extra, exceptis ascendentibus et excepta uxore defuncti et filiis et abiaticis ex linea masculina et, ipsis deficientibus, fratre[b] pro fratre et nepote pro patruo et genero pro socero et patruo pro nepote et e converso, sub poena librarum 50 planetarum[3] cuilibet contrafacienti et etiam heredi ipsius defuncti auferenda, et communi Brixiano applicanda ut infra.

De eodem[4]

[sig. aviiv] Aliqua persona, cuiuscunque conditionis et dignitatis existat, non habeat nec habere possit ad exequias alicuius defuncti nisi duas cruces grossas, nec expendere ultra soldos quinque pro qualibet cruce, computata mercede[c] portatoris, excepta cruce parrochiae et exceptis crucibus parvis regularum fratrum ad dictas exequias euntium, quibus dari possint soldi duo tantum pro qualibet cruce parva; nec habere possit ultra clericos et religiosos viginti quattuor, non computatis illis qui portant cruces, sub poena praedicta auferenda heredi defuncti et applicanda ut infra.

---

    [a] *correxi*: lugrubibus *cod.*
    [b] *correxi*: frater *cod.*
    [c] *correxi*: marcede *cod.*

Appendix 1[1]

General regulation for funerals of the dead.

In order to avoid ruinous costs and useless customs at obsequies for the dead, no one is to dress in hooded mourning[2] clothes, whether long or short, either in the house or outside, except for older relatives, the deceased's wife, his sons, his grandsons on the male side and, if those be lacking, a brother for a brother, a nephew for an uncle, a son-in-law for a father-in-law, an uncle for a nephew, and vice versa: subject to a fine of fifty *lire planet*[3] to be obtained from any offender, and also from the deceased's own heir, and to be assigned to the Commune of Brescia as below.

On the same topic[4]

No one, whatever his rank and position, is to have or be able to have more than two big crosses at any deceased person's obsequies, or to pay more than five *soldi* for any cross, including the carrier's fee, except for the parish cross and the small crosses of the Friars Regular attending the said obsequies, who may be given just two *soldi* for any small cross; nor may one have more than twenty-four clergy and religious, not including those who carry the crosses: subject to the previously stated fine, to be obtained from the deceased's heir and assigned as below.

---

[1] The sources for the text of this statute are discussed in the Introduction, n. 1. The text given in the *Quaestio* differs in several respects, notably in the omission of *capituli* three, four, and five (as they appear here): see Appendix 2.

[2] The version of the statute given in the *Quaestio* (sig. av) specifies that the clothes are "black".

[3] The *lira planet* (*libra planeta*), divisible into eleven *soldi*, was the Brescian form of the Lombard *lira imperiale*. The version of the statute given in manuscript specifies a fine of thirty *lire planet*: ASB, ASC 1528, fol. 134r.

[4] This clause and the next are given in reverse order in the manuscript version of the statute: ASB, ASC 1528, fol. 134r.

De eodem

Aliqua persona habere non possit, quando portatur cadaver ad sepulturam, nisi quattuor candellabra et dopleros sex ponderis librae unius cum dimidia pro quolibet doplero circa capsam, nec dare clericis et religiosis ultra onzias quattuor cerae et soldos duos pro quolibet, exceptis canonicis, presbitero parrochiano, praepositis praedicatoribus, quibus dari possint dopleri de libra una pro quolibet et soldi quattuor et non ultra; nec expendere possit pro mercede palii sive paliorum ponendorum super capsam defuncti ultra soldos sex planetae, sub poena auferenda et applicanda ut infra.

De eodem

Aliqua persona civitatis Brixianae vel districtus, cuiusvis conditionis et status existat, non audeat nec praesumat facere aliqua convivia pro exequiis septimis seu tricesimis defunctorum, sub poena cuilibet facienti dicta convivia librarum viginti planetarum, et cuilibet eunti ad dicta convivia soldos viginti, nisi sit affinis attinens vel sacerdos, auferenda et applicanda ut supra.

De eodem

Aliqua persona in civitate nec in districtu non vadat post funera mortuorum flendo alta voce nec percuciendo palmas vel pectus, sub poena librarum quinque cuilibet contrafacienti auferenda et applicanda ut supra.

De eodem

Sindici communis Brixiani vel alter eorum teneantur et debeant, sub poena librarum decem planetarum pro quolibet et qualibet vice, inquirere et denunciare dominae potestati seu alteri iusdicenti in civitate Brixiana contrafacientes[d] suprascripto statuto, et instare quod dictae poenae

---

[d] *correxi*: contrafacienti *cod.*

General regulation for funerals of the dead

On the same topic

No one, when a corpse is carried out for burial, is to be able to have around the coffin more than four candle-stands and six candlesticks, with a weight of one-and-a-half pounds for any candlestick, or to give the clergy and religious more than four ounces of candle-wax and two *soldi* each, except for the canons, the parish priest, and the preachers-in-charge, who may each be given one-pound candlesticks and four *soldi*, and no more; nor may one pay as the price of a pall or palls to be placed over the deceased's coffin more than six *soldi* of a *lira planet*: subject to a fine, to be obtained and assigned as below.

On the same topic

No one from the city or district of Brescia, whatever his rank and station, is to dare or presume to organize any feasts for masses said on the seventh or thirtieth day after people's decease: subject to a fine of twenty *lire planet*, to be obtained from any organizer of the said feasts, and one of twenty *soldi* from any attender at them, unless he be a close relative or a priest, and to be assigned as above.

On the same topic

No one is to go about in the city or district after funerals of the dead weeping loudly or beating his hands or breast: subject to a fine of five *lire*, to be obtained from any offender and assigned as above.

On the same topic

The syndics of the commune of Brescia, or one or other of them, are to be committed and obliged, subject to a fine of ten *lire planet* for anyone and any occasion, to investigate, and denounce to the *podestà* or the other magistrate in the city of Brescia, those who offend against the foregoing

exigantur, prout supra in unoquoque ex suprascriptis capitulis continetur; de quibus omnibus poenis suprascriptis tres partes quattuor partium applicentur communi Brixiano, et reliqua quarta pars dictis sindicis vel alteri eorum, et nihilominus quilibet possit esse accusator et habeat dictam partem ipsis sindicis praemissa inquirere omittentibus.

statute, and to insist that the said fines be enforced, as specified above in each of the foregoing chapters; of all the foregoing fines three-quarters are to be assigned to the commune of Brescia, and the remaining quarter to the said syndics, or to one or other of them, and anyone may nevertheless be their accuser and have the said quarter if the syndics themselves neglect to investigate the matters just mentioned.

Appendix 2

Quaestio an infrascripta statuta super mortuariis sint contra ecclesiasticam libertatem.

An enquiry as to whether the statutes about death disbursements quoted below go against church freedom.

Appendix 2

[SIG. AR] Quaestio an infrascripta statuta super mortuariis sint contra ecclesiasticam libertatem.

Ad Dei omnipotentis et huius inclitae civitatis honorem et gloriam, necnon ad animorum timentium Deum serenitatem et pacem, discutiendum est sequens statutum: an sit contra libertatem Ecclesiae, et per consequens cum papali excommunicatione annexa super statuentes non solum in mortuariis sed etiam in omnibus aliis contra ecclesiasticam libertatem, et servari facientes, scriptores, potestates, consules, rectores, consiliarios locorum ubi statuta vel consuetudines huiusmodi eduntur vel servantur, iudicantes vigore talium statutorum, redigentes iudicata in publicam formam, et amoveri non facientes talia de libris suis, iuxta capitulum "Noverit", *De sententia excommunicationis*,[1] a qua sententia non excusat, secundum Panormitanum[2] ibi, quod in fine statutorum aliquando scribitur ("Quae sunt contra ecclesiasticam libertatem habeantur pro non scriptis").

In cuius statuti examinatione ita procedetur. Nam primo posito statuto et tribus capitulis decretalis in quibus haec materia continetur, ponentur rationes ad partem falsam. Secundo veritas determinabitur. Tertio

Appendix 2

An enquiry as to whether the statutes about death disbursements quoted below go against church freedom.

For the honor and glory of almighty God and this renowned city, and also for the tranquility and peace of the minds that fear God, we must discuss the following statute: whether it goes against the Church's freedom, and consequently involves the papal excommunication incurred by those who make statutes against church freedom not only in regard to death disbursements but also in all other matters, by those who ensure their observance, by the scribes, podestà, consuls, rectors, and councilors of the places where these types of statutes or customs are promulgated or observed, by those who make judgments by the force of such statutes, those who issue the judgments in a public form, and those who do not have such statutes removed from their books. This is in accordance with the chapter "Noverit" of *On the sentence of excommunication*,[1] exemption from which sentence is not provided, as Nicholas de Tudeschis[2] says apropos, by what is sometimes written at the end of statutes ("Things that go against church freedom shall be held not to have been written").

The following method will be adopted in examining this statute. After the statute and three chapters of the decree containing this material have first been stated, the arguments for the wrong view will be stated. Secondly, the truth will be ascertained. Thirdly, the opposing arguments

---

[1] See n. 5 below.

[2] Niccolò de' Tudeschis (1386–1445), alias Abbas Siculus (born in Sicily, he became an abbot there in 1425) or Panormitanus (he was archbishop of Palermo from 1435), wrote extensively on canon law, including commentaries on the *Decretals of Gregory IX*, on the *Sext*, and on the *Clementines*: DDC 6: 1195–1215.

respondebitur rationibus oppositis. In hac autem quaestione Deus et sancti omnes invocantur ut haec scribentes [nihilo se] moveri nisi veritatis amore et culpae formidine arbitrentur omnes. Unde non minori studio in quaerendis oppositis rationibus quam in ve-[sig. av]ris scrutandis laboratum est quanta potuit fieri celeri fidelitate, praesertim quum mora omnis damnosa sit quando homines in peccato et excommunicatione detineantur.

Postquam (statuto incipiente) "ad evitandas damnosas expensas" prohibitum fuit "sub poena" quod non induantur de nigro in exequiis nisi tales personae, subiungitur aliud statutum in haec verba formaliter.

Statuta Brixiae super mortuariis.

Aliqua persona, cuiuscunque conditionis et dignitatis existat, non habeat nec habere possit ad exequias alicuius defuncti nisi duas cruces grossas, nec expendere ultra solidos quinque pro qualibet cruce, computata mercede portatoris, excepta cruce parochiae et exceptis crucibus parvis Regularum Fratrum ad dictas exequias euntium, quibus dari possint solidi duo tantum pro qualibet cruce parva; nec habere possit ultra clericos et religiosos viginti quatuor, non computatis illis qui portant cruces: sub poena praedicta, auferenda heredi defuncti et applicanda ut infra.

Aliqua persona habere non possit, quando portatur cadaver ad sepulturam, nisi quatuor candelabra et dopleros sex ponderis librae unius cum dimidia pro quolibet doplero circa capsam, nec dare clericis et religiosis [sig. aiir] ultra ontias quatuor cerae et solidos duos pro quolibet, exceptis canonicis, presbytero parochiano, praepositis praedicatoribus, quibus dari possint dopleri de libra una pro quolibet, et solidi quatuor et non ultra; nec expendere possit pro mercede palii sive paliorum ponendorum super capsam defuncti ultra solidos sex planetarum: sub poena auferenda et applicanda ut infra.

An enquiry as to whether the statutes 157

will be answered. In this enquiry, however, God and all the saints are called on to ensure that all those who write these things down believe they are influenced by nothing but love of truth and fear of blame. Hence no less trouble has been taken to consider the opposing arguments than to probe the true ones as speedily and reliably as possible, especially since all delay is harmful when people are in the grip of sin and excommunication.

After (at the beginning of the statute) "in order to avoid ruinous costs" it has been forbidden "subject to a fine" to dress in black at burials, except for specified people, another statute is added, in the following formal phrasing.

Brescia's statutes about death disbursements.

No one, whatever his rank and position, is to have or be able to have more than two big crosses at any deceased person's obsequies, or to pay more than five *soldi* for any cross, including the carrier's fee, except for the parish cross and the small crosses of the Friars Regular attending the said funeral, who may be given just two *soldi* for any small cross; nor may one have more than twenty-four clergy and religious, not including those who carry the crosses: subject to the previously stated fine, to be obtained from the deceased's heir and assigned as below.

No one, when a corpse is carried out for burial, is to be able to have around the coffin more than four candle-stands and six candlesticks, with a weight of one-and-a-half pounds for any candlestick, or to give the clergy and religious more than four ounces of candle-wax and two *soldi* each, except for the canons, the parish priest, and the preachers-in-charge, who may each be given one-pound candlesticks and four *soldi*, and no more; nor may one pay as the price of a pall or palls to be placed over the deceased's coffin more than six *soldi* of a *lira planet*: subject to a fine, to be obtained and assigned as below.

Decretales adversus statuentes contra ecclesiasticam libertatem.

Innocentius tertius, [*Liber*] *extra,* De constitutionibus: **capitulum "Ecclesia Sanctae Mariae."**[3]

"Ecclesia Sanctae Mariae" et infra: "Nos attendentes, quod laicis — etiam religiosis — super ecclesiis et personis ecclesiasticis nulla sit attributa facultas, quos obsequendi manet necessitas, non auctoritas imperandi, a quibus, si quid motu proprio statutum fuerit, quod ecclesiarum etiam respicit commodum et favorem, nullius firmitatis existit, nisi ab ecclesia fuerit approbatum . . ." Haec ibi.

Idem in concilio generali, [*Liber*] *extra,* De rebus Ecclesiae non alienandis: **capitulum finale.**[4]

"Cum laicis — quamvis religiosis — disponendi de rebus Ecclesiae nulla sit attributa potestas, quos subsequendi manet necessitas, non auctoritas imperandi: dolemus in quibusdam ex illis sic refrigescere caritatem, quod immunitatem ecclesiasticae libertatis, quam non tantum sancti patres, [sig. aiiv] sed etiam principes saeculares privilegiis multis munierunt,[a] non formidant suis constitutionibus — vel potius destitutionibus — impugnare, non solum de alienatione feudorum ac aliarum possessionum ecclesiasticarum, et usurpatione iurisditionum, sed etiam de mortuariis, necnon et aliis, quae iuri spirituali annexa videntur, illicite praesumendo. Volentes igitur super his indemnitatibus consulere ecclesiarum ac tantis gravaminibus providere, constitutiones et venditiones huiusmodi feudorum seu aliorum bonorum ecclesiasticorum sine legitimo personarum ecclesiasticarum assensu praesumptas occasione

---

[a] *correxi*: minuerunt *cod.*

The decretals aimed at those who make statutes against church freedom.

Innocent III, [*Liber*] *extra*, *On ordinances*: the chapter "Ecclesia Sanctae Mariae"[3]

"Ecclesia Sanctae Mariae" and below: "We note that laypeople — even devout ones — have been given no power over churches and church members, laypeople who still have the obligation to obey, not the authority to command; and any statute which they make on their own initiative and which also impinges on the convenience and favorable treatment of churches has no standing unless it has been approved by the Church . . ." These are the words used.

The same pope in the general council, [*Liber*] *extra*, *On not alienating the Church's property*: final chapter.[4]

"Since laypeople, however devout, have been given no power to deal with church property — for they still have the obligation to conform, not the authority to command — it irks us when love grows so cold in some of them that by their enactments (or rather annulments) they fearlessly attack the immunity of church freedom, which not merely holy fathers but even secular princes have buttressed with many privileges. This they do by their unlawful presumption, not only in alienating fiefs and other church possessions and in appropriating jurisdictions, but also in regard to death disbursements, and other things too, which are seen as adjuncts of spiritual authority. Wishing, therefore, to safeguard these immunities of churches and to provide against troubles so great, with the sacred council's approval we rule that such enactments and sales of fiefs or other church goods, taken up without the formal consent of ecclesiastics and

---

[3] X 1. 2. 10; *CIC* 2: 12–14.

[4] X 3. 13. 12; *CIC* 2: 516; *Decrees of the Ecumenical Councils*, ed. N. P. Tanner, S. J., 2 vols. (London and Washington, DC: Sheed & Ward and Georgetown University Press, 1990), 1: 254 (referring to the Fourth Lateran Council of 1215).

constitutionis laicae potestatis, cum non constitutio, sed destitutio vel destructio dici possit, necnon usurpatio iurisditionum, sacri approbatione concilii decernimus non tenere, praesumptoribus per censuram ecclesiasticam compellendis." Haec ibi.

Honorius tertius, [*Liber*] *extra, De sententia excommunicationis:* **capitulum "Noverit."**[5]

"Noverit fraternitas tua" et infra: "Excommunicamus omnes haereticos utriusque sexus, quocunque nomine censentur, et fautores et receptatores et defensores eorum, necnon et qui decetero servari fecerint statuta edita et consuetudines introductas contra Ecclesiae libertatem, nisi ea de capitularibus suis infra duos menses post huiusmodi publicationem sententiae fecerint amoveri. Item excommunicamus statutarios[b] et scriptores statutorum ipsorum, necnon potestates, consules, rectores et consiliarios locorum ubi decetero huiusmodi statuta et consuetudines editae fuerint vel servatae, necnon [sig. aiiir] et illos qui secundum ea praesumpserint iudicare, vel in publicam formam scribere iudicata." Haec ibi.

Rationes falsae ad probandum quod suprascripta statuta non sunt contra ecclesiasticam libertatem.

Quod valeant, arguitur rationibus Albrici de Rosate Bergomensis advocati[6] in opere *Quaestionum circa statuta* (parte secunda, circa principium), subtilissime adductis et[c] profundissime et optime per eum solutis.[7] Quae et in parte vulgo adducuntur, omissis ipsius Albrici allegationibus brevitatis causa: quas videre poterunt qui voluerint in dicto opere, nil ultra concludentes quam hic sit expressum, fundamentis rationum inhaerendo.

---

    [b] *correxi:* statuarios *cod.*
    [c] *correxi:* ad *cod.*

achieved by a lay power's enactment, do not hold, since it cannot be called an enactment — rather, an act of annulment or annihilation, and indeed an appropriation of jurisdictions. Those responsible for these things must be coerced by the Church's censure." These are the words used.

Honorius III, [*Liber*] *extra*, On the sentence of excommunication: the chapter "Noverit."[5]

"Noverit fraternitas tua" and below: "We excommunicate all heretics of both sexes, whatever category they fall into, and those who support, shelter, and protect them: also those who at other times ensure the observance of statutes which have been promulgated and customs which have been introduced against church freedom, unless they have them removed from their statute-books within two months after the publication of such a decision. Also we excommunicate those who make the statutes and those who write them down, and also the podestà, consuls, rectors, and councilors of the places where at other times such statutes and customs have been promulgated or observed, and also those who have presumed to make judgments based on them, or to write down the judgments in a public form." These are the words used.

False arguments to prove that the above statutes do not go against church freedom.

The claim that they are valid uses arguments of Alberico da Rosate, the lawyer of Bergamo,[6] in his work of *Enquiries about Statutes* (second part, near the beginning) — arguments very precisely adduced, and very thoroughly and excellently demolished by him.[7] And in fact they are given a partial public airing, with the omission (for brevity's sake) of the same Alberico's citations: those who so wish will be able to see these in the said work, and they imply no more than is stated here, concentrating on the core of his arguments.

---

[5] X 5. 39. 49; *CIC* 2: 910.
[6] See *Defense*, n. 8.
[7] Albericus de Rosciate, *Super statutis* (Venice, 1497), 2. 2, sigs. d6r–d8v.

Et primo pro parte quam tenet falsam sic arguit:
Quod agitur pro reipublicae conservatione ab hiis qui praesunt civitati tenet et robur habet: sed praedictum statutum est pro conservatione reipublicae et ad tollendas damnosas expensas. Ergo valet.

Secundo:
Non est minor auctoritas civitatis quam personarum privatarum: sed privatae personae possunt apponere conditiones diversas in contractibus. Ergo et in mortuariis; ergo et civitas hoc idem potest.

Tertio:
Per ius commune potest fieri statutum propter publicam utilitatem, ne fiat commercium certarum rerum cum personis non subditis. Ergo et per statutum, nec tamen censetur con-[sig. aiiiv]tra libertatem Ecclesiae. Ergo a simili de statuto praemisso.

Quarto:
Illa lex non videtur posse dici contra libertatem Ecclesiae, per quam subditi saeculares limitantur circa res suas, etiam si ex tali limitatione inducatur privatio lucri ecclesiasticarum personarum: sed statutum praemissum est huiusmodi. Ergo, etc.

Quinto:
Libertas est naturalis facultas eius quod cuique facere libet, nisi quod vi aut iure prohibetur, ut *Institutiones, De iure personarum*.[8] Ergo, quando non fit contra praedicta, non fit contra libertatem. Sed per statutum praedictum circa funera ponitur frenum tantum laicis et eorum rebus, quod est in naturali facultate communitatis; nec est attendendum quod ex consequenti sequatur, sed debet attendi principalis causa statuti. Ergo, etc. Item non prohibetur iure, quia hoc ius ad clericos non extenditur, sed ad saeculares. Non vi, quia quod non veniant nisi tot clerici, et non detur eis nisi tantum, non ex vi illata rebus, iuribus, aut personis

First, he puts this point in favor of the view he considers wrong:

What is done by those in charge of the city to preserve the state holds good and has power: but the aforesaid statute aims to preserve the state and to abolish ruinous costs. It is therefore valid.

Second:

The city's authority is no less than that of private persons: but private persons can impose various conditions for contracts. Therefore they can also do so for death disbursements; therefore the city can also do this.

Third:

Common law allows a statute to be made in the public interest, in order to prevent traffic in certain commodities with persons who are not subjects. Therefore statute law also allows it, nor is it deemed contrary to the Church's freedom. Similarly, therefore, with the foregoing statute.

Fourth:

A law which imposes restrictions on lay subjects' own property cannot, it seems, be called contrary to the Church's freedom even if such restrictions led to a loss of profit for ecclesiastics: but the foregoing statute is of this type. Therefore . . . etc.

Fifth:

Freedom is the natural power of doing what each person pleases, except what is prevented by force or by law, as stated in the *Institutes*, *On the law of persons*.[8] Anything, therefore, that does not go against those principles does not go against freedom. But the aforesaid statute about funerals curbs only laypeople and their property, as is within the natural power of a society; nor should one look at what may follow as a consequence: rather, the main reason for the statute should be looked at. Therefore . . . etc. Likewise, freedom is not prevented by law, because *this* law does not affect clergy, only laypeople.

Force is not an issue, because the stipulation that only *so* many clergy are to come, and that they be given only *so* much, does not result from force used against property, rights, or persons, but is due to laypeople's

---

[8] *Inst.* 1. 3. 1; *Justinian's Institutes*, trans. with an intro. by P. Birks and G. McLeod, with the Latin text of P. Krueger (London: Duckworth, 1987), 38–39 (*CICv* 1: 2). (Cf. n. 21 below.)

ecclesiasticis contingit, sed quia laici nolunt plures vocare: quod nolle manifestatur per statutum civium voluntate factum, a quo resiliri per singulos non potest, nisi novum condendo statutum.

Sexto:
Non videtur fieri aliquid animo iniuriandi nisi probetur, ubi etiam intervenit alicuius personae lucri pri-[sig. aivr]vatio, sed probari non potest cives animo iniuriandi fecisse statutum. Ergo non est dicendum hoc animo factum fuisse: quod si hoc animo non est factum, non videtur esse contra libertatem Ecclesiae.

Septimo:
Licitum in persona propria debet in alia licitum reputari: sed Ecclesia aequum putat ne bona clericorum devolvantur ad saeculares. Ergo etiam aequum putare debet ne saecularium bona devolvantur ad clericos in funeribus vel aliis casibus.

Octavo:
Statutum invitat ad bonum, quod est ne clerici ad exequias tanquam ad bonum et magnum lucrum pecuniarum vadant, et ad avaritiam provocentur. Ergo est licitum.

Nono:
Non est contra libertatem Ecclesiae quod non est contra eius privilegia: sed statutum afficit laicos tantum, non autem clericos vel eorum privilegia, ut videtur. Ergo, etc.

Decimo:
Ex ordine caritatis sibi ipsi prius subveniendum est quam aliis. Quum ergo fiat hoc ad sibi ipsis prius subveniendum et pro communi bono, videtur esse non contra Ecclesiae libertatem, sed secundum caritatis ordinem.

Haec sunt media tacta per dictum Dominum Albricum proposita pro parte negativa, quam tenet falsam: videlicet, quod non [sig. aivv] sit hoc statutum contra libertatem Ecclesiae. Ad quae omnia respondebitur infra per ordinem.

An enquiry as to whether the statutes

unwillingness to summon more — an unwillingness clearly shown by the statute made at the wish of the citizens, from which there can be no shrinking back by individuals, unless a new statute is enacted.

Sixth:
Nothing is deemed to be done with the intention of causing injury unless this be proved, even when the loss of someone's profit occurs, but it cannot be proved that the citizens made a statute with the intention of causing injury. Therefore it should not be said to have been made with this intention: but if it was not made with this intention, it is not deemed contrary to the Church's freedom.

Seventh:
What is lawful for a particular person must be considered lawful for another: but the Church thinks it fair that the goods of clergy should not fall into laypeople's hands. Therefore it must also think it fair that laypeople's goods should not fall into the hands of clergy at funerals or in other situations.

Eighth:
The statute encourages something good: that clerics should not attend funerals as a source of good, big financial profit, and be roused to rapacity. Therefore it is lawful.

Ninth:
What does not go against the Church's privileges does not go against its freedom: but the statute affects laypeople only, and not clergy or their privileges, as it seems. Therefore . . . etc.

Tenth:
The normal practice of charity is that one should help oneself before others. Since, therefore, this action is being taken for the citizens to help themselves first, and for the common good, it seems not to go against the Church's freedom but to accord with the normal practice of charity.

These are the assertions neutrally mentioned by the said Master Alberico in favor of the negative view which he considers wrong: namely, that this statute does not go against the Church's freedom. They will all be answered in order below.

Undecimo:

Arguitur ultra praedicta per textum iuris, capitulum "Animae defunctorum", ubi dicitur quod pompae exequiarum magis sunt solatia vivorum quam subsidia mortuorum, et est textus, [*Causa*] *xiii, quaestio ii*:[9] quem textum videre velint omnes, quia optime seipsum declarat, ut etiam infra patebit.

Duodecimo:

Arguitur etiam per auctoritatem Abbatis, quae hactenus quaesita nusquam potuit inveniri: dicunt enim quidam Abbatem ita sentire, cuius contrarium infra declarabitur.

Tertiodecimo:

Arguitur etiam ex dicto cuiusdam Rosellae sive Baptistinae Ordinis Minorum,[10] titulo *De excommunicatione*, paragrapho decimo-octavo,[11] quae [*sic*] videtur tenere quod ad resecandas pompas fieri possit statutum super mortuariis, nil aliud allegans quam Abbatem in quodam consilio incipiente, stante quadam constitutione, ubi ponit casum utrum sit contra libertatem Ecclesiae statutum disponens quod mater possit de bonis mobilibus ad pias causas pro tertia parte pro libito erogare, residuum autem tenebatur relinquere filiis. Ubi dicit dicta Rosella Abbatem concludere quod non est contra libertatem Ecclesiae.

An enquiry as to whether the statutes

Eleventh:

As well as the aforesaid points, a further claim rests on a legal text — the chapter "Animae defunctorum" — where it is said that mourners' processions give more comfort to the living than aid to the dead. The text is in [*Case*] *13, question 2*:[9] everyone may wish to see this text, for it is self-explanatory, as will also be seen below.

Twelfth:

A further claim rests on a pronouncement of De Tudeschis which a search has so far failed to find anywhere: some people say it is his view, but the opposite will be shown below.

Thirteenth:

A further claim stems from a statement by one Rosella or Battistina, of the Order of Friars Minor,[10] entitled *On excommunication* (par. 18).[11] He seems to maintain that a statute about death disbursements could be made so as to prune extravagance, citing only De Tudeschis: at the start of a certain debate, when a certain ordinance was in force, he posed the question whether a statute goes against the Church's freedom in enabling a mother to spend, if she wishes, the equivalent of a third of her movable goods on sacred causes, while being obliged to leave the rest to her children. The said Rosella states De Tudeschis's conclusion that it does not go against church freedom.

---

[9] C. 13 q. 2 c. 22; *CIC* 1: 728: "The souls of the departed are released in four ways: by the offerings of priests, by the prayers of saints, by the alms of loved ones, or by the fasting of relatives. Funeral arranging, burial preparation, a mourners' procession, do indeed give more comfort to the living than aid to the dead. If a costly burial is of some benefit to an ungodly person, a cheap burial — or none at all — will disadvantage a godly one. And yet the bodies of the departed, especially those of the righteous, are not for that reason to be scorned and cast away. There is a further saving lesson here: how great can be the recompense for alms we bestow on those with life and feeling, if even such service as in conscientiously rendered to people's lifeless limbs is not lost on God." Cf. above, xxxiii, 43.

[10] Baptista Trovamala de Salis (d. 1496), the Observant Franciscan who in 1483 completed *Summa Casuum Conscientiae* (a manual for confessors), the second edition of which, *Rosella Casuum* or *Summa Rosella* (Pavia and Venice, 1489) was much used well into the sixteenth century.

[11] *Summa Rosella* (Venice, 1495 edition), par. 18, fols. 180r–181v, in particular fol. 181r–v; *DDC* 2: 201–3.

Quartodecimo:

Arguitur per opinionem Bartholi[12] in lege finali *De pactis*,[13] qua tenet quod ingrediens religionem possit testari, et quod sta-[sig. br]tutum disponens quod non valeat testari non sit contra libertatem Ecclesiae, et quod si darent ingressus, tunc statutum non valeret. Ex quo aliquod argumentum videtur trahi posse, quod saeculares possint disponere de rebus Ecclesiae, quae tamen in praesentiarum non sint de Ecclesia.

Quintodecimo:

Arguitur quod servatur hoc statutum in quibusdam — licet paucis — civitatibus.

Determinatio per rationes quod praedicta statuta sunt contra ecclesiasticam libertatem.

Post falsas rationes adductas sequitur determinatio veritatis, quod erat secundo loco propositum.

Et primo praemitto, quod civitas potest constringere suos subditos, non autem personas ecclesiasticas, neque de eorum bonis temporalibus sive spiritualibus et spiritualibus annexis disponere, quia sunt omnino ab eorum iurisditione exempti, ut in capitulo "Ecclesia Sanctae Mariae," *De constitutionibus*,[14] et in capitulo "Cum laicis," *De rebus Ecclesiae non alienandis*,[15] cum similibus.

Secundo praemitto, quod inferior non potest statuere contra superiorem: [*Constitutiones*] *Clementinae*, "Ne Romani" in principio, *De*

An enquiry as to whether the statutes

Fourteenth:

A claim rests on the opinion of Bartolo[12] about the final law *On pacts*:[13] he maintains that someone entering the religious life can make a will, that a statute depriving him of the power to make one does not go against the Church's freedom, and that if [the statute-makers] granted that he *could* make one after entering, then the statute would be invalid. From this it seems possible to draw some evidence that laypeople could deal with church property which at the time, however, is no concern of the Church.

Fifteenth:

It is claimed that this statute is observed in certain — albeit few — cities.

Reasoned ascertainment that the aforesaid statutes do go against church freedom.

Citation of false arguments is followed by ascertainment of the truth, which was allotted second place.

By way of preface, I say first that a city can restrain its own subjects but not ecclesiastics, nor can it make rules about their temporal, spiritual, and spiritually-connected goods, for they are fully exempt from civil jurisdiction, as stated in the chapter "Ecclesia Sanctae Mariae" of *On ordinances*,[14] and in the chapter "Cum laicis" of *On not alienating the Church's property*,[15] together with similar statements.

My second prefatory remark is that an inferior cannot legislate against a superior, as stated in the *Clementines* (at the beginning of the

---

[12] The famous jurist Bartolo of Sassoferrato (ca. 1313–1357): see F. Calasso, "Bartolo da Sassoferrato," *DBI*, 6: 640–69. One of his *Aureae quaestiones* (Venice, 1471, unpaginated) is: "Quidam reliquit vel donavit aliquam rem monacho ea conditione & hoc pacto ut monasterio suo nullum ius acquiratur." (He disputed this in Perugia, February 1356.)

[13] X 1. 35. 8; *CIC* 2: 205–6: "Pactiones factae a vobis, ut audivimus, pro quibusdam spiritualibus obtinendis, quum in huiusmodi omnis pactio omnisque conventio debeat omnino cessare, nullius penitus sunt momenti . . ." etc.

[14] See n. 3 above.

[15] See n. 4 above.

electione,[16] in capitulo "Cum inferior," *De maioritate et obedientia*,[17] in capitulo "Inferior," *xxi Distinctio*,[18] cum concordantiis.

Tertio praemitto, quod illud statutum dicitur esse contra libertatem ecclesiasticam quod est contra privilegia indul-[sig. bv]ta Ecclesiae universali sive a Domino Deo, sive a papa, sive ab imperatore, secundum doctrinam Innocentii et omnium scribentium in dicto capitulo "Noverit," per Bartholum et alios in *Auctentica* ("Cassa"), *Codice, De sacrosanctis ecclesiis*.[19] Et Dominus Felinus[20] in capitulo "Noverit" circa finem ita inquit: "Et dicas generaliter quod illud statutum dicatur contra ecclesiasticam libertatem, per quod prohibetur personis ecclesiasticis illud quod neque de iure divino neque humano est prohibitum, quia ita suadet diffinitio libertatis, quae dicitur esse naturalis facultas faciendi quod alicui libet, nisi a iure prohibeatur: lex 'Libertas', *Digesta, De statu hominum*."[21] Quod bene nota; et addo ad maiorem declarationem, quod unum de privilegiis Ecclesiae est ipsam esse capacem ut possit ei donari in infinitum absque aliqua insinuatione, ut *Auctentica, De non alienandis aut permutandis rebus Ecclesiae*, paragrapho "Si minus" [*recte*, "Sinimus"],

chapter "Ne Romani" of *On election*),[16] in the chapter "Cum inferior" of *On superiority and obedience*,[17] and in the chapter "Inferior" of *Distinction 21*,[18] together with parallel instances.

My third prefatory remark is that the statute is said to go against church freedom because it goes against the privileges and indults granted to the universal Church, whether by the Lord God, or by the pope, or by the emperor, according to the doctrine of Innocent and all those commenting on the said chapter "Noverit", and as stated by Bartolo and others in the *Authenticum* (under "Cassa"), referring to the law of the *Code, On the inviolability of churches*.[19] Also Master Felino,[20] towards the end of his commentary on the chapter "Noverit", says this: "And you would normally say that a statute is called contrary to church freedom if it causes ecclesiastics to be prevented from doing what is prevented by no divine or human law, for that is what the definition of freedom suggests: it is described as the natural power of doing what anyone pleases to do unless it is prevented by law, as stated in the law 'Libertas' of the *Digest, On human status*."[21] Note this well; and, to make it clearer, I add that one of the Church's privileges is that it is big enough to enable gifts to be given to it unrestrictedly without any deviousness, as stated in the *Authenticum, On not alienating or exchanging church property*, in the paragraph "Si

---

[16] *Clem.* 1. 3. 2; *CIC* 2: 1135: "Ne Romani electioni Pontificis indeterminata opinionum diversitas aliquod possit obstaculum vel dilationem afferre: nos, inter cetera praecipue attendentes, quod lex superioris per inferiorem tolli non potest, ..." etc.

[17] X 1. 33. 16; *CIC* 2: 202: "Quum inferior superiorem solvere nequeat vel ligare, sed superior inferiorem liget regulariter et absolvat, et satis absonum videatur, ut filius potestatem habeat in parentem, ..." etc.

[18] D. 21. c. 4; *CIC* 1: 70: "Inferior sedes potiorem absolvere non potest. Sola enim potior inferiorem convenienter absolvit. Hinc liquido providetur, quia quem non potest absolvere, nec potest iudicio inferior potiorem ligare."

[19] See n. 33 below. Bartolo's comments are found in his *Super autenticis* (Nuremberg, 1481), collatio ii, *De non alienandis aut permutandis rebus ecclesiae*, under the rubric "Sinimus". (See also n. 22 below.)

[20] Felino Maria Sandeo (1444–1503), successively bishop of Penna and Atri, and of Lucca; also author of a commentary on the Gregorian decretals.

[21] *Dig.* 1. 5. 4 pr.; *The Digest of Justinian* (hereafter *DJ*), ed. T. Mommsen, P. Krueger, and A. Watson, 4 vols. (Philadelphia: University of Pennsylvania Press, 1985), 1: 15 (*CICv* 1: 35). (Cf. n. 8 above.)

Collatio ii.[22] Qui ergo prohibet illi fieri donationem, aut limitat nisi tantum dari aut donari posse, excusari non potest quod non veniat contra ecclesiasticam libertatem de directo, et non per accidens tantum aut indirecte.

His praemissis, nunc ad probationes transeundum est. Et probatur dictum statutum offendere ecclesiasticam libertatem, habitam:

a iure divino;

a iure imperatorio;

a iure pontificio;

a praeclarissimorum doctorum communi iudicio.

Ad primum, probatur dictum statutum esse contra ius divinum, quo iure indistincte et sine ulla limitatione suadetur [sig. biir] et aliquando praecipitur elemosina fieri indigentibus et in animae remedium: *Tobiae* quarto ("Elemosina ab omni peccato liberat, et morte");[23] *Danielis* quarto ("Peccata tua elemosinis redime");[24] *Lucae* xi ("Date elemosinam et, ecce, omnia munda sunt vobis");[25] item *Tobiae* iiii ("Panem tuum cum egenis comede");[26] [*Ad*] *Hebraeos* xiii ("Beneficentiae et communionis nolite oblivisci, talibus enim hostiis promeretur deus");[27] *Tobiae* iiii ("Ex substantia tua fac elemosinam, et ne avertas faciem tuam ab

An enquiry as to whether the statutes   173

minus" [*recte*, "Sinimus"] of *Collection 2*.²² Whoever, therefore, prevents a gift being given to it, or restricts the gift given or received to only *so much*, cannot be excused on the ground that he does not oppose church freedom directly, as distinct from just accidentally or indirectly.

After these prefatory remarks, we must now move on to the proofs, and it is proved that the said statute tramples on church freedom, which derives:

from divine law;
from imperial law;
from pontifical law;
from the shared judgment of the most illustrious doctors.

As to the first point, it is proved that the said statute goes against divine law which, with no distinction and without any restriction, urges and sometimes enjoins the giving of alms to help the needy and as balm for the soul: *Tobit*, chap. 4 ("Almsgiving delivers from every sin and from death");²³ *Daniel*, chap. 4 ("Atone for your sins with almsgiving");²⁴ *Luke*, chap. 11 ("Give alms and, look, everything is clean for you");²⁵ likewise *Tobit*, chap. 4 ("Share your bread with those who are hungry");²⁶ *Hebrews*, chap. 13 ("Do not forget to do good and to share things, for God is reconciled by such sacrifices");²⁷ *Tobit*, chap. 4 ("Draw from your substance to give alms, and do not turn your face from any

---

²² *Nov.* 7. 2. 1; *CICv* 3: 53: "Sinimus igitur imperio, si qua communis commoditas est et ad utilitatem reipublicae respiciens causa et possessionem exigens talis alicuius immobilis rei qualem proposuimus, hoc ei a sanctissimis ecclesiis et reliquis venerabilibus domibus et collegiis percipere licere, undique sacris domibus indemnitate servata et recompensanda re eis ab eo qui percepit aequa aut etiam maiore, quam data est. Quid enim causetur imperator, ne meliora det? cui plurima deus dedit habere et multorum dominum esse et facile dare, et maxime in sanctissimis ecclesiis, in quibus optima mensura est donatarum eis rerum immensitas."

²³ Tobit 4:11.
²⁴ Daniel 4:24.
²⁵ Luke 11:41.
²⁶ Tobit 4:17.
²⁷ Hebrews 13:16.

ullo paupere"[28] — quod bene nota, videlicet, "ab ullo paupere"); *Sanctus Iacobus* in canonica [*recte, Ecclesiasticus*] ("Sicut aqua extinguit ignem, ita elemosina extinguit peccatum"[29] — videlicet, tam nostrum quam defunctorum). Et innumera possent adduci quibus elemosina — et per consequens omnis et cuiusvis generis elemosina — divino iure et naturali aut praecipitur aut consulitur. Cum ergo statutum limitet elemosinas mortuorum in exequiis et minuat, clarum est quod et Ecclesiae et iuri divino contrariatur. Nec valet si dicatur: "Non prohibemus elemosinas fieri, sed hanc specialem," quia haec est elemosina, ergo prohibetur elemosina, et nullam possunt prohibere. Nam cum a Deo sit religiosis indigentibus concessum cuiusvis generis elemosinas recipere, et aliis saecularibus praeceptum vel consultum elemosinas dare, constituentes oppositum et iuri divino obsistunt, et religiosorum indigentium et pro animabus orantium libertatem offendunt. Ergo . . . etc. Item *Ecclesiasticus* [*recte, Proverbia*]: "Qui pronus est ad misericordiam benedicetur in populis."[30] Sed non est pronus qui prohibet aliquod[d] genus elemosinae: imo adversarius. Nec benedicetur in populis qui [sig. biiv] illam virtutem quae magnificentia vocatur et viros claros facit a sua civitate expellit — quae magis laudabiliter ostenditur in exequiis quam in ludis, conviviis, ac spectaculis, et vestium pompis. Quae ad magnificentiam pertinere pro qualitate personarum docuit Aristoteles in libro iiii *Ethicorum*,[31] quibus tamen nullum efficax unquam remedium adhibitum fuit, iuvenibus ac mulieribus impedientibus, religiosis eo facilius oppressis, quo pro reipublicae conservatione die noctuque orationibus vacant. Tempore quoque Domini nostri Iesu Christi, cum vidua in filii exequiis a Christo suscitati "erat turba multa"[32] — quod ad fidei protestationem, viventium consolationem est introductum, nec mirum si et elemosinae tunc convenientius erogentur.

---

[d] *correxi*: aliquot *cod.*

poor person"[28] — note this well, namely, "from any poor person"); *St. James* in his canonical letter [*recte, Ecclesiasticus*] ("Just as water quenches fire, so almsgiving quenches sin"[29] — namely, *our* sin as well as that of the departed). And countless cases could be cited where almsgiving — and consequently *all* almsgiving, of whatever kind — is either enjoined or advised by divine and natural law. Since, therefore, the statute restricts and reduces almsgiving for the dead at funerals, it is clearly opposed both to the Church and to divine law. Nor is this possible argument valid: "We do not prevent [all] almsgiving, only *this* particular type." It is still almsgiving, therefore almsgiving *is* prevented, and they cannot prevent any type of it. For since God allows religious who are in need to accept any kind of alms whatever, and enjoins or advises others who are laypeople to give alms, those who ordain the opposite are both obstructing divine law and trampling on the freedom of religious who are in need and who pray for souls. Therefore . . . etc. Again, in *Ecclesiasticus* [*recte, Proverbs*]: "Whoever is inclined to compassion (*misericordia*) will be blessed among the nations."[30] But whoever prevents some kind of almsgiving is *not* so inclined: indeed, he is against it. Nor will a person be blessed among the nations who drives out from his city that virtue which has the name "munificence" and makes men famous — a virtue which is more commendably displayed in funerals than in games, feasts, and shows, and in extravagance of dress. Aristotle taught in his *Ethics* (bk. 4) that the relevance of these things to munificence depends on people's status,[31] but no remedy for them has ever been successful, since youths and women are an obstacle, but the daily and nightly devotion of religious to prayer for the state's preservation has made *them* all the more easily put down. In the time of our Lord Jesus Christ, too, with the widow at the funeral of her son whom Christ raised up "there was a great crowd"[32] — a detail inserted as a declaration of faith and as a solace to the living. No wonder that alms too should quite fittingly be paid out then!

---

[28] Tobit 4:7.
[29] Ecclesiasticus 3:33.
[30] Proverbs 22:9, which, however, lacks the words "among the nations" (*in populis*).
[31] *Nicomachean Ethics* 1122a24–26.
[32] Luke 7:12.

Ad secundum, dicitur quod est contra leges ab imperatoribus Ecclesiae universali indultas; est enim contra legem primam, *Codice, De sacrosanctis ecclesiis*, ubi dicitur: "Habeat unusquisque licentiam sanctissimo catholicoque concilio decedens bonorum quod optaverit relinquere," etc.[33] "Quod enim facit heres pro anima defuncti per defunctum fieri dicitur, quum eius personam repraesentet," capitulo "A nobis," *De sententia excommunicationis*,[34] et per consequens eo modo quo voluerit relinquere poterit. Cuius oppositum sequitur ex statuto; non enim poterit paterfamilias in testamento disponere quod pro anima sua accipiantur tot fratres in suis exequiis, quod ipse magis expedire iudicabit pro anima sua quam alias elemosinas. Ergo statutum irrationabile est, ut destructivum ultimarum piarum voluntatum et con-[sig. biiir]tra ecclesiasticam libertatem attributam ab imperatoribus.

Ad tertium, primo dicitur quod est contra privilegia a domino papa indulta nam [*Causa*] *tertiadecima, quaestione ii* dicitur: "Animae defunctorum quatuor modis solvuntur, aut oblationibus sacerdotum, aut precibus sanctorum, aut carorum elemosinis, aut ieiunio cognatorum."[35] Isti autem agunt contra hoc privilegium et beneficium per suum statutum, ergo non valet; et est in derogationem ecclesiasticae libertatis et detrimentum animarum. Ad idem est textus, capitulo "Cum ex eo," *De poenitentiis et remissionibus*, ubi Innocentius in concilio generali dicit: "Monemus et exhortamur in Domino quatenus de bonis vobis a Deo collatis pias elemosinas erogetis, ut per haec bona et alia quae Domino inspirante feceritis ad aeterna gaudia possitis pervenire."[36] Et pulchre in

An enquiry as to whether the statutes

As to the second point, the statute is declared contrary to laws conceded by the emperors to the universal Church, for it goes against the first law in the *Code, On the inviolability of churches*, where it is stated: "May each individual have the freedom to bequeath at his death whatever portion of his goods he chooses to the most holy Catholic council, etc."[33] "For what an heir does for a deceased person's soul is said to be done *through* the deceased, since the heir serves as his proxy," according to the chapter "A nobis" of *On the sentence of excommunication*.[34] Consequently, too, the testator will be able to bequeath his property by whatever method he wishes. The statute has the opposite effect, for the head of a family will not be able to prescribe in his will that for his soul's sake so many brothers be admitted to his funeral, if he himself judges this more profitable for his soul than other types of alms. The statute is therefore unreasonable, as being destructive of people's last devout wishes and contrary to church freedom granted by the emperors.

As to the third point, first, the statute is declared contrary to the privileges conceded by our lord the pope, for in [*Case*] 13, *question 2*, it is stated: "The souls of the departed are released in four ways: by the offerings of priests, by the prayers of saints, by the alms of loved ones, or by the fasting of relatives."[35] *Those* people, however, are attacking this privilege and benefit through their statute, which is therefore invalid; and it threatens to diminish church freedom and cause harm to souls. The same point is made by a passage in the chapter "Cum ex eo" of *On penances and remissions*, where Innocent says in the general council: "We warn and urge you in the Lord to use some of the goods God has granted you for devout almsgiving, so that through these goods and through other actions inspired by the Lord you may attain everlasting joys."[36] It

---

[33] *Cod.* 1. 2. 1; *CICv* 2: 12.

[34] X 5. 39. 28; *CIC* 2: 899–900, ending with: "Heredes quoque ipsius [*sc.* qui mortuus est absolvendus sed non absolutus] ad satisfaciendum pro ipso, si monitione praemissa noluerint, per districtionem ecclesiasticam compellantur."

[35] See n. 9 above.

[36] X 5. 38. 14: *CIC* 2: 888–89.

capitulo "Non estimemus,"[37] et [in] capitulo "Tempus,"[38] et in aliis multis eiusdem [*Causae*] *tertiaedecimae, quaestionis ii*. Et quum innumerabiles quasi sint modi elemosinas faciendi, diversique diversis placeant, velle limitare modos, et clericis favorabiles prohibere, est homines ab elemosinis retrahere et divinis inspirationibus resistere — quod supra damnatur — et sic ecclesiasticam libertatem violare.

Secundo, est contra canonem expressum *De rebus Ecclesiae non alienandis*, capitulo ultimo.[39] Pro cuius intelligentia et efficaci probatione, quae non facile aut nullo modo solvi potest, praesuppono primo quod nemo summi pontificis auctoritatem neget aut concilii circa spiritualia vel an-[sig. biiiv]nexa spiritualibus et circa eorum declarationem. Praesuppono secundo quod in decidendis omnibus quaestionibus et disputationibus sit devenire ad nominum significationem (iuxta doctrinam Aristotelis), nisi disputantes sunt concordes in eis. Tunc sic: est apertissime prohibitum quod saeculares non disponant circa mortuaria per summum pontificem et concilium, et apertissime manifestatum hoc esse contra ecclesiasticam libertatem, ut est textus clarissimus, et qui nulla expositione potest operiri, in capitulo ultimo, *De rebus Ecclesiae non alienandis*, supra posito in principio. Et communiter doctores intelligunt per mortuaria numerum clericorum, candelas, denarios, et alia

is also beautifully stated in the chapter "Non estimemus,"[37] in the chapter "Tempus,"[38] and in many other passages of the same [*Case*] 13, question 2. And since there are almost countless ways of giving alms, and different ways appeal to different people, the desire to restrict those ways, and to prevent the ones favorable to clergy, amounts to deterring people from almsgiving and opposing godly inspirations — something which is condemned above — and thus trespassing on church freedom.

Secondly, the statute goes against the clearly stated canon *On not alienating the Church's property*, final chapter.[39] In view of this canon's discernment and its powerful argument, which cannot easily, or in any way at all, be invalidated, I first assume that no one denies the authority of the supreme pontiff or of the council concerning spiritual matters or their adjuncts, and concerning their definition. I assume, secondly, that (following Aristotle's teaching) the settlement of all enquiries and disputes involves recourse to the meaning of words, unless the disputants agree on them. So, then: it is very plainly forbidden by the supreme pontiff and the council for laypeople to deal with death disbursements, and it is made perfectly obvious that this practice goes against church freedom. The text in the final chapter (quoted above at the beginning) of *On not alienating the Church's property* is very clear, and cannot be hidden by any explanation. And in general the doctors understand by "death disbursements" a number of clergy, and candles, money, and

---

[37] C. 13 q. 2 c. 19; *CIC* 1: 727: "Non estimemus ad mortuos, pro quibus curam gerimus, pervenire, nisi quod pro eis sive altaris, sive orationum, sive elemosinarum sacrificiis solempniter supplicamus, quamvis non omnibus prosint pro quibus fiunt, sed his tantum, pro quibus, dum vivunt, cooperantur ut prosint. Sed quia non discernimus, qui sint, oportet ea pro regeneratis omnibus facere, ut nullus eorum pretermittatur, ad quos hec beneficia possint et debeant pervenire. Melius enim supererunt ista his, quibus nec obsunt, nec prosunt, quam eis deerunt, quibus prosunt."

[38] C. 13 q. 2 c. 23; *CIC* 1: 728: "Tempus, quod inter hominis mortem et ultimam resurrectionem interpositum est, animas abditis receptaculis continet, sicut queque digna est vel requie, vel erumpna, pro eo quod sortita est in carne dum viveret. Neque negandum est, defunctorum animas pietate suorum viventium relevari, cum pro illis sacrificium mediatoris offertur, vel elemosinae fiunt in ecclesia. Sed eis hec prosunt, qui, cum viverent, hec sibi ut postea possent prodesse meruerunt."

[39] See n. 4 above.

ad exequias pertinentia. Sic tenuit Hostiensis,[40] Ioannes Andreae,[41] Petrus de Ancharano,[42] Abbas Siculus, Ioannes de Imola,[43] et communiter scribentes. Est etiam clarum tales esse ipso facto excommunicatos per capitulum "Noverit" (supra positum in principio), [*Liber*] *extra, De sententia excommunicationis*, non obstante capitulo "Gravem" in verbo "promulgare", quia exponitur ("id est, promulgatam publicare"); ut ibi glossa Petri, et sic nota Hostiensis.[44]

Nec potest evitari haec doctrina, nisi aut dicendo quod in exequiis sunt aliqua ad divinum cultum et clericos nullo modo pertinentia, et quo ad illa nullam esse prohibitionem (quod conceditur, ut infra latius patebit); aut dicendo per hoc nomen mortuaria aliquid significari quod doctoribus communiter in hac materia scribentibus fuerit incognitum — quod est valde absurdum! Ideo [sig. biv^r] indubitanter tenendum

An enquiry as to whether the statutes 181

other things related to funerals. That was the view of Henricus de Segusio,[40] Giovanni d'Andrea,[41] Peter of Ancharano,[42] Nicholas de Tudeschis, Johannes ab Imola,[43] and of writers in general. It is also clear that such offenders are by that very fact excommunicate, according to the chapter "Noverit" (quoted above at the beginning), [*Liber*] *extra, On the sentence of excommunication,* notwithstanding the chapter "Gravem" at the word "proclaim", for it is explained ("that is, proclaim and publish") in Peter's gloss apropos; so, too, in De Segusio's note.[44]

Nor can this teaching be avoided, except by saying that some aspects of funerals are totally irrelevant to divine worship and clergy, so that no prohibition applies to them (a point which *is* granted, as will be more fully shown below); or by saying that by this term "death disbursements" something is meant that was not known to the doctors who generally wrote on this subject — which is totally ridiculous! One

---

[40] Henricus de Segusio (ca. 1200–1271), alias Hostiensis (cardinal-bishop of Ostia from 1261), best known as a canonist for his *Summa aurea* (Venice, 1570) and *Lectura in quinque libros decretalium* (Venice, 1581); DDC 5: 1211–27.

[41] Giovanni d'Andrea (ca. 1270–1348), professor of canon law at Bologna and Padua, and such an admired and prolific writer that Baldus called him *iuris canonici fons et tuba*: see S. Kuttner, ed., *Ioannis Andreae in quinque decretalium libros novella commentaria* (Venice: Franciscus Senensis, 1581; repr. in 4 vols., Turin: Bottega d'Erasmo, 1963), 1: viii and n. 24; DDC 6: 89–92.

[42] Peter of Ancharano (ca. 1333–1416), author of *In quinque libros decretalium fecundissima commentaria,* 5 vols. (Bologna, 1580–1581); DDC 6: 1464–71.

[43] Johannes ab Imola (ca. 1367/72–1436), teacher of law at Ferrara and Bologna, and author of *Commentaria super tres libros decretalium* (Venice, 1498 and 1500); DDC 6: 107–10.

[44] X 5. 39. 53; CIC 2: 911: "Gravem venerabilis fratris nostri Pisani archiepiscopi recepimus quaestionem, quod quidam cives Pisani, deputati a potestate ac populo ad statuta civitatis edenda, in derogationem apostolicae sedis et subversionem ecclesiasticae libertatis edere praesumpserunt, quod, si quis clericus vel laicus contra quemcunque laicum Pisani districtus ad iudicem ecclesiasticum literas apostolicas impetraverit, in mille solidis, nisi renunciaverit literis, condemnetur, nec reditus possessionum suarum reddantur eidem, vel agri excolantur illius, sed banno potius subiaceant potestatis ... Ideoque fraternitati tuae mandamus, quatenus in consiliarios et officiales civitatis ipsius, nisi statuta ipsa de capitularibus suis deleri fecerint, et idonee, sicut exigit res, caveri, quod similia de cetero non debeant attentare, excommunicationis sententiam promulgare procures."

est per dictum textum disponentes circa exequias manifeste agere contra ecclesiasticam libertatem et per consequens excommunicatos esse, cum omnibus qui consilium vel auxilium praestiterint, et ceteris qui in dicto capitulo "Noverit" et glossa penultima dicti capituli continentur, quae dicit quod dantes auxilium vel consilium[e] sunt excommunicati, et sunt privandi feudo Ecclesiae.[45]

Determinatio per auctoritates doctorum quod praedicta statuta sunt contra libertatem Ecclesiae.

Ad quartum — videlicet, commune doctorum iudicium — dicitur infrascriptos scripsisse et tenuisse antedictum statutum esse contra ecclesiasticam libertatem, et verisimile esse, si alii scripserunt aut aliquando sint scripturi, a veterum tramite non deviaturos.

Dominus Abbas Siculus.

Et primo adduco Dominum Abbatem Siculum in capitulo finali, *De rebus Ecclesiae non alienandis*, supra allegato[46] sic dicentem: "Aut enim statutum concernit cultum divinum vel refrigerium animae defuncti, et

---

[e] *omisi*: praestiterint *cod.*

must therefore steadfastly maintain, in accordance with the said text, that [laypeople] who deal with funerals plainly attack church freedom and are consequently excommunicate, together with all who have given them advice or help, and the other people included in the said chapter "Noverit" and in the penultimate gloss on the said chapter, which says that those who give such help or advice are excommunicate, and should be stripped of the Church's fief.[45]

Ascertainment by the doctors' pronouncements that the aforesaid statutes go against the Church's freedom.

As to the fourth point — namely, the shared judgment of the doctors — it is declared that those mentioned below wrote and maintained that the aforesaid statute goes against church freedom, and it is probable that any other past or future writers on the subject are unlikely to swerve from the path of their elders.

Master Nicholas de Tudeschis.

First, I cite Master Nicholas de Tudeschis who, commenting on the final chapter (adduced above)[46] of *On not alienating the Church's property*, says: "For *either* the statute relates to divine worship, or the relief of a deceased

---

[45] Bernard of Parma (d. 1263) compiled the *glossa ordinaria* on the Gregorian *Decretals*.

[46] See n. 4 above. The following passage paraphrases rather than quotes his *Lectura super quinque libros decretalium* (5 vols., Basel, 1477), III: *De rebus ecclesiae alienandis*, "Cum laicis." The full text of his gloss runs: "In contrarium facit quia pompae exequiarum sunt potius consolationes vivorum quam suffragia mortuorum nec ecclesia approbat ut in c. animae defunctorum et in c. quam preposterum xiii. q. ii. dicerem quod circa concernentia cultum divinum et refrigerium animae defuncti non valeant statuta laicorum quia illa proprie sunt annexa iuri spirituali et ita generaliter intelligo istum textum. Si circa concernentia pompas mundanas valeant statuta et credo specifice quod valeat statutum illud de pannis nigris passim non utendis quia de mortuis non est multum tollendum secundum fidem Christianam tum propter spem futurae vitae, tum ut vivi acquiescant dispositioni divine ut dicit textus. In dicto. c. quam preposterum."

tunc non valet quia, cum sint spiritualia ista, aut annexa iuri spirituali sicut officium sepulturae, non habent potestatem statuentes disponere (per dictum capitulum finale et capitulum 'Ecclesia' supra allegatum)[47] et consequenter incurrunt excommunicationem, quia agunt contra libertatem Ecclesiae; aut ergo statutum concernit pom-[sig. bivv]pam quandam (ut in pannis nigris et huiusmodi), et tunc tenet valere statutum, quia nec ad cultum divinum nec suffragium mortuorum hoc pertinet — sed potius sunt consolationes vivorum, nec Ecclesia talia approbat, ut in capitulo 'Quam preposterum,' [*Causa*] *xiii, quaestione ii*),[48] et ideo statuere possunt."

Dominus Antonius Corsetus Siculus.[49]

Dominus quoque Antonius Corsetus Siculus in *Repertorio* suo ita inquit: "Statutum non possunt facere laici super mortuariis quia illa sunt annexa iuri spirituali, nam de annexis idem est iudicium: capitulum 'Quanto,' *De iudiciis*.[50] Neque circa contingentia cultum divinum vel refrigerium animae defuncti statutum laicorum valet, ut in capitulo finali, *De rebus Ecclesiae non alienandis*,[51] et ibi Abbas[f] facit capitulum 'Quam

---

[f] *correxi*: et ibi Abbas de rebus Ecclesiae non alienandis *cod*.

person's soul, and in those cases it is invalid because, since these are spiritual matters, or adjuncts of spiritual authority such as the burial service, statute-makers have no power to deal with them (according to the said final chapter and the chapter 'Ecclesia', adduced above)[47] and consequently incur excommunication, because they attack the Church's freedom; or, on the other hand, the statute relates to a certain extravagance (as with black clothes and the like) and in that case," he maintains, "the statute is valid, since this matter concerns neither divine worship nor supplication for the dead — rather, these are solaces for the living, and the Church discountenances such things (as stated in the chapter 'Quam preposterum' of [Case] 13, question 2),[48] so those referred to may make statutes about them."

Master Antonio Corsetto of Sicily.[49]

Master Antonio Corsetto of Sicily, too, says in his *Repertorium*: "Laypeople may not make a statute about death disbursements, as they are adjuncts of spiritual authority, for the same judgment applies to the adjuncts, as stated in the chapter 'Quanto' of *On judgments*.[50] And a laypeople's statute about the appurtenances of divine worship or the relief of a deceased person's soul is also invalid, as stated in the final chapter of *On not alienating the Church's property*,[51] and in De Tudeschis's gloss on

---

[47] See (respectively) notes 4 and 3 above.

[48] C. 13 q. 2 c. 25; CIC 1: 729: "Quam preposterum est quamque perversum, ut cum Dei voluntatem fieri postulemus, quando evocat nos et accersit de hoc mundo, non statim voluntatis eius imperio pareamus, obnitimur et reluctamur, et pervicacium more servorum ad conspectum Domini cum tristitia et merore perducimur, exeuntes istinc necessitatis vinculo, non voluntatis obsequio, et volumus ab eo premiis celestibus honorari, ad quem venimus inviti."

[49] Antonio Corsetto (1450–1503), lecturer in canon law at Bologna and Padua, and a prolific writer: see A. Mazzacane, "Antonio Corsetto," *DBI*, 29: 540–42. The passage quoted is from his *Repertorium in opera Nicolai de Tudeschis* (Venice, 1499), fol. 236v.

[50] X 2. 1. 3; CIC 2: 239 (second sentence): "Causa vero iuris patronatus ita coniuncta est et connexa spiritualibus causis, quod non nisi ecclesiastico iudicio valeat definiri."

[51] See n. 4 above.

preposterum,' [*Causa*] *xiii, quaestio ii*.⁵² Circa concernentia tamen pompas mundanas valet statutum laicorum, et specifice factum, ut de pannis nigris in mortuariis non utendis, et de similibus." Haec ille.

Dominus Ioannes de Imola.

Dominus Ioannes de Imola in capitulo finali saepe dicto sic ait: "Nota quod laici non possunt facere statutum super alienatione rerum ecclesiasticarum, neque super mortuariis vel iuribus ipsius Ecclesiae, neque super annexis iuri spirituali. Et facit iste textus, secundum Dominum Petrum, quod non valeat statutum civitatis dispo-[sig. cr]nens quod circa funus non debeantᵍ portari nisi tot funalia seu dupleria, vel [non] debeant indui de nigro nisi tot, vel non debeant invitari nisi tot clerici. Dicit tamen quod in Tuscia talia statuta servantur." Neque aliter declarat: "Potes dicere quod tolerari posset statutum, quatenus disponat de his quae non applicantur ecclesiis, sicut sunt vestes nigrae quas portant aliqui associantes funus, et ut etiam sunt funalia, quae non remanent penes Ecclesiam. Sed quatenus disponunt quod non possint invitari nisi tot clerici, vel quod non possit offerri nisi tantum pro mortuariis, vel quod non dentur nisi tot candelae vel nisi tot denarii, videtur quod tale statutum non valeat per hunc textum." Haec Ioannes de Imola, qui etiam subiicit: "Dicit tamen Ioannes Andreae post Hostiensem quod multi praelati, quaerentes transitoriam pacem, tanquam canes muti non audent procedere contra tales — contra quos loquitur Gregorius in capitulo 'Sit rector,' *xliii Distinctio*;⁵³ facit etiam quod habetur in capitulo

---

ᵍ *correxi*: debent *cod.*

it, supported by the chapter 'Quam preposterum' of [*Case*] 13, *question* 2.*⁵²* But a laypeople's statute about things relating to worldly extravagance *is* valid, and so is a specific measure concerned, for example, with the non-wearing of black clothes as part of death disbursements, and similar matters." These are his words.

Master Johannes ab Imola.

Master Johannes ab Imola says this about the oft-mentioned final chapter: "Note that laypeople may not make a statute about alienating church property, nor about death disbursements or the Church's own jurisdictions, nor about the adjuncts of spiritual authority. And that text, according to Master Peter, invalidates a civic statute which prescribes that at a funeral only *so* many torches or candle-stands must be carried, or that only *so* many people must be dressed in black, or that only *so* many clergy must be invited. He says, however, that such statutes are observed in Tuscany." Similarly Johannes states: "You may say that a statute could be tolerated insofar as it dealt with things not assigned to churches, such as black clothes worn by some of the funeral party, and also torches, which do not remain in the Church's possession; but insofar as statute-makers prescribe that only *so* many clergy can be invited, or only *so* much money offered as death disbursements, or only *so* many candles or *so* many coins given, it appears that according to this passage such a statute is invalid." These are Johannes ab Imola's words. He also adds: "Giovanni d'Andrea, however, states (after De Segusio) that many prelates, seeking a temporary peace, like dumb dogs are afraid to proceed against such people — prelates against whom Gregory speaks in the chapter 'Sit rector' of *Distinction 43*[53] — and he is supported by the

---

[52] See n. 48 above.

[53] D. 43 c. 1; *CIC* 1: 153: "Sit rector discretus in silentio, utilis in verbo, ne aut tacenda proferat, aut proferenda reticescat. Nam sicut incauta locutio in errorem pertrahit, ita indiscretum silentium hos qui erudiri poterant, in errorem derelinquit. Sepe namque rectores inprovidi, humanam amittere gratiam formidantes, loqui libere recta pertimescunt, et iuxta veritatis vocem nequaquam iam gregis custodiae pastorum studio, sed mercenariorum vice deserviunt, quia veniente lupo fugiunt, dum se sub silentio abscondunt." A quotation from Gregory the Great, *Pastoral Care* 2. 4 (*PL* 77. 30).

'In canonibus,' [*Causa*] *xvi, quaestio i.*[54] Dicit etiam quod quidam Dominus Bert[r]andus ait:

> 'Pontifices muti de iure suo male tuti;
> Cum sint cornuti, non audent cornibus uti.'"[55]

Dominus Petrus de Palude, patriarcha Hierosolimitanus, iuris utriusque peritissimus.[56]

Petrus quoque de Palude, theologiae professor ac iuris utriusque peritissimus, in iiii sententia, *Distinctio xviii, quaestio iii, argumentum iii* sic ait: "Videtur esse contra ecclesiasticam libertatem quod rustici statue-[sig. cv]runt quod nullus offerat nisi in magnis festis, aut nisi tantum, aut quod super mortuum non sit nisi talis pannus vel tot cerei, et huiusmodi: quia libertas Ecclesiae est habere liberas oblationes et liberas sepulturas."[57] Haec Petrus de Palude.

contents of the chapter 'In canonibus' of [*Case*] *16, question 1.*[54] He also mentions the saying of a certain Master Bert[r]and:

> 'Priests who are dumb are at risk: their rights they may lose;
> Though they have horns, they're afraid these weapons to use.'[55]

Master Pierre de la Palu, patriarch of Jerusalem, expert in canon and civil law.[56]

Pierre de la Palu, too, teacher of theology and expert in canon and civil law, says this in the fourth sentence of *Distinction 18, question 3, article 3*: "It appears to go against church freedom when country folk have decreed that no one may make an offering except at high feasts, or offer more than *so* much, or that only *such* a shroud or *so* many wax tapers, and the like, may be placed over a dead person: for the Church's freedom means having unlimited offerings and unlimited burials."[57] These are Pierre de la Palu's words.

---

[54] C. 16 q. 1 c. 57; *CIC* 1: 779–80 (end of first paragraph): "Valde ergo iniquum et ingens sacrilegium est, quecumque vel pro remedio peccatorum, vel pro salute, aut requie animarum suarum unusquisque venerabili ecclesiae contulerit aut certe reliquerit, ab his, a quibus maxime servari convenit, id est Christianis et Deum timentibus hominibus, et super omnia a principibus et primis regionum, in aliud transferri vel converti." From a letter of Pope Symmachus, *PL* 129. 1219D.

[55] D'Andrea's comments on the chapter "Cum laicis" (see n. 4 above) occur in his *Novella* (see n. 41 above), 3: fol. 74r–v. The passage quoted here (cap. xii 5, fol. 74v) follows a reference to De Segusio, and identifies Bertrand as bishop of Grasse in France — probably the Bertrandus de Aquis who was bishop there 1218–1246: see Eubel, *Hierarchia catholica*, 1: 267.

[56] Pierre de la Palu (1270~80–1342), Dominican theologian, doctor of law, Latin patriarch of Jerusalem (1329–1342), and author of a commentary on the fourth book of Peter Lombard's *Sentences*: see Eubel, *Hierarchia catholica*, 1: 276; *DDC* 6: 1481–84.

[57] *Petrus de Palude in quartum sententiarum* (Venice, 1492), fol. 94r.

Summa Angelica Ordinis Minorum.[58]

Summa Angelica Ordinis Minorum in verbo "Immunitas", paragrapho xlvii sic ait: "Utrum laici possint statuere super mortuariis, respondet Ioannes de Imola in dicto capitulo finali quod sic, quatenus disponunt in his quae non applicantur Ecclesiae. Addit Panormitanus ibidem: Aut concernunt divinum cultum aut refrigerium animae: quia, cum haec sint annexa iuri spirituali, non valent — ut puta quod non dentur nisi tot cerei, vel non invitentur nisi tot clerici et huiusmodi — igitur solum valent in concernentibus pompas mundanas, quae sunt potius consolationes vivorum quam suffragia mortuorum, nec Ecclesia talia approbat, ut in capitulo 'Quam preposterum,' [*Causa*] *xiii, quaestio ii*.[59] Et sic transeunt communiter omnes doctores in dicto capitulo finali."[60] Et bene nota quod hic Frater Minor allegat Abbatem pro hac opinione.

Et quia dicit Baldus[61] (lex in *Codice, De Latina libertate tollenda*, per ipsum textum)[62] quod equi et arma ducti ad sepulturam militis, et cerei,

Fra Angelo Carletti of the Order of Friars Minor.[58]

Fra Angelo Carletti of the Order of Friars Minor says this at the word "Immunitas" (paragraph 47): "Johannes ab Imola's answer to the question raised by the said final chapter, as to whether laypeople can make statutes about death disbursements, is that they may, insofar as they are dealing with things not assigned to the Church. De Tudeschis, commenting on the same chapter ('*Either* the statutes relate to divine worship or the relief of the soul'), adds that, since these things are adjuncts of spiritual authority, statutes about them are invalid — for instance, the stipulation that only *so* many wax tapers be given, or that only *so* many clergy be invited, and the like — and are therefore valid only in matters relating to worldly extravagance, which are solaces for the living rather than supplications for the dead, and the Church discountenances such things (as stated in the chapter 'Quam preposterum' of [*Case*] *13, question 2*).[59] All the doctors alike are coming round to this opinion on the said final chapter."[60] And note well that this Friar Minor adduces De Tudeschis's example for this view.

"Also," he says, "since Baldus[61] states (quoting verbatim the law in the *Code, On abolishing Latin freedom*)[62] that horses and weapons brought to

---

[58] Fra Angelo Carletti (ca. 1414–1495), doctor of theology and of canon and civil law at Bologna who entered the Franciscan Order in 1441, rising high in its ranks and founding several *monti di pietà*: see S. Pezzella, "Angelo Carletti," *DBI*, 20: 136–38.

[59] See n. 48 above.

[60] *Summa Angelica* (a handbook for Franciscans), s. v. "Immunitas" (par. 47).

[61] Baldus de Ubaldis (ca. 1327–1400), a respected teacher of law at six universities (his pupils included Peter of Ancharano, Johannes ab Imola, and the future pope Gregory XI), and the author of an important *Commentary* on the first three books of the Gregorian *Decretals* (Lyon, 1585); *DDC* 2: 39–52. The passage cited here is from his *In Justiniani Corpus*, 9 vols. (Venice, 1577), 9: *In vii. viii. ix. x. & xi. codicis libros commentaria*, tit. *De Latina libertate tollenda*, fol. 7r: "Item collige arg. Ad equos, qui ducuntur ad sepulturam militum. Item ad cereos, quod debeant remanere fratribus sepelientibus: quasi sequela cadaveris, argu. Contra, ff. de aur, & arg. l. medico."

[62] *Cod.* 7. 6. 1. 5; *CICv* 2: 296: "Sed et qui domini funus pileati antecedunt vel in ipso lectulo stantes cadaver ventilare videntur, si hoc ex voluntate fiat vel testatoris vel heredis, fiant ilico cives Romani. et ne quis vana liberalitate iactare se concedatur, ut populus quidem eum quasi humanum respiciat multos pileatos in funus procedentes adspiciens, omnibus autem deceptis maneant illi in pristina servitute publico testimonio defraudati: fiant itaque et hi cives Romani, iure tamen patronatus patronis integro servando."

debent remanere apud clericos vel fratres sepelientes, quasi sint sequela cadaveris (argumentum lex, medio paragrapho finali, *Digesta, De auro et argento legando*),[63] ideo non valet statutum laicorum. Haec ibi.

Dominus Antoninus, Archiepiscopus Florentinus.[64]

Dominus [Antoninus] archiepiscopus Florentinus in *Tractatu censurarum*, in capitulo xviii sic ait: "Nota etiam (secundum quosdam) quod si qui statuerunt quod nullus offerat nisi in magnis festivitatibus, vel nisi tantum, vel quod super mortuariis [non] sit nisi talis pannus vel tot cerei, vel huiusmodi, hoc esset contra libertatem ecclesiasticam." Et infra: "Officiales vero et consiliarii tunc ligantur,[65] si scientes ea esse contra ecclesiasticam libertatem consenserint delicto, ut quia ea servaverunt vel dederunt consilium quod ea serventur, vel quod negligentes fuerunt ea de suis capitularibus delere, vel officium dimittere, quam cito de eis certificati sciunt et cognoscunt esse ea contra libertatem Ecclesiae concessa — aliquo tamen medio intervallo ad arbitrium boni viri. Aliae vero personae nominatae in hac decretali, licet servent huiusmodi statuta, non sunt excommunicati, secundum Innocentium et Ioannem Andreae."[66] Haec ille, quae quidem dicit de facientibus contra libertatem seu privilegium universalis Ecclesiae.

An enquiry as to whether the statutes 193

a soldier's burial, and wax tapers, must stay with the clergy or brothers who bury him, as if they were the corpse's escort (see the middle of the final paragraph in the law of the *Digest, On bequests of gold and silver*),[63] for that reason a laypeople's statute is invalid." These are his words.

Master Antonino, archbishop of Florence.[64]

Master [Antonino], archbishop of Florence, says this in his *Treatise on censures* (chap. 18): "Note also (following certain authorities) that if any people have decreed that no one may make an offering except at high festivals, or offer more than *so* much, or that, in the matter of death disbursements, there may only be *such* a shroud or *so* many wax tapers or the like, this would go against the Church's freedom." And below: "But officials and councilors are bound by the Church[65] from the moment when, knowing that those statutes go against church freedom, they have connived at the crime by, for example, observing them or advising that they be observed, or by neglecting to remove them from their statute-books, or to resign their position, as soon as they are certain about them, and know and recognize that they have been allowed contrary to the Church's freedom — though they are given what a gentleman would deem a moderate period of grace. But other persons named in this decretal, though they observe such statutes, are not excommunicate, according to Innocent and Giovanni d'Andrea."[66] These are his very words about those who act against the worldwide Church's freedom or privilege.

---

[63] *Dig.* 34. 2. 40. 1; *DJ* 3: 157 (*CICv* 1: 527): "Uxori suae testamento ita legatum est: "Semproniae, dominae meae, hoc amplius argentum balneare": quaesitum est, an etiam id argentum, quo diebus festis in balineo uti consuevit, legato cedat. Respondit [*sc.* Scaevola] omne legatum videri."

[64] Antonino Pierozzi (1389–1459), Dominican canonist who became archbishop of his native Florence in 1446 and was canonized in 1523: see A. d'Addario, "Antonino Pierozzi, santo," *DBI*, 3: 524–32.

[65] Cf. Matthew 16:19 (Christ's words to Peter): "Et quodcumque ligaveris super terram, erit ligatum et in caelis."

[66] Antonino, *Tractatus super censuras* (Mantua: Paul of Butzbach, 1475), where the two passages quoted here are preceded by: "[Capitulum xviii:] Excommunicamus omnes qui de cetero servari fecerint statuta edita et consuetudines vel potestatis abusiones introductas contra ecclesiasticam libertatem, nisi ea de capitularibus suis infra

Dominus Petrus de Monte, episcopus Brixiensis, praecessor Domini Dominici de Dominicis.[67]

Repertorium quoque Brixiense, id est, Domini Petri de Monte, episcopi Brixiensis, in litera statutum sic refert: "An valeat statutum laicorum quod pro exequiis mortuorum non expen-[sig. ciiv]datur nisi tantum, dico quod non, per capitulum finale, *De rebus Ecclesiae non alienandis*, per quem textum feci revocari Brixiae quoddam statutum."[68]

Dominus Bertachinus.[69]

In *Repertorio* quoque Bertachini in litera statutum sic scribitur: "Statutum quod pro mortuariis non possit expendi supra decem [solidos] non valet, quasi attingat annexa spiritualibus: capitulum 'Cum laicis,' *De rebus Ecclesiae non alienandis*, et Ludovicus in *Singularibus*, versus 'Reverendus Cardinalis Sancti Marcelli.'"[70] Haec ibi.

Master Pietro de Monte, bishop of Brescia and predecessor of Master Domenico de Dominicis.[67]

The Brescian *Repertorium*, too, namely, that of Master Pietro de Monte, Bishop of Brescia, has this manuscript reference to the statute: "As to whether a laypeople's statute prescribing that only *so* much be spent on funerals for the dead is valid, I say it is *not*: see the final chapter of *On not alienating the Church's property*. This text was my reason for having a certain statute of Brescia annulled."[68]

Master Bertachini.[69]

In Bertachini's *Repertorium*, too, there is this manuscript note about the statute: "A statute prescribing that no more than ten [*soldi*] can be spent on death disbursements is invalid, inasmuch as it touches on adjuncts of spiritual matters: witness the chapter 'Cum laicis' of *On not alienating the Church's property*, and Ludovicus, at the line 'Reverendus Cardinalis Sancti Marcelli' in *Unusual cases*."[70] These are his words.

---

duos menses post huiusmodi publicationem sententiae fecerint amoveri." The decretal referred to is the chapter "Noverit" (see n. 5 above), and D'Andrea's commentary on it (*Novella*, vol. 4, fol. 147r–v) includes the words: "[Statutarii et scriptores] iudicantes secundum ea [*sc.* statuta] et iudicata scribentes statim sunt excommunicati secundum Hostiensem nec excusari possunt a toto, licet interdum a tanto, supra, quod metus causa, sacris. Officiales vero secundum Innocentium & Hostiensem non sunt excommunicati, nisi servaverint, vel negligentes fuerint in eis delendis. [Consiliarii locorum] si consilium dederint, quod servetur: idem dicunt quidam, & si dederint contrarium consilium, quia debent dimittere dignitatem, vel officium, nisi destruant statutum, si habent potestatem destruendi . . ." (cap. xlix 2–3, fol. 147r).

[67] See *Defense*, n. 84.

[68] Pietro de Monte, *Repertorium*, 2 vols. (Padua, 1480), vol. 2, sig. n3r, s. v. "Statutum".

[69] Giovanni Bertachini (ca. 1448–ca. 1500), Padua-trained jurist called to Rome as Consistorial Advocate by Sixtus IV, for whom (after 1471) he wrote a vast legal compendium, the *Repertorium iuris*, 3 vols. (Rome, 1481): see M. Caravale, "Giovanni Bertachini," *DBI*, 9: 441–42.

[70] Johannes Bertachinus, *Prima pars . . . solennis repertorii*, 3 vols. (Nuremberg, 1483), 3: fol. cciir.

Dominus Ludovicus Romanus.[71]

Ludovicus in *Singularibus* suis,[h] [capitulo] cccliii incipiente "Reverendus," ita scribit: "Reverendus Cardinalis Sancti Marcelli scripsit mihi super duobus volens consuli. Primo, statutum est Romae quod pro exequiis fiendis non possit nisi tantum expendi; quaeritur an valeat, cum sit factum a laicis. In sero reperi textum rotundum quod non. Licet enim non sit factum super spiritualibus, tamen est factum super connexis eisdem: argumentum lex 'Quod si nolit' in fine, *Digesta, De aedilicio edicto*;[72] in capitulo 'Cum laicis,' *De rebus Ecclesiae non alienandis*, ibi, 'sed etiam de mortuariis'. Et ita consulam, plura adducendo."[73] Haec Ludovicus.

Dominus Felinus.

Dominus quoque Felinus, capitulo "Ecclesia Sanctae Mariae," *De constitutionibus*, columna xxvi sic dicit: "Et ad praedicta facit quae notat Ludovicus Romanus in *Singularibus*, [capitulo] cccliii incipiente 'Reverendus,' ubi dicit quod non valet statutum laicorum quod pro exequiis defunctorum non possit nisi tantum expendi, per dictum capitulum finale, *De rebus Ecclesiae non alienandis*, et dicit se ita respondisse uni cardinali, et se ita consulturum. Memini tamen legisse Baldum — sed locus non occurrit — limitantem praedicta: '. . . nisi statutum limitet impensam funeris concernentem pompam funeris inutilem clericis, puta circa vestes lugubres et similia'. Sed praedicta procedunt in concernentibus clerum,

---

[h] *omisi*: in sing. *cod.*

Master Ludovicus of Rome.[71]

In his *Unusual cases* (no. 353 [364], beginning "Reverendus") Ludovicus writes thus: "The Reverend Cardinal of San Marcello has written to me requesting advice on two matters. First, there is a statute at Rome prescribing that only *so* much be spent on funeral arrangements; he asks whether it is valid, since it was made by laypeople. At a late hour I found a well-phrased text saying it is *not*. For although the statute did not concern spiritual matters, yet it *did* concern their adjuncts: see the law of the *Digest, On the aedile's edict*, at the end of 'Quod si nolit';[72] it is included in the chapter 'Cum laicis' of *On not alienating the Church's property*, at the phrase 'but also in regard to death disbursements'. This will be my advice, with further citations."[73] These are Ludovicus's words.

Master Felino.

Master Felino, too, commenting on the chapter "Ecclesia Sanctae Mariae" of *On ordinances*, says this (col. 26): "And the preceding statements are supported by Ludovicus of Rome's remarks in *Unusual cases* (chap. 353 [364], beginning 'Reverendus'), where he says that, according to the said final chapter of *On not alienating the Church's property*, a laypeople's statute prescribing that only *so* much can be spent on funerals of the departed is invalid, and says that this was his answer to a cardinal, and this would be his advice. Yet I remember reading — *where*, I do not recall — Baldus's qualification of the preceding statements : '. . . unless the statute restricts funeral expenditure relating to funerary extravagance which is no use to clergy: for instance, expenditure on mourning clothes and the like'. The preceding statements still apply, however, in matters

---

[71] Ludovicus Pontanus de Roma (1409–1439), precocious commentator on the *Digest* and the *Decretals* who, despite his youth and his training in civil law, played an important role in the Council of Basel, where he died of the plague.

[72] *Dig.* 21. 1. 31. 24–25; *DJ* 2: 613 (*CICv* 1: 310): "In his autem actionibus eadem erunt observanda quae de partu fructibus accessionibus quaeque de mortuo redhibendo dicta sunt. Quod emptioni accedit, partem esse venditionis prudentibus visum est."

[73] Ludovicus Pontanus, *Singularia juris* (Venice, 1471), chap. 364 [note different number].

ut in cera et similibus, et cum invenero denuo Baldum, dicetur vobis."[74] Haec ibi.

Idem Dominus Felinus in capitulo i, *De sponsionibus*, ibi: "Pro quibus non incongrue adduci potest quod notat Bartholus in lege 'Inficiando,' paragrapho finali, *Digesta*, *De furtis*,[75] dum dicit valere statutum puniens eum qui ad nuptias suas invitaret ultra duodecim puellas, non enim potest impugnari qui statuat super materia spirituali — quia hoc non detrahit vinculo matrimonii neque solemnitatibus, sed immoderatis pauperum expensis. Bene fateor quod non valeret statutum quod sponsa, dum benedicitur, non donet ultra certam summam sacerdoti, et induco quod notat Ludovicus Romanus in *Singularibus*, [capitulo] cccliii, quod incipit 'Reverendus Dominus Cardinalis,' ubi refert se consuluisse [sig. ciiiv] ad instantiam cuiusdam cardinalis quod non valet statutum laicorum quod pro exequiis fiendis non possit nisi tantum expendi, quia istud concernit bursas clericorum, et allegat textum singularem secundum eum in capitulo finali — ibi, 'sed etiam de mortuariis', supra — *De rebus Ecclesiae non alienandis*."[76] Haec Felinus.

Dominus Andreas Barbatia.[77]

Dominus quoque Andreas Barbatia in dicto capitulo finali dicit sic: "Nota quod laici non possunt statuere super alienatione rerum Ecclesiae, nec super mortuariis, nec super annexis iuri spirituali; et dicit

relating to the clergy, such as candle-wax and the like. And when I find the Baldus reference again, I will tell you."[74] These are his words.

The same Master Felino says concerning *On betrothals* (chap. 1): "In their favor [i.e., in favor of sumptuary statutes] it may not be inappropriate to cite Bartolo's remark about the law in the *Digest*, *On thefts*, at 'Infitiando' (final paragraph),[75] when he says that a statute penalizing someone who invites more than twelve girls to his wedding is valid, since whoever makes the statute cannot be attacked for dealing with a spiritual matter — for the statute is not detrimental to the bond of marriage or its ceremonies, but to excessive expenditure by the poor. I quite agree that a statute would be invalid which prescribed that, when a bride-to-be is blessed, she is not to give the priest more than a specified amount, and I cite Ludovicus of Rome's remark in *Unusual cases* (chap. 353, which begins 'Reverendus Dominus Cardinalis'). There he reports his advice, given at the instance of a certain cardinal, that a laypeople's statute which prescribes that only *so* much can be spent on funeral arrangements is invalid, since *that* affects the pockets of clergy, and he adduces a passage (remarkable, according to him) from the final chapter — at the phrase 'but also in regard to death disbursements', near the top — of *On not alienating the Church's property*."[76] These are Felino's words.

Master Andrea Barbazza.[77]

Master Andrea Barbazza, too, makes this comment on the said final chapter: "Note that laypeople may not make a statute about alienating the Church's property, nor about death disbursements, nor about

---

[74] Untraced.

[75] *Dig.* 47. 2. 68 pr.; *DJ* 4: 755 (CICv 1: 822): "Infitiando depositum nemo facit furtum (nec enim furtum est ipsa infitiatio, licet prope furtum est): sed si possessionem eius apiscatur intervertendi causa, facit furtum. Nec refert, in digito habeat anulum an dactyliotheca quem, cum deposito teneret, habere pro suo destinaverit."

[76] Felino is discussing *On betrothals* in the *Liber extra*: X 4. 1; CIC 2: 661–72.

[77] Andrea Barbazza (d. 1480), Sicilian-born canon lawyer who from 1430 studied at Bologna, later becoming a respected and influential lecturer and teacher there, and numbering among his pupils Antonio Corsetto (see n. 49 above) and Rodrigo Borgia, the future pope Alexander VI: see F. Liotta, "Andrea Barbazza," *DBI*, 6: 146–48.

Dominus Petrus non valere statutum laicorum disponens quod circa funus non debeant portari nisi tot funalia vel dupleria, vel non debeant indui de nigro nisi tot, vel invitari nisi tot clerici. Dicit tamen quod in Tusia talia statuta servantur. Ioannes de Imola dicit tale statutum posse tolerari, quatenus disponit de his quae non applicantur Ecclesiae, ut sunt vestes nigrae quas portant aliqui associantes funus, ut etiam sunt funalia[i] quae non remanent penes Ecclesiam; sed quatenus statutum dicit non posse invitari nisi tot clericos, vel non dentur nisi tot candelae vel denarii, quia tale statutum non valet per ipsum textum, et ita transeunt moderni scribentes hic. Et hoc est pulcrum ad doctrinam Baldi in lege in *Codice, De Latina libertate tollenda*, ubi per illum textum dixit quod equi et arma ducti ad sepulturam [sig. civr] militis debent remanere fratribus sepelientibus, quasi sint sequela cadaveris: argumentum lex, medio paragrapho finali, *Digesta, De auro et argento legando*, quod est bene notandum."[78] Haec Barbatia.

Idem tenet Dominus Ioannes Baptista Severianus[79] in repetitione legis "Omnes populi," *Digesta, De iustitia et iure*.[80]

Facit etiam optime pro supradictis textus in capitulo "Eos," *De immunitate ecclesiarum, Liber vi*,[81] arguendo a minori ad maius. Si enim incurrunt excommunicationem statuentes ne quis vendat, aut emat, aut

---

[i] *correxi*: funeralia *cod*.

the adjuncts of spiritual authority; and Master Peter pronounces invalid a laypeople's statute prescribing that only *so* many torches or candlestands must be carried at a funeral, or only *so* many people dress in black, or only *so* many clergy be invited. He says, however, that such statutes are observed in Tuscany. Johannes ab Imola says that such a statute may be tolerated insofar as it deals with things not assigned to the Church, such as black clothes worn by some members of the funeral party, and also torches which do not remain in the Church's possession; but insofar as the statute says that no more than *so* many clergy can be invited, or only *so* many candles or coins given, he states (quoting the chapter verbatim) that such a statute is invalid, and present-day writers here are coming round to this opinion. This fits in beautifully with Baldus's teaching about the law in the *Code, On abolishing Latin freedom*, where (quoting it verbatim) he said that horses and weapons brought to a soldier's burial must stay with the brothers who bury him, as if they were the corpse's escort: see the middle of the final paragraph in the law of the *Digest, On bequests of gold and silver*, and one should note this well."[78] These are Barbazza's words.

The same view is held by Master Johannes Baptista Severianus[79] in recapitulating the law "Omnes populi" of the *Digest, On justice and law*.[80]

The above statements are also excellently supported by words written in the chapter "Eos" of *On the immunity of churches* in the *Sext*,[81] arguing "from lesser to greater". If those who decree that no one is to sell to,

---

[78] See nn. 62 and 63 above for Barbazza's references to Baldus.
[79] Unidentified.
[80] *Dig.* 1. 1. 9; *DJ* 1: 2 (*CICv* 1: 29): "Omnes populi, qui legibus et moribus reguntur, partim suo proprio, partim communi omnium hominum iure utuntur. Nam quod quisque populus ipse sibi ius constituit, id ipsius proprium civitatis est vocaturque ius civile, quasi ius proprium ipsius civitatis: quod vero naturalis ratio inter omnes homines constituit, id apud omnes peraeque custoditur vocaturque ius gentium, quasi quo iure omnes gentes utuntur."
[81] VI 3. 23. 5; *CIC* 2: 1064: "Eos, qui, temporale dominium obtinentes, suis subditis, ne praelatis aut clericis seu personis ecclesiasticis quicquam vendant, aut emant aliquid ab eisdem, neque ipsis bladum molant, coquant panem, aut alia obsequia exhibere praesumant, aliquando interdicunt, quum talia in derogationem libertatis ecclesiasticae praesumantur, eo ipso excommunicationis sententiae decernimus subiacere."

molat[j] granum aut coquat panem clericis, fortius hoc debent incurrere statuentes ne intersint exequiis mortui nisi tot clerici, et dentur singulis candela una tot unciarum, et solidi duo tantum. Quia haec magis sunt contra ecclesiasticam libertatem et in derogationem eius (ut ibi dicitur), cum haec proprie sint spectantia ad mortuaria: de quibus supra per doctores et capitulo "Cum laicis." Quod capitulum omnes doctores allegant ad probandum statutum laicorum super mortuariis non valere, et ita intelligunt Innocentium voluisse, ut patet in responsionibus eorum.

Ultimo, pro corroboratione[k] praedictorum dico quod istud statutum, ex quo factum est, nunquam servatum est; et sic per non usum et contrariam consuetudinem sublatum est, nec amplius valet. Nam sunt fere triginta quinque anni quod fuit institutum, et nemo est qui recordetur illud pra-[sig. civv]ticatum et observatum fuisse — imo revocatum fuit, ut apparet supra in *Repertorio* Brixiensi,[82] quare de novo non potest praticari, cum vires nullas habeat (iuxta notata per Cinum[83] in lege "Rem non novam," paragrapho "Patroni," *Codice, De iudiciis*,[84] [et] per Angelum Aretinum[85] in prohemio *Institutionis* [recte, *Institutorum*], in versu "Dissuetudinem"), nisi ut ex nunc per illustrissimum ducale dominium confirmetur et innovetur. Quia et si civitas statuere possit, tamen non valet nisi fuerit per superiorem confirmatum cui subiecta est; et si confirmaretur, adhuc tamen non teneret, quia est contra concilium generale, de quo in dicto capitulo finali, quod huiusmodi constitutionem sive[l] statutum decernit non tenere in quo expresse fit mentio de mortuariis. Et

---

[j] *correxi*: molam *cod*.
[k] *correxi*: corrobatione *cod*.
[l] *correxi*: fuit *cod*.

An enquiry as to whether the statutes 203

buy from, or mill grain or bake bread for clergy incur excommunication, there is an even stronger reason why those who decree that only *so* many clergy are to attend a dead person's funeral, and each is to be given one candle of *so* many ounces, and just two *soldi*, should incur this sentence. For these things go even more against church freedom and towards diminishing it (the phrase used there), since they specifically concern death disbursements: on the latter, see the doctors' views and the chapter "Cum laicis" above. All the doctors adduce this chapter to prove that a laypeople's statute about death disbursements is invalid, and that is what they understand Innocent to have meant, as is clear from their responses.

Finally, as confirmation of the preceding statements I say that your statute has never been observed ever since it was passed; it has thus been abolished by disuse and contrary custom, and is no longer valid. For it is almost thirty-five years since it was established, and there is no one who remembers it having been practiced and followed — rather, it has been annulled, as is clear from the Brescian *Repertorium* mentioned above.[82] It cannot, therefore, be practiced *anew*, for it is powerless (according to the remarks of Cino[83] on the law "Rem non novam" of the *Code, On judgments*, at the paragraph "Patroni,"[84] and according to Angelo d'Arezzo[85] in the preface to his *Institutes*, at the line "Dissuetudinem"), except it be ratified and restored from now on by the illustrious ducal dominion. For even if the city *could* make a statute, it is still invalid unless it has been ratified by the superior to which the city is subject; even if it *were* ratified, it would still be invalid, since it goes against the general council, as seen in the said final chapter, which prescribes that the kind of ordinance or statute where death disbursements are expressly mentioned

---

[82] See n. 68 above.

[83] Cino (Sighibuldi) da Pistoia (ca. 1270–1336/37), a poet admired by Dante, and a leading jurist and law-teacher (Bartolo was among his pupils) whose *Lectura in Codicem* — a commentary on the first nine books of Justinian's *Code* — earned him a doctorate at Bologna in 1314.

[84] *Cod.* 3. 1. 14. 4; *CICv* 2: 122.

[85] Angelo (Gambiglioni) d'Arezzo, *Instituta cum divisionibus et summariis* (Venice, 1503), bk. 1, *De iustitia et iure* (commenting on the words "et quod postea desuetudi[n]e inumbratum est ab imperiali remedio illuminatum est"): "nota legem tolli per desuetudinem: vel per contrariam consuetudinem vel per supervenientem legem tolli."

non potest inferior[m] concilio disposita per concilium generale anullare, tollere, aut contrafacere, cum inferior legem superioris tollere non possit iuribus supra allegatis: et glossa Abbatis et scribentes in capitulo "Cum dilecti," [*recte*, "Ne Romani,"] *De electione*,[86] [et] idem Abbas in capitulo "Quod dilectio tua," *De consanguinitate et affinitate*.[87] Et propterea dicit Hostiensis in dicto capitulo ultimo, in versu 'sacri approbatione concilii':[88] "Quis ergo praesumet venire contra? Neque enim potest errare Ecclesia generalis ([*Causa*] *xxiiii, quaestione i*) a recta fide."[89]

Dominus Iason de Papia.[90]

Addo dictum Domini Iasonis, qui requisitus super hac materia pro habenda veritate respondit manu propria [sig. dr] Reverendo inquisitori Brixiae dicens: "Vidi quam plurima[n] circa materiam funeralium collecta et ad me transmissa. Ea laudo et approbo, quoniam ex eis ostenditur clare et vere statutum ipsum contra libertatem ecclesiasticam esse, et ob hoc statuentes ac illud observari facientes in excommunicationis sententiam incidisse."[91] Haec ille.

Ex quibus omnibus clare patet quod erat probandum: videlicet, statutum praedictum contra ecclesiasticam libertatem esse cum excommunicatione annexa; et requiri statuti huius et aliorum similium si qua in statutis Brixiensibus — quod est bene investigandum, ne liberi ab uno in alio sint irretiti — deletionem, ut ex textibus[o] in principio positis patet; et omnes in dictis capitulis contentos hac[p] poena ligari.

---

[m] *omisi*: et *cod.*

[n] *correxi*: plura *cod.*

[o] *correxi*: testibus *cod.*

[p] *correxi*: ac *cod.*

An enquiry as to whether the statutes 205

does not hold. And the council's inferior cannot nullify, abolish, or oppose things prescribed through the general council since, owing to the rules cited above, an inferior cannot abolish a superior's law: see also De Tudeschis's gloss, and commentators on the chapter "Cum dilecti" [*recte*, "Ne Romani"] of *On election*.[86] The same De Tudeschis writes about the chapter "Quod dilectio tua" of *On consanguinity and affinity*,[87] and that is why De Segusio, commenting on the words "with the sacred council's approval" in the said final chapter,[88] asks: "Who then will presume to oppose it? For indeed the Church as a whole cannot stray ([*Case*] 24, question 1) from the true faith."[89]

Master Jason of Pavia.[90]

I append the statement of Master Jason who, when questioned on this subject as to what one should regard as the truth, gave this hand-written answer to the reverend inquisitor of Brescia: "I have seen as many items as possible that were gathered and passed on to me on the subject of funeral expenses, and I praise and approve them, since they show clearly and truly that this particular statute goes against church freedom, and that therefore its makers and those ensuring its observance have fallen under the sentence of excommunication."[91] These are his words.

All these facts supply clear evidence for what needed proving: namely, that the aforesaid statute goes against church freedom (an offence which incurs excommunication); that removal of this statute and of any other similar Brescian statutes — this should be examined well, lest in being rid of one they have been ensnared in another — is required, as is obvious from the texts cited at the beginning; and that all those included in the said chapters are bound by this sentence.

---

[86] See n. 16 above.
[87] X 4. 14. 3; *CIC* 2: 701–2.
[88] See n. 4 above.
[89] C. 24 q. 1 c. 9; *CIC* 1: 969: "A recta fide ergo et apostolico tramite propter ullam perturbationem nolite recedere, scientes, quoniam iuxta Salvatoris sentenciam beati sunt qui persecucionem patiuntur propter iusticiam [Matthew 5: 10]."
[90] Unidentified.
[91] Untraced.

Quapropter diligentissime advertendum est an absolvi aliqui potuerint, aut in futurum possint: et qui observari[q] fecerunt, et qui de consilio sunt, quamvis non sint operati quod observaretur, nam textus capituli "Noverit" includit consiliarios locorum et non consiliarios in hoc negocio. Attento praecipue quod semper pontifex summus intendit adhiberi remedia, et ligare in perpetuum successores — ut apparet ex supra notatis. De hoc scribens Dominus Abbas Siculus in capitulo ultimo, *De rebus Ecclesiae non alienandis*, dicit: "Conclude ergo quod statutarii, et alii de quibus in textu, sunt excommunicati ipso facto, sed successores eorum non sunt excom-[sig. dv]municati, nisi quamprimum sciverint,[r] non fecerint statuta deleri de libris."[92] Haec ille. Et disputatur subtiliter ab eo et ab aliis doctoribus utrum illud "quamprimum" intelligatur "in primo quasi instanti", etc. Item attento quod consilium magnificae civitatis Brixiae de longe maioribus disponere potest non recusante illustrissimo dominio, quod semper affectat rem gratam facere fidelissimae huic et magnificae civitati. Nec dubium est quin illustrissimum atque serenissimum dominium nostrum hac in re omnia per consiliarios gesta gratissima habeat, quemadmodum et ante gratum habebat quicquid fiebat contra tale statutum — et hoc dictum sit ne impotentia allegetur.

Nec est oblivioni tradendum quod excommunicati non possunt a peccatis absolvi nisi prius ab excommunicatione absolvantur, secundum rationabilem et magis approbatam doctorum sententiam. Maximus enim effectus excommunicationis est a sacramentis separatio, et absolutio facta nullius est roboris.

Est etiam ad hoc praecipue advertendum, quod nulla ratio adduci potest quin absoluti de facto, non de iure, reincidant in eundem canonem post absolutionem, non exequendo quae summus pontifex mandat in capitulis supra allegatis — aut verius nunquam valuerit absolutio. Et si in aliquo casu valuit, non providendo in futurum iterum reincidunt.

---

[q] *correxi*: observare *cod.*
[r] *omisi*: et *cod.*

Very careful thought must therefore be given to the question whether some people can have been, or can in future be, absolved: both those who ensured the statute's observance, and members of the council, even though they did not bring about its observance, for the passage in the chapter "Noverit" mentions "councilors of the places", and not "councilors involved in this business". One should especially note that, as is clear from the above quotations, the supreme pontiff's intention is for remedies to be applied *always*, and to bind *for ever* such people's successors. Writing about this, De Tudeschis says apropos the final chapter of *On not alienating the Church's property*: "Conclude, then, that statute-makers, and others listed in this passage, are automatically excommunicate; but their successors are not excommunicate unless, immediately they realized the situation, they did not have the statutes removed from the books."[92] These are his words. And there is an abstruse debate between him and other doctors as to whether the word "immediately" should be understood as "at the first instant or so", etc. One should also note that the council of the splendid city of Brescia can deal with far greater matters without any objection from the illustrious dominion, which always strives to do what pleases this most loyal and splendid city. And there is no doubt that in this affair our illustrious and serene dominion will be extremely grateful for all that the councilors do, just as earlier it was grateful for whatever steps were taken against such a statute — let this be said to counter any imputation of weakness!

Nor must it be forgotten that, according to the reasonable and more favored opinion of the doctors, those excommunicated cannot be absolved from their sins without first being absolved from excommunication. For excommunication's greatest effect is exclusion from the sacraments, and absolution of sins, if it is performed, has no power.

Special thought must also be given to this fact: no reason can be advanced why those absolved *de facto*, not *de jure*, would not fall under the same canonical sentence again after absolution, by not carrying out the supreme pontiff's commands in the chapters cited above — or, more truly, why their 'absolution' was not always invalid. And if in some situation it *was* valid, through lack of forethought they fall under the sentence again.

---

[92] Not in his *Lectura super quinque libros*, III: *De rebus ecclesiae alienandis*, "Cum laicis."

Nec ignorantia potest excusare, cum sit ignorantia iu-[sig. diir]ris, quae regulariter neminem excusat exceptis paucis, de quibus in lege prima, *Codice, De iuris et facti ignorantia,* in paragrapho "Nondum."[93] Et hoc tenet Ioannes de Lignano[94] et glossa in dicto capitulo "Noverit," per regulam "Ignorantia," *De regulis iuris, Liber vi.*[95]

Et maxime cum res sit in dubium deducta a principio, quod debuit esse causa bene recogitandi super male actis; nec excusare posse videtur quod aliqui teneant oppositum, qui pro re hac dillucidanda modico studio incubuerunt, et volumina pauca revolverunt in tam grandi ac periculosissimo negocio, ad animam totiusque reipublicae salutem pertinente. Additur quod nullo modo nulloque ingenio effici potest quin casus sit saltem, etiam apud pertinacissimos, dubius, cum communis ac rationabilis opinio, quae supra posita est et probata, etiam saxa trahere sufficiat in dubium. Concludunt autem omnes theologi quod in dubio, non eligendo tutiorem partem, exponit se homo periculo peccati mortalis, et per consequens mortaliter peccat.

An autem qui incurrerunt excommunicationem suprascriptam possint ab alio quam a summo pontifice absolvi non est temere procedendum, praecipue cum in facto consistat. Et videtur absolutio papae reservata:

primo, per dictum Rosellae in titulo *De excommunicatione*, paragrapho xviii, cui Minores plurimum deferre videntur;[96]

secundo, per bullam Sixti (quae videri potest in fine eiusdem Rosellae), in qua voluit, concedendo auctoritatem confitendi [sig. diiv] quibuscunque,

Nor can their ignorance excuse them, since it is ignorance of the law, which by rule excuses no one except a few people: see the first law of the Code, *On ignorance of law and fact*, in the paragraph "Nondum"[93] — a view also taken by Giovanni da Legnano,[94] and in the gloss to the said chapter "Noverit," following the rule "Ignorantia" of *On rules of law* in the *Sext*.[95]

And this is particularly true since, from the start, their position has been thrown into doubt, which should have caused a radical rethink about misdeeds; nor does it seem a possible excuse that *some* people hold the opposite view — people who in fact have applied themselves with slight enthusiasm to explaining this matter, and have perused few books in such a huge and hazardous business, which concerns the soul, and the well-being of the state. An added point is that no means and no cleverness can make their case other than doubtful at the least, even amongst the most persistent of them, since the shared and reasonable opinion set out and proved above would be enough to drag even stones into doubt. But all the theologians conclude that in doubt, in not choosing the safer side, a person exposes himself to danger of mortal sin, and consequently sins mortally.

Nor should one rashly proceed to ask whether those who have incurred the excommunication mentioned above can be absolved by someone other than the supreme pontiff, especially since it is a matter of *fact*. And it does seem that absolution is reserved for the pope:

first, because of Rosella's statement — to which the Friars Minor seem to attach much importance — entitled *On excommunication* (par. 18);[96]

second, because of Sixtus's bull (it may be seen at the end of the same Rosella's statement) where, while delegating the power of confession to

---

[93] *Cod.* 1. 18. 1; *CICv* 2: 74: "Quamvis, cum causam tuam ageres, ignorantia iuris propter simplicitatem armatae militiae adlegationes competentes omiseris, tamen si nondum satisfecisti, permitto tibi, si coeperis ex sententia conveniri, defensionibus tuis uti."

[94] Giovanni da Legnano (ca. 1320–1383), doctor of canon and civil law at Bologna best known for his treatises on the laws of war and peace, but also author of a *Commentary* on the Gregorian *Decretals* and of a *Lectura* on the *Clementines*; *DDC* 6: 111–12.

[95] VI 5. 12. reg. 13; *CIC* 2: 1122: "Ignorantia facti, non iuris, excusat."

[96] See n. 11 above.

servatum esse casum violationis Ecclesiae libertatis, et alia quae in Cena Domini servari consueverunt;[97]

tertio, videtur esse practica curiae talia reservare;

quarto, est diligenter considerandum an reservatio facta per alios summos pontifices duret (etiam concesso quod hoc anno non fuerit posita in casibus Cenae Domini), cum praecipue Sixtus (ubi supra) auctoritate apostolica statuat quod decetero nunquam intelligantur tales casus esse concessi, cum clausulis strictissimis quas videre est facile (ubi supra). Hic autem omittuntur brevitatis causa.

Responsiones ad argumenta falsa circa principium posita.

Ad argumenta quae tertio loco sunt solvenda, quamvis per antedicta veritas satis elucescat, praemitto de mente suprascripti Domini Albrici — quod ad cognoscendum statutum esse contra ecclesiasticam libertatem ex tribus, et eorum singulis, deveniri potest:

et primo, quando universaliter prohibentur saeculares deservire ecclesiis aut cum eis contrahere, ut capitulo ultimo, *De immunitate ecclesiarum, Liber sextus*;[98]

secundo, quando de clericis vel religiosis in statuto fit expressa mentio et specialis — hoc innuit etiam dictum capitulum;

tertio, quando apponitur poena in ipso statuto, per quam excluduntur religiosi ab eorum perceptione quorum sunt [sig. diiir] de iure capaces.

Duo autem ultima clare ponuntur in statuto Brixiensi, quibus non potest excusari quin statutum sit contra libertatem Ecclesiae et in eius odium factum. Quod forte non praesumeretur si nulla mentio fieret aut

whomsoever, he wished the case of trespassing on the Church's freedom to be reserved, along with other cases relating to Holy Communion which are usually reserved;[97]

thirdly, it seems to be curial practice to reserve such things;

fourth, one should think carefully whether a reservation made by other supreme pontiffs still endures (even granting that in this year it was *not* counted among the 'Holy Communion' cases), especially since Sixtus (as above) decrees with apostolic authority that "at other times such cases are never to be understood as delegated", with very strict stipulations which are easily seen (as above). Here, however, they are omitted for brevity's sake.

Answers to the false claims listed near the beginning.

I preface the false claims which — in third place — must be demolished (although, thanks to previous statements, the truth is already dawning) with a remark about the thinking of the above-mentioned Master Alberico. From three factors, and from each separately, one may come to recognize that the statute goes against church freedom:

first, because by it laypeople are universally forbidden to minister to churches or do business with them — see *Liber sextus*, *On the immunity of churches* (final chapter);[98]

second, because the statute makes express and special mention of clergy and religious — as also implied by the said chapter;

third, because the statute itself fixes a penalty which causes religious to be barred from receiving those benefits for which they are legally qualified.

The two last factors are clear components of the Brescian statute, and make it impossible for the statute *not* to go against the Church's freedom and *not* to have been motivated by hatred of it. That motive would perhaps not be assumed if there were no mention made or penalty

---

[97] The bull *De auctoritate majoris poenitentiarii Sanctae Romanae Ecclesiae*, issued by Sixtus IV on 9 May 1484: see *Magnum Bullarium Romanum* (Lyons, 1682), 1:440–42.

[98] See n. 81 above.

poena imponeretur, tantum verbis generalibus utendo, non enim viderentur per verba generalia offendere voluisse quos non nominassent: ergo . . . etc.

Item praemitto quod verbum 'videtur', si in supra aut infrascriptis reperitur, non est verbum dubitativum, sed affirmativum. Nam per verbum 'videtur' fertur sententia diffinitiva, ut est textus notabilis Ulpiani iurisconsulti in lege "Quid tamen," paragrapho "Si arbiter."[99]

Ad primum ergo dicitur quod non est ad conservationem reipublicae, imo est ad destructionem, quia fit contra clericos, qui sunt principalis pars reipublicae. Sed instant: "Non prohibemus dari elemosinas aliis modis." Respondetur: "Satis est ad impietatem, si multis modis possint fieri elemosinae erga clericos, et tu unum modum aut omnino prohibeas, aut diminuas, qui forte multis placet plusquam ceteri modi." Et dicit Albricus quod illae leges non ligant clericos, quia etiam leges conditae in favorem ecclesiarum robur non sumunt nisi approbatae per Ecclesiam: *De constitutionibus*, capitulo "Ecclesia Sanctae Mariae."[100]

Ad secundum dicitur falsum esse quod quicquid possunt privatae personae, hoc possit communitas generaliter, nam certum est per Hostiensem et Ioannem Andreae, *De iure iurando*, capitulo "Venientes,"[101] quod licet per pactum possit renunciari appellationi [sig. diiiv] inter duos litigantes, non tamen posset fieri statutum generale quod non possit appellari. Similiter

An enquiry as to whether the statutes

set, with just *general* terms being used, for general terms would make their users seem not to have wished to offend those they had not named: therefore ... etc.

I add this prefatory remark: that the word 'seems', if used in the comments above or below, is a word expressing not doubt, but affirmation. For the word 'seems' carries a definitive meaning, as seen in a noteworthy text of the jurist Ulpian on the law "Quid tamen," in the paragraph "Si arbiter."[99]

The reply to the first claim, therefore, is that the statute is aimed, not at the state's preservation, but at its ruination, since it goes against clergy, who are the main part of the state. "But," they insist, "we do not ban almsgiving by other methods." The answer is: "It is tantamount to impiety if many ways of giving alms to clergy were possible, and you either banned outright, or reduced, one way which many people happen to like more than the others." And Alberico says that *those* laws do not bind clergy, because even laws established in favor of churches assume no power unless ratified by the Church: see *On ordinances*, the chapter "Ecclesia Sanctae Mariae."[100]

The reply to the second claim is that it is false to say the community in general can do whatever private persons can, for it has been established by De Segusio, and by Giovanni d'Andrea, commenting on the chapter "Venientes" of *On taking an oath*,[101] that although between two litigants the right of appeal can by agreement be renounced, yet a general statute could not be passed making an appeal impossible. Similarly in

---

[99] *Dig.* 4. 8. 21. 1; *DJ* 1: 153 (*CICv* 1: 98). In fact, neither of the ways Ulpian uses *videtur* in this passage conveys 'doubt' or 'affirmation': in the clause *nihil videri Titium debere Seio* it means 'appears' (as a matter of fact on the evidence), while in the clause *videri contra sententiam arbitri fecisse* it means 'it is taken to be' (as a matter of law). We are indebted to Emeritus Professor Anthony M. Honoré for advice on this point.

[100] See n. 3 above.

[101] X 2. 24. 19; *CIC* 2: 366. D'Andrea's commentary on this chapter (*Novella*, vol. 2, fols. 190v–191r) includes the sentence: "& licet cives possint condere legem municipalem contra ius; non tamen in praeiudicium principis, vel alterius, de quo remittit Innocentius ... fatetur tamen, quod sine constitutione litigantes possunt appellationi renunciare ..." (cap. xix 6, fol. 191r).

in proposito: licet Ticius[102] possit ita disponere in testamento suo quod non vocentur nisi xxiiii clerici ad suum funus, non tamen civitas generaliter potest hoc statuere, quia primum nullius derogat libertati, sicut secundum derogat. Nam dominium in civitate non est despoticum, quo videlicet domini regunt servos, sed politicum, videlicet, quo domini regunt cives liberos in multis super paene omnibus negociis suis.[103]

Ad tertium dicitur: cum Ecclesia possit recipere elemosinas in infinitum et habere[s] liberas oblationes, apparet quod statutum per quod talis facultas et libertas [tolluntur] — saltem per indirectum, per poenam appositam vocantibus plures clericos quam xxiiii — sit contra libertatem Ecclesiae.

Ad quartum respondetur quod imo illa limitatio facta saecularibus, ne dent ecclesiis plusquam statutum dicit, est contra libertatem Ecclesiae, quia aufert per poenas appositas libertatem donandi ecclesiis, in casu valente ad suffragia animarum, ad divinum cultum honorandum, et ad religiosorum sustentationem, et in casu praecipue concesso a iure communi (tam civili et canonico quam etiam divino et naturali) — quae iura religiosos capaces faciunt elemosinarum cuiuscunque generis. Item fit praecipue contra dispositionem capituli ultimi, *De rebus Ecclesiae non alienandis*, ut latius supradictum est.

Ad quintum respondetur quod imo facultas Ecclesiae tol-[sig. divr]litur, ne possit recipere liberas elemosinas, nec [non] hoc sequitur ad statutum, sed quod plus est directe est materia statuti, cum dicatur non possint habere nisi clericos vigintiquatuor, et non possint eis dari nisi duo solidi pro quolibet. Neque principale intentum potest esse bonum, quoniam via et media ad illud[t] sunt mala — ut si quis furetur ut possit facere elemosinam. Similiter hic: ut consulant et prospiciant (ut ipsi dicunt) paupertati civium, vetant dari elemosinas funerales clericis. Falsum etiam est quod talia statuta non prohibeantur iure, ut patet

---

[s] *correxi*: habeat *cod*.
[t] *correxi*: illam *cod*.

An enquiry as to whether the statutes   215

the present instance: although Titius[102] can prescribe in his *will* that only twenty-four clergy be invited to his funeral, yet a city in general cannot make a *statute* to this effect, because the first procedure diminishes no one's freedom, as the second does. For power in a city is not the despotic type where masters rule over *slaves*, but the statesmanlike type where masters rule over *citizens*, who in many ways are free as regards nearly all their own affairs.[103]

The reply to the third claim is this: since the Church can receive alms unrestrictedly and have unlimited offerings, obviously a statute which abolishes such a power and such a freedom — indirectly at least, by imposing a penalty on those who summon more than twenty-four clergy — *does* go against the Church's freedom.

The answer to the fourth claim is that certainly the restriction placed on laypeople's giving churches more than stated by the statute *does* go against the Church's freedom, because by the penalties imposed it removes the freedom to make gifts to churches. There is a strong case in favor of prayers for souls, respect for divine worship, and subsistence for religious, and a case especially allowed by common law (both civil and canon law, and divine and natural law too) — laws which qualify religious for alms of whatever sort. Also, the statute especially contradicts the terms of *On not alienating the Church's property* (final chapter), as more fully explained above.

The answer to the fifth claim is that certainly the Church's power is abolished, rendering it unable to accept unlimited alms, and this is also a corollary of the statute; but more to the point is the statute's content, for it says that people cannot have more than twenty-four clergy, who can be given no more than two *soldi* each. And its main aim cannot be good, for the ways and means to it are bad — as if one were to steal in order to give alms. Likewise here: in order to show concern and consideration (their own words) for the poverty of their citizens, they forbid the giving of funeral alms to clergy. It is also false to claim that

---

[102] A typical name used (especially for the judge) in Roman legal *formulae*: A. Borkowski, *Roman Law*, 2nd ed. (London: Blackstone Press Ltd, 1997), 75–76. See also n. 99 above.

[103] Cf. Aristotle, *Politics* 1252a7–16, where the statesman (*politikos*) is contrasted with the ruler of a kingdom (*monarkhos*), or of a household (*oikonomikos*), or of a group of slaves (*despotês*). Cf. above, xxxix n. 68.

per doctores superius adductos. Imo et vi prohibentur clerici, undique minando volentibus invitare plures.

Ad sextum: quo animo hoc faciant, ipsi viderint. Diceret tamen Albricus quod est praesumptio doli et odii contra tales statu[t]arios, per superius notata: "Nam clericis opido sunt infesti," [*Causa*] *ii, quaestio vii*;[104] "[Cum] laicis," [*Liber*] *extra*;[105] *De immunitate ecclesiarum*, capitulo "Clericis," *Liber vi*.[106] Nam videntes se non posse ligare clericos directe, per indirectum poenam apposuerunt in fraudem.

Ad septimum: saecularis potest transire ad sacros ordines, non tamen clericus in sacris potest redire ad vitam laicalem. Item — cum quicquid habent clerici pauperum sit — sicut Ecclesia iudicat iustum ut omnia bona clericorum praeter sustentationem suam in pauperum usum aut in reparationem ecclesiarum veniant, ita iustum iudicat quod saeculares possint dare in infinitum elemosinas. Unde hoc argumentum potius concludit oppositum [sig. divv] quam propositum.

Ad octavum: cum de facti natura agitur, non oportet transire ad intentionem, quia solus Deus occultorum est cognitor.[107] Dicitur etiam quod quanto plures (praesertim religiosi) conveniunt, tanto plures dicuntur orationes — et tanto plures etiam saeculares conveniunt, et euntes ad domum luctus monentur de fine cunctorum. Item non spectat ad laicos corrigere peccata clericorum, etiam si oblationibus male utantur.

Ad nonum: patet ex praedictis quod dicta statuta sunt contra privilegia Ecclesiae et communia iura.

Ad decimum: hoc est secundum caritatis ordinem — ut quilibet pro anima sua relinquat quantum et quomodo velit, et faciat quod de se

An enquiry as to whether the statutes 217

such statutes are not prevented by law, as the doctors cited above make clear. Certainly clergy are banned by force too, with widespread threats against those wishing to invite more.

As to the sixth claim: they themselves will know their intention in doing this. Alberico, however, would say that against such statute-makers there is a presumption of guile and hatred, according to the views quoted above: "For in the town are people who are hostile to clergy", in [*Case*] 2, question 7;[104] "[*Cum*] laicis," in the [*Liber*] *extra*;[105] and the chapter "Clericis" of *On the immunity of churches*, in the *Sext*.[106] For, seeing that they cannot bind clergy directly, they have imposed a penalty in order to cheat them indirectly.

As to the seventh claim: a layperson can transfer to holy orders, yet a clerk in holy orders cannot return to a secular life. Also — since whatever clergy possess belongs to the poor — in the same way as the Church pronounces it just for all the clergy's goods except their subsistence to be used for the benefit of the poor or for the repair of churches, so it pronounces it just for laypeople to be able to give alms unrestrictedly. Hence, this claim does not prove its point but, rather, the opposite.

As to the eighth claim: when an issue is essentially factual, it is not right to transfer one's attention to motive, because God alone knows secrets.[107] It is also said that the more people (especially religious) congregate, the more prayers are said — and also the more laypeople congregate and, as they go to the house of mourning, are warned about everyone's end. Again, it is no concern of laypeople to correct clergy's sins, even if they were to misuse offerings.

As to the ninth claim: it is obvious from what has been said that the said statutes *do* go against the Church's privileges and corporate rights.

As for the tenth claim: *this* is what accords with the normal practice of charity — that anyone you please should leave behind for his soul's sake whatever, and in whatever way, he wishes, and devote what

---

[104] C. 2 q. 7 c. 14; CIC 1: 485: "Laici in accusatione episcoporum audiendi non sunt, quia oppido quidam eis infesti sunt, et indignum est ut ab eis accusentur, qui eorum gravitatem nolunt imitari."

[105] See n. 4 above.

[106] VI 3. 23. 3; CIC 2: 1062–63: "Clericis laicos infestos oppido tradit antiquitas, quod et praesentium experimenta temporum manifeste declarant . . ." etc.

[107] Cf. Psalms 43: 22: "Nonne Deus requiret ista? Ipse enim novit abscondita cordis."

est ad honorem Dei; et ut quisque bene advertat quid expediat, et quid possit statuere. Et concludit Albricus statutum esse fundatum super iniquitate, non super caritate.

Ad undecimum (ubi allegatur[u] capitulum "Animae defunctorum"): rogando responsionem bene [noti] notarii, sic dicitur. Primo, quod textus ille loquitur de pompis saecularibus quae in exequiis fiunt pro vivorum solatio, non autem de spiritualibus vel annexis spiritualibus; quod patet, nam numerando quibus modis animae defunctorum solvantur dicit quod "aut oblationibus sacerdotum, aut precibus sanctorum, aut carorum elemosinis, aut ieiunio cognatorum." Quorum tria consequuntur ipsae animae per invitationem [sig. er] multorum religiosorum, qui rogant Deum in processione funebri, et demum, etiam dum celebrant pro elemosinis datis, elemosina quoque ipsa subvenit defunctis, tam ex parte operis operati quam etiam operantis, ut dicunt theologi. Demum subiungit: curatio vero funeris [et] pompa exequiarum magis sunt vivorum solatia quam subsidia mortuorum, quae profecto sic debent intelligi ut non contrarientur hiis quae supra dixit esse ad animarum sublevationem.

Item ad idem respondetur: dato quod esset pompa illa quae est circa funera, et tamen esset circa spiritualia aut annexa spiritualibus, adhuc nullo modo possent saeculares disponere. Alioquin sequeretur quod possent in omnibus esse iudices clericorum et summi pontificis, cum facile possint omnia in malum et pompam interpretari; et fierent iudices secretorum quae a solo animo dependent. Quae omnia sunt valde absurda. Inspiciant ergo facta ipsa, quae spiritualia sunt aut annexa spiritualibus.

Item, cum (teste Augustino) superbia bonis operibus insidietur, ut pereant,[108] pari ratione possent omnia bona opera prohiberi, ut constructio

---

[u] *correxi*: alligatur *cod*.

he has to the honor of God; and that each person should heed well what is profitable, and what he *can* decide. And Alberico concludes that the statute is based on unfairness, not on charity.

As to the eleventh claim (where the chapter "Animae defunctorum" is adduced): to a request for the reaction of a well-known notary this is the reply. First, the text speaks of secular extravagance occurring at funerals for the comfort of the living, not about spiritual matters or spiritual adjuncts; this is plain, for in listing the ways in which the souls of the departed are released it says: "Either by the offerings of priests, or by the prayers of saints, or by the alms of loved ones, or by the fasting of relatives." The souls themselves pursue three of these ways by inviting many religious who entreat God in the funeral cortège, and finally, even when they celebrate the Mass in return for alms given, the alms themselves also aid the departed, with respect both to the deed done and to the doer, as theologians say. Finally, the notary adds, funeral arranging and a mourners' procession do indeed give more comfort to the living than aid to the dead, but they should surely be understood in such a way that they are not opposed to the things which he previously called conducive to the relief of souls.

A further answer to the same claim is this: given that the extravagance which exists in regard to funerals *did* exist, and that it nevertheless existed in regard to spiritual matters or spiritual adjuncts, still laypeople would by no means be able to deal with funerals. Otherwise it would follow that in everything they could be the judges of clergy and of the supreme pontiff, since they could easily interpret everything as evil and extravagant; and they would become judges of hidden thoughts which derive from the mind alone. All these things are absolutely ridiculous. Let them, therefore, examine the actions themselves, which are spiritual or spiritually connected.

Again, since (as Augustine attests) pride infiltrates good works so that they perish,[108] by the same token *all* good works could be banned,

---

[108] Augustine, *Regula*: Praeceptum 1. 7 (PL 32. 1379); see G. Lawless, O. S. A., *Augustine of Hippo and his Monastic Rule* (Oxford: Clarendon Press, 1987), 82–83: "Alia quippe quaecumque iniquitas in malis operibus exercetur ut fiant, superbia vero etiam bonis operibus insidiatur ut pereant."

ecclesiarum, monasteriorum, hospitalium — et cetera similia — cum ex pompa fieri possint.

Ad auctoritatem Abbatis, quae allegari videtur satis publice, non datur responsio, quia aliter invenitur quam allegetur, ut supra notatum est. Et hoc in capitulo ultimo, *De rebus Ecclesiae non alienandis*.

Ad Rosellam respondetur quod aut nullius aut modi-[sig. ev]cae auctoritatis est, ideo eadem facilitate relinquitur qua allegatur. Ad fundamentum suum dicitur quod est valde dissimilis casus, item quod argumentum suum tractum a simili potest faciliter centum pedibus claudicare. Item dicitur non esse allegandum Abbatem a simili, quoniam invenitur doctrina eius praecise ad casum nostrum contraria huic similitudini, ut supra est notatum in capitulo ultimo, *De rebus Ecclesiae non alienandis*. Item advertendum est ad ea ex quibus cognoscatur violari ecclesiasticam libertatem, ut supra dictum est ante principium responsionum, et notatum per Dominum Albricum.

Ad opinionem Bartholi dicitur quod communis doctorum opinio est in contrarium, qui volunt quod tam ingrediens quam ingressus non possunt proiberi testari saeculari statuto.

Ad id quod dicitur, [statutum] servari in aliquo loco, respondetur malum quod alibi est factum non est allegandum et in consequentiam trahendum. In aliquibus enim locis maiores inhonestates, maiores factiones, maiores iniusticiae, maiores pompae, maiores ecclesiarum pessundationes fiunt quam Brixiae, quae tamen imitanda non sunt. Et alicubi institutus est mons pietatis, aut cum usura aut cum maximo dubio; quod tamen Brixiae impugnatum est, et aliter Brixiani cives disposuerunt, volentes omni periculo reiecto aere publico providere officialibus montis — cum totius Italiae commendatione.[109]

[sig. eiir] Haec ad Dei laudem collecta sunt et excogitata, ne civitatis huius — quam magnificae! — cives ignorent quae ad statuta sua condenda aut manutenenda requiruntur, cum Ecclesiam tangunt. Dignentur igitur

such as the building of churches, monasteries, hospitals — and other similar things — since they *may* result from extravagance.

To De Tudeschis's pronouncement, which seems to be cited quite publicly, no answer is given, because it is found to be otherwise than may be alleged, as mentioned above. This is in relation to *On not alienating the Church's property* (final chapter).

The answer to Rosella is that he has no, or slight, authority, so it is as easy to ignore as to cite him. The reply to his core argument is that it is a very different situation, and also that his claim, drawn as it is from similarity, can easily be wrong-footed a hundred times. A further reply is that De Tudeschis should not be cited on the basis of similarity, since his teaching is found exactly to negate this resemblance in regard to our own situation, as mentioned above apropos of *On not alienating the Church's property* (final chapter). Attention should also be paid to the reasons for recognizing that the statute trespasses on church freedom, as stated above before the start of these answers to the claims, and as mentioned by Master Alberico.

The reply to Bartolo's view is that the shared view of doctors is the opposite: they maintain that, both *when* entering and *after* entering the religious life, religious cannot be banned from making a will by a secular statute.

The answer to the claim that the statute is observed in some place is that evil done elsewhere should not be cited and taken to its consequence. For in some places greater disgraces, greater power struggles, greater injustices, greater extravagances, greater ecclesiastical disasters happen than at Brescia, but they must not be copied. Also, somewhere a *monte di pietà* was established, either charging interest or using a very doubtful system; but this was opposed at Brescia, and Brescian citizens arranged matters differently, wishing to cast all danger aside and subsidize officials of the *monte* with public money — to the applause of all Italy.[109]

These comments have been assembled and thought out in praise of God, lest the citizens of this city — what a splendid one it is! — be unaware of the prerequisites for establishing and preserving their own statutes,

---

[109] See *Defense*, n. 21.

qui reipublicae gubernandae aut praesunt, aut praeesse in futurum poterunt, cum affectu veritatis cognoscendae[v] praemissa a principio usque ad finem attentius legere, donec alia superaddi possint ad maiorem evidentiam — si maior esse potest quam per praemissa colligitur.

FINIS.

Ex conventu Sancti Dominici Brixiae, Angelo Britan[n]ico impressore, M. D VI. Aprilis prima luce.

---

[v] *correxi*: cognoscere *cod.*

when they affect the Church. Let those, therefore, who are, or who may in future be, in charge of the state's government deign to read the above paper quite carefully from start to finish with zeal to learn the truth, until further facts can be added to give stronger proof — if it *can* be stronger than is assembled above.

THE END.

Published by the convent of St. Dominic at Brescia, and printed by Angelo Britannico, on the first of April, 1506.

INDEX

Note: Arabic page numbers refer only to the English text since the original Latin may conveniently be found facing the translation throughout.

A

Accolti, Benedetto, xlii
Acts of Mercy, Seven, xlvi
Aelius Aristides, xli
Ajax, 59
Alberico da Rosciate, xxxiii, 11, 83, 161, 163, 165, 213, 221
Alexander VI, Pope, xlii
alms, xvii, xxviii, xxxii, xxxvi–xxxviii, xlvi, lix, 13–21, 37, 45, 69, 97
Angelo (Gambiglioni) d'Arezzo, 203
Aquila, lx
Aquinas, *see* Thomas Aquinas, St
Aristotle,
　Economics, liv
　Nicomachean Ethics, xxxiii, 175
　Politics, 113
Arrian, xliii
Arrigoni, Francesco:
　Panegyric of Brescia, xxvi
Augustine, St, (Augustinianism), xvii, xxxiv, li, lxii, 21, 219
　De cura pro mortuis gerenda, xxxiii n. 56
　De moribus ecclesiae catholicae, 15
Augustinian order, xvi
Averoldi, Bartolomeo, xlii

B

Baldus de Ubaldis, 191, 193, 197, 201
Bale, John, l
Barbaro, Francesco, xxvi
Barbatia (Barbazza), Andreas, 39 n. 33, 199, 201
Baron, Hans, lii, liii–liv
Bartolus, 169, 171, 199, 221
bastards, 135
Becichemo, Marino, xxv, xxvi, xli, lvi–lvii n. 119
Bellona, 63
bells, li, lviii, lx
　see also funerals
Bergamo, lx
Bern, l
Bernardino da Feltre, xxiii, lxii, lxiii
Bernardino of Siena, St, lxii, lxiii
Bertachino, Giovanni, 39 n. 33, 195
Bertrand, (bishop of Grasse), 189
Bible (texts):
　Old Testament, Proverbs 22: 9, 175; Daniel 4: 24, 173
　New Testament, Acts 4: 34–37, 49; Acts 5: 29, 27; Matt. 5: 45, 139; Matt. 6: 3–4, 125; Matt. 6: 34, 59; Matt. 7: 21, 23; Matt. 13: 46, 77; Matt. 16: 24, 93; Mark 8: 34, 93; Luke 3: 11, 59; Luke 7: 12, 175; Luke 9: 23, 93; Luke 11: 41, 173; John 10: 12, 67; 1 Cor. 12: 12–28, 137; Heb. 13: 16, 173
　Vulgate, Tobit 4: 7, 175, 4: 11, 173, 4: 17, 173; Ecclus. 3: 33, 175
Bologna, xxvi

Borghese, Giovanni Battista, xlviii
Borgia, Cesare, xlii
Borgia, Giovanni, xlii
Borgia, Rodrigo, *see* Alexander VI, Pope
Bracciolini, Poggio, liv
Bragadin, Francesco, xviii–xix, 31, 31–3 n. 26, 33
Brescia:
  academy of *Vertunni* in, xlii
  archbishop of, xxx, xxxi n. 46, lxx, 87
  architecture of, xxiv–xxv
  bishop of, xxx, xxx n. 46, xxxi, xxxiv, xl, lxx, 83, 85, 87
  churches in, xxv, 9
  epidemics in, xvi, xxviii, 31
  famine in, xxviii, xxxvi, 31
  hospitals in, 9, 27, 53
  humanism and humanists in, xxiv–xxvii
  inquisitor in, 205
  monasteries in, 27
  patron saints of, xxv
  political state of, xviii–xxii
  preachers in, lxiii
  San Domenico in, xv, xxx
    and bequests, xxxviii n. 64, xlvii n. 90
  see also Jews; *monte di pietà*; sumptuary legislation
Bresciano, Giovanni Antonio, lxx
Britannico family, lxx
Britannico, Angelo, xli, xliii, lxx, 223
Britannico, Giovanni, xxv, xxvi
Bruni, Leonardo, liv

C

Calderini, Antonio, xlii
Calfurnio, Giovanni, xxv, xli
  tomb of, Frontispiece, liv
candles, xv, lviii, lx, 21, 65, 67, 71, 81
  see also funerals; mortuaries

canon law:
  citations of,
    Decretum Gratiani, C. 2 q. 7 c. 14, 217; C. 13 q. 2 c. 19, 179, 219; C. 13 q c. 22, xxxiii, 43, 45, 47, 167, 177; C. 13 q. 2 c. 23, 179; C. 13 q. 2 c. 25, 185, 187, 191; C. 16 q. 1 c. 57, 189; C. 24 q. 1 c. 9, 205; D. 21 c. 4, 171; D. 43 c. 1, 187
    Liber Extra, 1.2.10, xxxiii, 159, 169, 185, 197, 213; 1.33.16, 171; 2.1.3, 185; 2.24.19, 213; 3.13.12, xxxiii, xxxix, 55, 69, 159, 161, 169, 179, 183, 185, 187, 195, 197, 199, 201, 203, 205, 207, 215, 217, 221; 4.1, 199; 4.14.3, 205; 5.38.14, 177; 5.39.28, 177; 5.39.49, 155, 161, 171, 181, 183, 207, 209; 5.39.53, 181
    Liber Sextus, 3.23.3, 217; 3.23.5, 201, 211; 5.12, reg. 13, 209
    Clem. 1.3.2, 169, 171, 205
Capaneus, 129
Capriolo, Elia:
  life and career of, xxxv
  as possible author of *Defensio*, xiv, xxxv
  writings of:
    Chronica de rebus brixianorum, xxxv, lxiii–lxiv
    De confirmatione Christianae fidei, xxxv, lxvii n. 146
Carletti, Fra Angelo, 191, 193
Carmelite order, xvi
castrators, xx, 135
Catullus, 131
Cavalcanti, Giovanni, xlii
Cereta, Laura, xxvi
Charybdis, 39, 39 n. 32
Chiari, xxvi

Index

Christian virtues, xxxvi, xliv
   charity as one of the, xlvi, xlvii
   see also Valgulio, writings of
Chrysostom, Dio, xli
Cicero (Ciceronianism), xxvi, lvii, 33 n. 27; 35 n. 28; 97 n. 11; 99 nn. 12, 13; 101 nn. 14, 15; 103 n. 16; 107 n. 21; 109 n. 23; 111 n. 26; 119 n. 33; 143 n. 55
   and concept of *res publica*, xvii
Cigole, lxx
Cino (Sighibuldi) da Pistoia, 203
civil law:
   citations of:
      Code, 1.2.1, 171, 177; 1.18.1, 209; 3.1.14.4, 203; 7.6.1.5, 191, 193
      Digest, 1.1.9, 201; 1.5.4 pr., 171; 4.8.21.1, 213; 21.1.31.24–25, 197; 34.2.40.1, 193, 201; 47.2.68 pr., 199
      Institutes, 1.3.1, 163
      Novellae, 7.2.1, 171, 173
Cleomedes, xli, xlii
Cleopatra, 77
clothing, *see* funerals; sumptuary legislation
coats of arms, liii, 61
Codagnello, Martino:
   as possible author of *Defensio*, xxxi n. 49
   as author of *Oratio ad serenissimum Venetorum principem Leonardum Lauredanum*, xxxi–xxxii n. 49
commemoration of the dead, xlvii, liv
   see also images
Concoreggio, Gabriele, xxv, xxvi, xli
confraternities, xvi, xxvii, xlvi–xlvii
Cornaro, Caterina, queen of Cyprus, xli
Corsetto, Antonio (Siculus), 39 n. 33, 185, 187
Cortesi, Paolo:
   De Cardinalatu, lv

Crates, 77 n. 75
Cremona, lxv
Cricca, 133
Cyprian, lxii

D

Dante, xxvii
da Rosciate of Bergamo, Alberico, *see* Alberico da Rosciate
De Dominicis, Domenico, 83
Defensio populi Brixiani rei violatae ecclesiasticae libertatis ob decretum ab eo factum de ambitione et sumptibus funerum minuendis, accusantibus Fratribus Sancti Dominici, xxxv–xl, lxix, lxx, 1–87
   attacks St Thomas Aquinas, 5
   on bequests, 37
   on Dominican
      behavior at funerals, 21, 73
      doctors, 57, 59
      excommunication of Brescians, 11, 49
      greed and pride, 2–5, 7, 9, 17, 39, 47, 49, 67, 77, 81
      alliance with Jews, 7
      ingratitude towards Brescia, 9, 49
      inquisition, 49
      riches, 15, 23, 33
      sickliness, 17
   on famine and fever in Brescia, 7
   on Jewish moneylending, 7
   on printing and distribution of *Quaestio*, 5, 7, 9, 33
   on sumptuary legislation, 7, 33
   see also Brescia; Capriolo; funerals; Jesus Christ; sumptuary legislation
de Monte, Pietro, 39 n. 33, 83, 85 n. 84, 195
   see also bishop of Brescia

De sumptibus funerum, see Valgulio, Carlo, writings of
dentists, xx, 135
de Vitalibus, Bernardinus, xliii
Die Totenfesser, l
Dionysius the Areopagite, pseudo-, xlix, 123
Dominican order, xvi–xvii
   attacked, xxxvi, xliv
   conventuals in:
      object to statute regulating funerals, xv, xxix
   observants in, lxii
   persecute witches in Valcamonica, xxxvi
   practice magic, xxxvi, 55
   resents *monte di pietà*, xxiii
   see also *Defensio populi Brixiani rei violatae ecclesiasticae libertatis ob decretum ab eo factum de ambitione et sumptibus funerum minuendis, accusantibus Fratribus Sancti Dominici*; *Questio an infrascripta statuta super mortuariis sint contra eccesiasticam libertatem*
Don Agostino de Moris (prior of San Domenico), xxx–xxxi, xliv n. 85

E

ecclesiastical liberty, xv
Egidio of Viterbo, lxvi
Egyptians, 127, 129
England, xxviii n. 37
   funerals in, li
Epictetus, xlix, 107 n. 19; 109 n. 24; 111 n. 25
Erasmus, Desiderius, lvi, 133–5 n. 48
   Praise of Folly, xiv, lvi
   The Funeral, xiv, xxviii n. 37, xlviii, lvi

F

Fabius, xxvi
Faenza, lx
Ferdinand of Aragon, King, lix
Ficino, Marsilio, xxv, xlii
Filipino de' Sali, xliii
flautists, 135
Florence, xxi, xli, lxi, lxiii
   funeral orations in, liv
   funerals in, xlvii, xlviii, lviii
   moneylending in, xxxix–xl, 67
Fra Girolamo (Dominican), xxx, xliv n. 85
Francis, St, 53
Franciscan order, xvi–xvii, xlvii, 29, 53, 71
   observants of, xvii, lxii
Franciscanism, lii
funerals:
   confraternal attendance at, xxvii
   criticism of expense of, xiv–xv
   mourning clothes for, xiv, xxxiv, lix
   mourning customs of ancients at, xlix, 33 n. 27, 127
   processions of, xvi, xlvii
   regulated by statute, xv, xv n. 1, xvi, xxvii–xxxi
   social function of, xv, lxviii
   see also England; Florence; Leipzig; Protestantism; Spain; Venice

G

Gandino, lxx
Gavardo, 83
Ghibellines, xxi–xxii, xxi n. 18
Giovanni da Imola, 39 n. 33, 181, 187, 201
Giovanni da Legnano, 209
Giovanni d'Andrea, 181, 187, 193, 213
Giustiniani, Tommaso, lv

Index

Gravina, Pietro, xlii
Guelfs, xxi–xxii, xxi n. 18, xl, xliii

H

Henricus de Segusio, *see* Hostiensis (cardinal)
honor, xviii, xlv
horses, 61, 71, 129, 201
Hostiensis (Henricus de Segusio), cardinal, xxxiii, 181, 187, 213
humanism,
   and virtue, xvii
   and wealth, liv
   see also Brescia; Capriolo, Elia; Valgulio, Carlo
Hyrcanians, 127

I

images:
   in churches, 63
   of Jesus Christ, xlviii
   of mourning, xlviii n. 91
   on tombs, Frontispiece, liv
indults, xxxviii, 25, 27, 37, 43, 79
Inquiry as to whether the statutes about death disbursements quoted below go against church freedom, see *Questio an infrascripta statuta super mortuariis sint contra eccesiasticam libertatem*
inquisition, 49
Irus, 133
Isabella of Castile, Queen, lix

J

James, St, 59, 175
Jason of Pavia, 205
Jerome, St, lxii

Jesus Christ, xlv, xlviii, lvi, 23, 51, 53, 55, 59, 79, 87, 93, 103, 175
Jews, xxii–xxiv, 87
Joseph, St, 53
Julius II, Pope, xxix–xxx
Justinian, Emperor, xxxviii
Juvenal, xxvi

L

Laertius, Diogenes, 77
Lapiths, 83
Lateran Council, Fifth, lxvi
Lateran Council, Fourth, xxxiii
law, xliv–xlv, 31, 37, 59, 69, 71, 95, 101, 103, 105
League of Cambrai, War of the, lxv
Leipzig, li
Leno, xlii
Leo X, Pope, lv
Livy, xxvi
Longinus, 51
Louis XII, King, lxvi n. 145
Luther, Martin, l, li

M

Machiavelli, Niccolò,
   The Prince, xxi
Malatesta, Pandolfo, xviii
Mantua, xxvi
Manuel, Nickolaus, l
Marone, Andrea, xli
marriage, 199
Mars, 63
Mary, Virgin, 51, 53
masses, xliv, lviii, lix
Melga, Giacomo, xl n. 69
Midas, xxxix, 75
Milan, lx
Minelli, Antonio, Frontispiece

Minerbetti, Tommaso, xlii
Misinta, Bernardino, xli
Molinari, Giovanni Battista, xxvii
monte di pietà, xxiii–xxiv, 27, 53, 221
Moreto, Antonio, xliii
mortuaries, xvi, 41, 65, 69, 179, 181
   see also candles; canon law; civil law
Mount Olympus, 85

N

Nebuchadnezzar, 129
Niccolò de' Tudeschis, see Panormitanus

O

Olivieri, Giovanni, xxvi

P

Padua, xxvi, liv, lx
Panormitanus (Niccolò de' Tudeschis), xxxiii, 39 n. 33, 155, 167, 181, 183, 185, 191, 205, 207, 221
Parma, lx
Paul, St, 59
Pazzi, Cosimo, xlviii
Persians, 127
Persius, xxvi
Perugia, xxvi, lix–lx
Peter, St, 59
Peter of Ancharano, 181
Petrarch, xxvii, lii
   De Remediis, xiii
   'Insepultus abiicar', liii
Pharaohs, 129
Pierozzi, Fra Antonino, 39 n. 33, 193
Pierre de Palu, 39 n. 33, 189
Pilate, 51
Pisa, lx
Pius III, Pope, lv

Plato, xlii, 35, 35 n. 28, 43 n. 37, 109, 113
Pliny, xxvi
Plutarch, xli, xlii
Pluto, 55
Poliziano, Angelo, xxv, xli
Pontano, Ludovico, 39 n. 33, 195, 197, 199
Posculo, Ubertino, xxv
prodigies and portents, lxiii, lxv–lxvi
Protestantism, l–li
Pseudo-Plutarch, xliii
purgatory, xvi, l–li

Q

Querini, Vincenzo, lv
Questio an infrascripta statuta super mortuariis sint contra eccesiasticam libertatem, xxix, xxxi–xxxiv, 155–223
   and disuse of funerary statute, 203
   and papal excommunication, 155, 183, 207
   see also canon law; civil law

R

reason, 35, 101, 103
Rosella, see Trovamala de Salis, Baptista
Rusconi, Giorgio de', lxx

S

Sandal, Ennio, lxx
Sandeo, Felino Maria, 39 n. 33, 171, 197, 199
Sanuto, Marino, xviii n. 9
Saraco, Marco, xxx
Sardanapalus, 129
Sasso, Panfilo, xxvi

Index

Savonarola, Fra Girolamo, lxii–lxiii
Scala dynasty, xviii
Scotus, Johannes Duns, 5, 5 n. 2
Scutari, xxvi
Severianus, Johannes Baptista, 201
Simon of Trent, xxiii n. 21
Sinibaldo, Falco, xlii
Sixtus IV, Pope, 209, 211
slaves, 215
Solon, lvii, 33 n. 27, 35
Spain:
    funerals in, xlviii, lix
Spalato, xlii
Stoicism, xlix, lvii
Summa Angelica, 191
sumptuary legislation:
    in Brescia, xiv–xv, lx–lxii, 146–51, 157, 203
    in Italy, lviii, lix–lx
    in Venice, lxv

T

Talmud, lxiii
Taverio di Rovato, Giovanni, xxv, xxvi, xxvii
tax farmers, xx, 135, 141
tears, liii, lviii
Tertullian, lxii
Thomas Aquinas, St, xxxiv n. 59, 59
    see also *Defensio populi Brixiani rei violatae ecclesiasticae libertatis ob decretum ab eo factum de ambitione et sumptibus funerum minuendis, accusantibus Fratribus Sancti Dominici*
Titius, 215
tombs, xlvii, liii
Tommaso Seneca di Camerino, xxvi
Torriani dynasty, xviii
Totenfesserei, l
traitors, xx, 135
Trent, xxiii n. 21
Trovamala de Salis, Baptista, 167, 209, 221
trumpeters, 135

U

Ulpian, 213
unlearned, the, 135
usury, 97

V

Valcamonica, xxxvi, 49
Valgulio, Carlo, life and career of, xl–xliii
    and humanism, xxv
    writings of, xliii
        as possible author of *Defensio*, xxxv
        Contra vituperatorem musicae, lxx
        De sumptibus funerum, xliii–xlvi, lxix–lxx, 91–143
        disdain for wealth and wordly honors in, 97, 105, 115, 121, 131
        and bonds of civil association, 137
        four classical virtues in, 103, 107, 109
        honor in, xlv, 91, 105, 107, 137
        inequality in funerals in, 95
        Jesus Christ in, xlv
        misericordia (compassion) in, xlv, 97
        natural equality of men in, 99, 101
        pietas (loyalty) in, xlv
        seven deadly sins in, 133, 135
        theological virtues, 111
    see also alms; Brescia; funerals; Jesus Christ; law; mortuaries; sumptuary legislation

Valgulio, Stefano, xl
Valgulio, Tristanus de, xxx n. 42
Venice, lxx
   funerals in, xlvii n. 90, lxi
   and government in Brescia, xviii–xxii, 31, 207
   under attack, lxv
Vergil, xxvi, 131, 139 n. 53
Vio, Tommaso (Cajetan), xxiii
Visconti family, xviii, xxi, xxv
Visconti, Filippo Maria, xviii, lx
Vittorino da Feltre, xxvi

W

weapons, liii, 61, 63, 63, 71, 191, 193, 201
widows, liii, 17
witches, xxxvi, 49, 51

Z

Zane, Paolo, *see* Brescia, bishop of